Change and continuity in the North Atlantic Alliance

SPEECHES BY
THE SECRETARY GENERAL OF NATO
MANFRED WÖRNER

PUBLISHED BY
THE OFFICE OF INFORMATION AND PRESS
NATO
1110 BRUSSELS

L'Alliance de l'Atlantique Nord:
le changement dans la continuité

DISCOURS
DU SECRETAIRE GENERAL DE L'OTAN
MANFRED WÖRNER

PUBLIE PAR
LE BUREAU DE L'INFORMATION ET DE LA PRESSE
OTAN
1110 BRUXELLES

Table
of contents
Table
des matières

Page

Manfred Wörner

CHAIRMAN OF THE NORTH
ATLANTIC COUNCIL
AND SECRETARY GENERAL OF NATO

Manfred Wörner was born in Stuttgart on September 24, 1934. He attended the Universities of Heidelberg and Paris and then pursued legal studies at the University of Munich. He received a doctorate in international law in 1958, his dissertation having dealt with the defence relations of allied countries.

Mr. Wörner worked as an administrator in the State of Baden-Würtemberg, before becoming parliamentary adviser at the State Diet of Baden-Würtemberg in 1962. Elected to the German Bundestag in 1965, he remained a member of parliament until becoming Secretary General of NATO. His special interests as an elected representative have been parliamentary reform and security policy.

Chairman of the Working Group on Defence of the Christian Democratic Union/Christian Social Union (CDU/CSU) parliamentary party until 1976, Mr. Wörner was Chairman of the Defence Committee of the German Bundestag until 1980; and Deputy Chairman of the CDU/CSU parliamentary party with special responsibility for foreign policy, defence policy, development policy and internal German relations until 1982. During this period he was also a member of the Federal Executive of the CDU and Deputy Chairman of the Konrad Adenauer Foundation.

From October 1982 until May 1988, Mr. Wörner was Minister of Defence of the Federal Republic of Germany. He took up his appointment as Secretary General of NATO on July 1, 1988.

□

*M*anfred *Wörner*

PRESIDENT DU CONSEIL
DE L'ATLANTIQUE NORD
ET SECRETAIRE GENERAL DE L'OTAN

Manfred Wörner est né à Stuttgart le 24 septembre 1934. Après avoir suivi les cours des universités de Heidelberg et de Paris, il poursuivit des études de droit à l'université de Munich. Il a obtenu un doctorat en droit international en 1958, sa thèse ayant porté sur les relations des pays alliés en matière de défense.

Après avoir été administrateur du Land de Bade-Wurtemberg, M. Wörner fut nommé, en 1962, conseiller parlementaire auprès de la Diète de ce même Land. Elu au Bundestag en 1965, il siégea au parlement allemand jusqu'à sa nomination au poste de Secrétaire général de l'OTAN. La réforme du parlement et la politique de sécurité retinrent tout particulièrement son attention de parlementaire.

Président du Groupe de travail sur la défense du groupe parlementaire de l'Union chrétienne démocrate et de l'Union chrétienne-sociale (CDU/CSU) jusqu'en 1976, M. Wörner a en outre rempli les fonctions de président de la Commission de la défense du Bundestag jusqu'en 1980 et de vice-président du groupe parlementaire de la CDU/CSU jusqu'en 1982. A ce titre, il assuma des responsabilités particulières en matière de politique étrangère, de politique de défense, de politique de développement et de relations interallemandes. Au cours de la même période, il fut également membre de l'Exécutif fédéral de la CDU et vice-président de la Fondation Konrad Adenauer.

M. Wörner a été ministre de la Défense de la République fédérale d'Allemagne d'octobre 1982 à mai 1988 et a pris ses fonctions de Secrétaire général de l'OTAN le 1er juillet 1988.

❑

Foreword

The speeches included in the present volume were delivered by the Secretary General of NATO, Mr. Manfred Wörner, between November 1988 and November 1990. The first anticipates the 40th anniversary of the Atlantic Alliance. Towards the end of the collection appear speeches which mark Mr. Wörner's historic visit to Moscow and his unprecedented address to the Hungarian Parliament. In the 24 short months which are thus covered by this collection, Europe has witnessed its most radical transformation in half a century. Communism in Central Europe has collapsed, for the most part in the wake of peaceful revolutions soon followed by democratic elections; the Soviet Union has begun a strategic retreat from its forward position in the heart of Europe, thereby completely transforming the East-West security equation; and German unity, once a distant hope, has suddenly become a reality, the end of Germany's division also signalling the end of Europe's unnatural division.

Change in Europe has been matched by change in the Atlantic Alliance itself. In three momentous summit meetings and many ministerial sessions, some regular, some exceptional, NATO has been able to realise its political destiny as an instrument of cooperation and partnership in the building of the new Europe. Two landmark declarations issued by the Alliance's Heads of State and Government mark this transformation and the end of an era of confrontation between irreconcilable political systems: the first resulting from the Brussels Summit of May 1989 and the second from the London Summit of July 1990. These documents have not only established guidelines for NATO's quest for a new quality of relationship with its erstwhile adversaries, but have also proved invaluable in convincing the Soviet Union that the Alliance's vision of a Europe whole and free would be fully compatible with its own legitimate security interests. The declarations have thus not merely set out objectives but also contained the decisions and proposals that have brought those objectives ever closer.

Readers wishing to understand the genesis of NATO's transformation, and to follow the thinking that has led from confrontation to cooperation in European security in a period of little more than a year, will have useful source material in the speeches of Manfred Wörner. The collection reproduced in the following pages begins at a time when the Cold War was still very much alive and takes the reader through the period of sudden and dramatic change, including Soviet acceptance of the participation of a united Germany as a full member of NATO - a notion which might previously have been regarded as unthinkable - and culminating in the signature in Paris of the Treaty on Conventional Armed Forces in Europe, the Joint Declaration on peaceful relations between the members of NATO and of the Warsaw Treaty Organisation, and other important developments to further the CSCE process. They reveal a gradual shift from the visionary to the more operational role of the Alliance as it moves to take advantage of its opportunities and to appeal to a new, receptive audience among its former adversaries. In demonstrating from one speech to the next the dynamic interaction of Alliance policies and external events, this collection stands by itself as an important historical record of a unique period whose consequences are in many cases still unresolved and will be with us for many years yet. In looking ahead to the new challenges of the Alliance in the 21st century, as well as explaining the reasons for its past successes, Mr. Wörner's speeches establish beyond all doubt an image of a living and creative institution which is rising to meet the challenges it now faces in a constantly changing world. For the reader who seeks to obtain a coherent view of NATO's enduring value, this collection offers an indispensable guide.

*A*vant-propos

Les discours reproduits dans le présent volume ont été prononcés par le Secrétaire général de l'OTAN, M. Manfred Wörner, entre novembre 1988 et novembre 1990. Le premier discours annonce le 40ème anniversaire de l'Alliance atlantique et les derniers marquent la visite historique de M. Wörner à Moscou et son discours devant le Parlement hongrois. Durant la brève période de vingt-quatre mois couverte par ce livre, nous avons assisté à la transformation la plus radicale qu'ait connue l'Europe en un demi-siècle. Le communisme s'est effondré en Europe centrale sous l'effet de révolutions, pour la plupart pacifiques, suivies d'élections démocratiques; l'Union soviétique a entamé un repli stratégique en quittant graduellement les positions avancées qu'elle occupait au centre de l'Europe, ce qui modifie complètement l'équation de la sécurité Est-Ouest; l'unité allemande qui n'avait longtemps été qu'un lointain espoir est devenue brusquement une réalité, la fin de la division de l'Allemagne signifiant du même coup la fin de la division contre nature de l'Europe.

Le changement en Europe est allé de pair avec un changement à l'intérieur même de l'Alliance atlantique. Trois réunions au sommet d'une extrême importance et de nombreuses sessions ministérielles, ordinaires ou extraordinaires, ont permis à l'OTAN d'assumer pleinement son destin d'instrument de coopération et de partenariat dans la construction d'une Europe nouvelle. Les chefs d'Etat et de gouvernement de l'Alliance ont ainsi publié, d'abord à l'issue du sommet de Bruxelles, en mai 1989, puis du sommet de Londres, en juillet 1990, deux déclarations qui font date et qui marquent à la fois cette profonde transformation et la fin de l'ère de confrontation entre des systèmes politiques inconciliables. Si ces documents ont tracé les lignes directrices que l'OTAN devait suivre pour imprimer une qualité nouvelle aux relations avec ses adversaires d'hier, ils ont aussi grandement aidé à convaincre l'Union soviétique que la vision alliée d'une Europe entière et libre était tout à fait compatible avec les intérêts légitimes de sa propre sécurité. Ainsi, ces déclarations n'ont pas simplement fixé des objectifs, mais énoncé les décisions et propositions qui les ont rendus beaucoup plus proches.

Le lecteur qui souhaite comprendre la genèse de la transformation de l'OTAN et suivre le cheminement d'une pensée qui a permis, en un peu plus d'un an, de faire passer la sécurité européenne du stade de la confrontation à celui de la coopération pourra utilement se référer aux discours de Manfred Wörner. Les textes conduiront le lecteur d'une époque où la guerre froide était une réalité encore bien vivante à la période d'événements inattendus et spectaculaires - notamment l'acceptation par l'Union soviétique d'une Allemagne unie, membre de l'OTAN à part entière - qui aboutira à la signature à Paris du Traité sur les forces conventionnelles en Europe, la Déclaration commune sur les relations pacifiques entre l'OTAN et l'Organisation du Traité de Varsovie, ainsi que d'autres développements majeurs dans le cadre du processus de la CSCE. Les discours de M. Wörner permettent aussi de voir comment l'Alliance prend peu à peu un rôle moins "visionnaire" et plus actif alors qu'elle s'attache à tirer parti des chances qui s'offrent à elle et qu'elle s'adresse à un auditoire nouveau, plus réceptif, chez ses anciens adversaires. En montrant d'un discours à l'autre quel est le jeu des influences réciproques entre les orientations de la politique de l'Alliance et le cours des événements extérieurs, ce recueil constitue en soi un important témoignage historique sur une période exceptionnelle dont les conséquences, dans bien des cas, ne nous sont pas encore apparues mais resteront sans doute sensibles de longues années. En cherchant à discerner les nouveaux défis qui attendent l'Alliance au 21ème siècle, aussi bien qu'en expliquant les raisons de ses succès antérieurs, les discours de M. Wörner donnent sans conteste l'image d'une institution vivante et créatrice, capable de relever les défis auxquels elle se trouve confrontée dans un monde en constante évolution. Le lecteur qui cherche à bien saisir ce qui fait la pérennité de la valeur de l'Alliance y trouvera un guide indispensable.

*A*lastair Buchan Memorial Lecture

London
23 November
1988

It is a particular privilege for me to have been invited to deliver the 1988 Alastair Buchan Memorial Lecture in a year which marks the 30th anniversary of the I.I.S.S. Not only this series of lectures, but the Institute itself, are fitting memorials to one of the outstanding strategic thinkers of post-war era. We are also on the threshold of celebrating the 40th anniversary of the North Atlantic Alliance. There is a natural link between these two anniversaries. The Alliance, composed of sixteen independent sovereign democratic states, relies on the continued support of its publics. The Institute, since its inception, has sought to contribute to the necessary development of an enlightened public consensus on Western security policy.

This distinguished occasion is called a "lecture", which is commonly understood as an informative talk before an audience, or a lengthy scolding. My purpose is neither. My purpose is to ask your help in maintaining the solid platform which is the only conceivable basis, in my opinion, for the political progress we seek over the next decade in East-West relations. The basic challenge which threatens our success, above all, is that of nurturing public understanding and support for our strategy - political and military - and thus preserving public confidence. It is people like you in this audience who play such an important rôle in shaping that opinion. I hope that my remarks tonight will stimulate your thinking about new ways to address things we dare not take for granted.

Anniversaries are traditionally a time to reflect on the past, and to try to draw conclusions which may better equip us to meet the demands of the future. If you will, a twin process of recollection and reorientation. It is almost a truism to suggest

15

that throughout its existence the Alliance has been faced with challenges to its cohesion; indeed, a casual reading of the public commentaries of the last 40 years might create the impression that it has been in a state of recurrent crisis. Of course, there is no doubt that there have been periods of major upheaval, often focussed on nuclear issues. The Institute was founded at a time when the launch of the Sputnik had marked the beginning of the end of unchallenged American strategic nuclear superiority. This ultimately led, some ten years later and after a highly charged emotional debate over the rôle of nuclear weapons in Europe, to the adoption of the strategy of flexible response.

The nuclear debate resurfaced again after another decade had passed with the controversy over the modernisation of intermediate nuclear forces and the so-called double track decision. Nevertheless, the Alliance has survived - indeed more than survived, it has demonstrated a political solidarity and steadfastness that has led us to a situation where our peace and freedom rests on sounder foundations than ever. We have good reasons to be proud of our success of the past, and to be optimistic about the future.

Yet we now face a new challenge. For the first time we face a Soviet Leader who is moving to a more pragmatic approach to international affairs. I firmly believe that Mr. Gorbachev's attempts at reform, internal and external, are a response to **our** success, and the manifest failure of the Soviet system. His policies of reform have changed the East-West equation, and we must both welcome and encourage this. But at the same time they are designed to prevent the collapse of the Soviet economy on which the political system - and in the longer term the military strength - of the Soviet Union depends. This attempt cannot be successful without political reform, with the consequences that we are already seeing.

Across the whole spectrum of East-West relations there is a process of change which presents both challenges and risks to the Alliance. As Alastair Buchan himself wrote in the concluding lines of *The End of the Post War Era*: "A profound responsibility for this (orderly) process of evolution lies on the shoulders of the West.... It has been the West that has been the cradle of political ideas.... If the springs of political improvisation in the West dry up then the new agenda of world politics will be a barren one".

These are words that ring true even in today's much changed circum-stances. Our springs have not dried up. It is our agenda which is on the advance, and it is far from barren. We can no longer afford to set the process of East-West developments in the framework of a mutual *status quo*. We must go beyond this and create a dynamism with which we can establish a new political order in Europe, taking advantage of the prospects for change before us. The political competition in Europe is one in which the future of both Europe and the Western Alliance is at stake. As my distinguished predecessor Lord

Carrington proposed in this lecture five years ago, the Alliance must have a clear vision of the future European security order in the years up to the end of the century, and a positive political strategy to pursue that vision. I believe we have a unique opportunity to create a new security framework, but this can only be achieved if we couple the process of dynamic political change to the creation of military stability incorporating a nuclear component.

Failure to define where our policies are leading and an inability to articulate them clearly has been in part, I suggest, a reason for our relative lack of success in convincing the younger generation, in particular, of the need to maintain our defence support. Our strategy must be capable of accommodating both the changing political relationships within the Alliance as well as with the Soviet Union. We must be prepared to seek actively to draw the Soviet Union more closely into the global community. What we are searching for is a shared concept of security that will provide the necessary basis for pursuing political change which may ultimately lead to a new peaceful, stable and more humane international order. The key to this process will be to maintain - and indeed enhance - stability while at the same time creating the conditions for promoting and accommodating the change on our terms.

In politics and in public discourse we tend to focus on tactics, and lose sight of our strategy and goals. Our vision of Europe's future security and political order is already well defined. It is based on our values, and on the lessons we have learned from a bitter history. It is driven by the historic effort to build an East-West relationship in which we recognize that military forces are an inescapable reality, but in which the resort to armed force is no longer an option for the conduct of international relations. But it is equally based on the clear premise that defence, including nuclear defence, must be a precondition for stability. Realization of our ambitious political agenda, and management of our rapidly changing political environment, is not possible in a situation of military instability.

In developing this theme I must first say something about the political background, for we must not forget that the challenges we face are first and foremost political. Indeed, NATO is essentially a political Alliance. It was forged as much to consolidate the battered democracies of post-war Europe as to defend against the communist threat of aggression. This is reflected in the preamble to the Washington Treaty: "We are determined to safeguard the principles of democracy, individual liberty and the rule of law". In the end, the continued vitality of the Alliance depends on maintaining our collective will to preserve our democratic heritage.

Not only do we have to adjust to a process of rapid change in international relations, but also to changes in the relative economic strength and political potential of the West European partners. However I will not dwell today on the question of the sharing of rôles, risks and responsibilities - the so-called burden-sharing debate - save to say that the resurgence of Europe must be seen as reinforcing the Alliance as a whole. Intensified economic co-operation not only strengthens the economic base necessary to sustain our collective military effort, but it directly facilitates the rationalisation of defence production and standardization of equipment. The Alliance will need to adjust to greater European integration in the defence field. But whatever form future European co-operation in security and defence matters takes, it must display transparency of activity and compatibility with Alliance goals. Ultimately the transatlantic partnership must remain the guarantor of our collective security.

It is only on the basis of that partnership that we will be able to build military stability, and be able to exploit the opportunities and manage the risks in the field of East-West relations. There is a great deal to welcome in Mr. Gorbachev's policies of reform. We should applaud the declared intent to expand the rights of Soviet citizens, to increase the free flow of information, to restructure the legal system. Of more direct concern to our security policy, we must also encourage the apparent priority of co-operation over confrontation and common human interests over antagonism between political ideologies. Being an optimist, I hope these signs reflect a greater acknowledgement of common values in international affairs. We are challenging Mr. Gorbachev: to the extent he responds, he should earn our co-operation.

But we should not forget that these reforms are the result of necessity, not altruism. Mr. Gorbachev's aim is to make the socialist system more effective: to release, as he puts it, its hidden potential. His goal is to ensure the Soviet Union's continued rôle as a world superpower. To achieve his economic and political reforms at home he requires a stable international environment both to avoid distracting his internal efforts, and to ensure that the West does not interfere with, and if possible assists, the process. But our aim, beyond giving him reassurance, should be to ensure that the Soviet reforms lead to a major degree of military self-restraint. A crucial question is whether or not Soviet military capabilities, after a period of change and reform, will still remain a key determinant of the European political order. It has been a primary goal of the Alliance throughout its existence to loosen this stranglehold over our future, and there are signs that it may now be attainable.

We must also not lose sight of the fact that so far there has been little change in the might of the Soviet military machine or in its offensive nature. Modernisation programmes across the whole spectrum of Warsaw Pact equipment continue unabated. The Soviet Union's claim to superpower status rests almost entirely on their military strength. Even if the Soviet leadership is prepared to draw down this strength to some extent, at least in the short to medium term, there are likely to be considerable limitations on their freedom of actions. For if the Soviet Union ceases to deploy an intimidating array of military forces, how will it compensate in order to maintain its superpower status?

Herein lies a crucial dilemma for Western leaders. Faced with a continuation of the existing military imbalance, and the need for strength and credibility as the foundation of our political agenda, we have no option but to maintain our own defensive capabilities, and justify this to our publics. But in the defence community we tend to use the word "threat" as a term of art well understood by all the professionals. Maybe we use it too often, and too simplistically. The public may not perceive it the same way. The military threat to the Alliance is, of course, a combination of capability and intention. While we may assess that the Soviet Union has no present intention of attacking the West - and indeed the policies of the new Soviet leadership certainly appear a good deal more benign than those of even a decade ago - there is no doubt that the military capability to do so remains unabated. Moreover, intentions can change much more rapidly than armoured divisions.

But in the mind of the layman, "threat" is more associated with intention. The image of Mr. Gorbachev - a "man with whom one can do business" - demonstrating unheard of flexibility in foreign policy, opening up new opportunities for co-operation, does not suggest to the public that we need to worry about the "Soviet threat". An attenuation of international adventurism, withdrawal from Afghanistan, and willingness to compromise in arms control all increase the pressures on the West increasingly to lower its guard, politically and militarily. The prospects - which are not yet realities - of fundamental political change in the East make it harder to justify the requirements of deterrence. Our task is to legitimise our continued defence efforts at a time when the public perception is that a robust defence posture is less necessary.

Of course the defence effort of the West is not a simple matter of a response to a military threat. The concept of maintaining security and stability encompasses the preservation of political and national sovereignty; ensuring continued freedom; maintaining international confidence, including an assurance of predictability in international relations; and demonstrating our collective political will. If the West should begin a process of abandoning its competitiveness, political and military, the Soviet reforms could succeed without the desired reduction in Soviet military might, and the profound Soviet military restraint which we seek. Thus we would forfeit our own political success.

How should we respond to this challenge? I make no apologies for taking the Harmel doctrine as my starting point. Although the Harmel report was undertaken in very different circumstances from those which prevail today - the Alliance had just undergone the twin shocks of the withdrawal of France from the integrated military structure and its strategy had undergone a radical

19

transformation, leading some even to doubt NATO's continued existence - its prescription remains sound, and in my view requires no revalidation. But as I have already made clear, this is not a call to maintain the *status quo* ; we must be active in developing our policies on the sound basis of Harmel to meet the new challenge. We should seize opportunities to build on the traditional bases of Alliance strength - military co-operation and political solidarity.

Arms control will naturally play an important part in this process. The INF treaty, involving heavily asymmetric reductions and extensive verification arrangements, and achieved only as a result of Alliance determination and cohesion, has pointed the way. There are now clear opportunities in the fields of strategic nuclear forces, chemical weapons and, perhaps most challenging of all, in the prospective Conventional Stability Talks. But our central objective must remain clear: to seek enhanced stability at lower levels of forces. To manage this process effectively, we must ensure the various negotiations are set firmly within an agreed process for arms control, and are pursued in consonance with our security requirements.

But political dialogue, encompassing arms control, is only half of Harmel. We must equally maintain a strong defensive posture. That posture rests crucially on the rôle of nuclear weapons, and it is the rôle of nuclear weapons that lies at the heart of the strategic dilemma which has taxed the Alliance from almost its earliest days. It is to this theme which I would now like to turn.

I started this lecture by mentioning two anniversaries. This year also marks a third, one of major significance to the Alliance. Last January was the 20th anniversary of the publication of the final version of MC 14/3, the document which enshrines our strategy of flexible response. With the abandonment of the old "tripwire" strategy of massive retaliation, flexible response gave theatre nuclear forces a central rôle in providing the essential link to ensure the continued coupling of the United States strategic deterrent to the security of Europe, a crucial element of reassurance to the European members of the Alliance.

Nevertheless the sensitivities over coupling remained. Almost ten years later my distinguished predecessor as German Defence Minister, and by then Chancellor of the Federal Republic, Helmut Schmidt, gave what became perhaps the most widely-quoted Alastair Buchan Memorial Lecture. In this he drew attention to the political implications for Alliance security of the advances that had been made in limiting central strategic systems in the SALT negotiation, in contrast with the total lack of progress in reducing conventional arms in MBFR. While he did not call for additional nuclear deployments - he rather concentrated on the way ahead in arms control - he highlighted the disparity that had arisen between East and West in theatre nuclear weapons. At almost the same time, NATO Defence Ministers meeting in the Nuclear Planning

Group agreed to set up the High Level Group to examine the need for the modernisation of the Alliance's theatre nuclear forces.

The rest, as they say, is history. The HLG subsequently recommended the modernisation of NATO's intermediate range nuclear forces, and in December 1979 Alliance Foreign and Defence Ministers endorsed the "double-track" decision. Following the Alliance proposal of the "zero option" in 1981 this ultimately led to the historic INF agreement, finally ratified earlier this year.

But despite the success of the INF agreement the nuclear dilemma remains; indeed the agreement, by creating an expectation of further stages of nuclear disarmament, has in some ways increased the problems for NATO. I say problems because they are essentially threefold.

The first, the rôle of the non-nuclear European nations in the nuclear decision-making process, was in large measure solved by the creation of the Nuclear Planning Group some 20 years ago. The Group has elaborated the political framework for NATO's nuclear planning, which culminated in the agreement in 1986 on the General Political Guidelines for the possible use of theatre nuclear weapons in the defence of the Alliance. It has dealt with the specific modernisation and deployment decisions which have to be faced from time to time. Through both efforts, the European Allies have been able to participate fully in the decision-making process.

The result has been a very responsible collective approach to the political treatment of nuclear planning, including a considerable degree of self-restraint in force structures. Moreover, while the basic strategy of MC 14/3 has in no sense been modified, the work in the NPG leading up to the General Political Guidelines finally resolved the debate between those who argued that theatre nuclear forces could be used decisively as a means of winning a conflict in Europe, and those who saw their rôle as essentially one of conveying a political signal: a political signal with a powerful military impact, but nevertheless one intended to convey a clear message to the Soviet leadership about NATO's resolve. The Guidelines unambiguously support this latter elaboration of the strategy.

But the very success of these policies, allied with achievements in arms control, have led to the second problem: the renewed public questioning of the strategy of deterrence just at the time, ironically, when responsibility and rationality govern the nuclear policies of the Alliance more than ever before. We are faced with the problem that sometimes it appears that every citizen is his own strategist - but a strategist who sometimes tends to disregard the solid foundation of thought and judgement on which the rôle of nuclear weapons in our security is based.

Fortunately, the founding members of this Institute - Alastair Buchan himself, Michael Howard, the current President and many others - have sought to ensure that our security needs are defined in their relationship to our political purposes in a way that people can understand. Nobody has made it clearer than Michael Howard that participation and enlightenment, those vital needs of our democracies, have their price. Deterrence cannot endure without reassurance, and without the awareness of the citizens that all the measures necessary to preserve peace in the nuclear age are taken responsibly and purposefully.

Let us be in no doubt: nuclear deterrence has underpinned the deterrent strategy of NATO throughout its existence and created a form of stability which could not have existed with conventional forces alone. Moreover recent Soviet pronouncements indicating an acceptance of the doctrine that a nuclear war is not winnable by either side suggest a possible doctrinal consensus. It would be very odd if the Alliance were to jeopardise its policy of deterrence just at a time when there are prospects of making the Soviet leadership understand the importance of its contribution to maintaining the sort of stability in Europe which is the necessary precondition for peaceful change.

But if we are to convince the Soviet Union, we must first be secure in the support of our own publics. We therefore have to disabuse them of the notion that such weapons are peace-threatening rather than peace-keeping. During a time when our theatre nuclear stockpile in the West has been reduced by over a third to its lowest level in 20 years - tangible evidence of our intentions, however much the public ignores it - the armoury of conventional forces that we face has been dramatically enhanced. And in addition to the devastating power that even non-nuclear forces now command, the Soviet Union has available to it a vast array of modern chemical weapons. Without the deterrent provided by our nuclear forces, these capabilities might well be regarded as much more readily usable, with predictable consequences for stability and confidence.

It is of course a natural reaction to seek immunity from nuclear weapons. None of us like them, but none of us in the Alliance, under any circumstances that I can now foresee, can do without them. Given that they cannot be "disinvented", we must be clear that no area of the Alliance can be made immune from the threat they pose. Wherever nuclear weapons are deployed in East and West, for the foreseeable future the ingenuity of defence planners will see to it that none of the members of NATO, or of the Warsaw Pact, is beyond their reach. So, immunity is not possible. But can we in the Alliance secure greater safety, both from nuclear weapons and from warfare in general? The two cannot be separated. Here the answer is not only "yes", but that we are making progress. The sheer numbers and types of nuclear weapons matter far less than factors like stability, vulnerability, credibility and the conventional imbalance. Our defence goals have been repeated so often that they are often lost from sight, but they are crucial: low levels of forces, conventional and nuclear; stability; and the certainty that no aggressor could conclude that the gains of possible aggression could possibly outweigh the risks.

We must therefore seek to convince Western public opinion that the vision of a nuclear-free Europe, far from reducing the risks to our security, would in practice entail the much greater risk of leading to a greater instability and to conflict that, quite apart from its consequences for the continued survival of the Western democracies, would inflict a devastating degree of damage. The chimera of a non-nuclear world held out by Mr. Gorbachev would not lead to a safer world. Successive Governments in all the NATO countries have considered this balance of risk and invariably concluded that the best way of ensuring continued security is a strategy of deterrence based on some mix of nuclear conventional forces.

An inescapable corollary to this - and one which we must not shrink from - is that this means even if we succeed in achieving heavily asymmetric reductions in conventional arms control negotiations, leading to a broad balance of conventional forces in Europe, we shall still need to rely on a modern theatre nuclear element to underpin our deterrent. Naturally we should keep our nuclear stockpile at the lowest possible level consistent with the needs of deterrence, and conventional stability at lower levels of forces could considerably assist the process of further reducing the number of nuclear weapons.

This is not an easy message to convey. But deterrence, and particularly nuclear deterrence, cannot endure unless our citizens are convinced not only that it is as a direct result of our policies that we have maintained our security in the past, but that the measures we are now taking are designed further to promote peace and security. So long as the deep political divide exists between East and West, and both sides retain the capability to inflict devastating destruction on the other, we must maintain a balance of conventional and nuclear forces. Allied governments must thus first be satisfied we have the right strategy, and then convince our publics.

The third problem is how we should deal with the Soviet Union. During a period when we may continue to see rapid political change within the Warsaw Pact, how should we conduct our policies so as both to continue to deter any possibility of aggression, but also to seek a more stable security relationship? If my thesis that the prospects exist for a degree of doctrinal convergence on the principles of nuclear deterrence is accepted, then I believe we need to work towards some form of political recognition by the Soviet leadership of our way of seeking military stability at lower levels of forces, but including a nuclear component.

Both sides need to acknowledge the need for strategic stability in order to promote political change. This stability can be enhanced by lower force levels, both nuclear and conventional, providing there is agreement on the need to maintain a nuclear force structure that preserves what some have described as a "just deterrent". In other words we seek to make our current strategy of nuclear deterrence an accepted *modus vivendi*. The elaboration of MC 14/3 that has been developed over the last 20 years and enshrined in the General Political Guidelines would thus be endorsed as a principle of international security that has stood the test of time.

In this approach the continuing process of arms control can play a role. But while such a process can contribute to reducing tension, it is only an adjunct to the development of a political dialogue, not a substitute for it. Ultimately we must hope that the development of such a *modus vivendi*, while providing enhanced security and stability, can be an essential step towards a very different world order. The post-war era has seen a dramatic change in favour of democracy. Most importantly the winds of change have begun to blow in Eastern Europe and the Soviet Union. What the consequences will be we do not yet know. Our hope must be that the East will conclude that they must avoid a military conflict with the West, not because of the risk and penalties that it would entail, but because of shared rules of responsible conduct, and wider sharing of values, which make the thought of conflict ever less imaginable, as it has become among the nations of the West themselves.

This I believe to be the real meaning of the Harmel doctrine. To quote Alastair Buchan again: "The modern international system springs primarily from the minds and experience of Western man and Western civilization.... The intellectual challenge of the next decade is both to use and to modify this great historical tradition, flawed but enriched by sporadic failure, to provide an interim accommodation with other civilisations and ideologies in an intractable social order which limits our ambitions but must not suspend our efforts".

The decade Buchan was referring to was the 1970s. If we have fallen short of his aspirations, it was perhaps less due to our own failings than our inability to sustain the necessary dialogue with a regime imprisoned in the iron cage of its own history. Now at last, we may have the opportunity to realize that dialogue. We can do so with confidence in the success of our political and economic systems, and the continued vitality of our Alliance. But we must be united, strong and clear in our purpose. Two hundred years ago John Curran noted that the condition of liberty is eternal vigilance; the Alliance has shown that vigilance for the past 40 years and we must not neglect it now.

□

Stability in Europe -NATO's way forward

Davos,
Switzerland
1 February
1989

In a few weeks from now, on April 4, the Atlantic Alliance will be forty years old. On that day we shall celebrate the achievements of the past, and who would deny us this right? With pride we will look back on forty years of peace with freedom for the peoples of Western Europe; we will remind ourselves of an economic prosperity which on the day the Treaty of Washington was signed would have seemed nothing more than a dream; and we will salute the transatlantic partnership which has led to a stronger and more self-reliant Western Europe and to a North America that is now actively engaged in world affairs. Today we look to the future not with fear but with confidence.

Forty years ago it was different. We were struggling to build a defence against the military threat from without, and to re-build our societies after the destructions of war. Yet the Treaty of Washington clearly shows that even in those dark days we looked beyond the immediate danger towards a dual purpose: first to create a permanent military stability in Europe that would not only reduce but indeed eradicate the threat of war; and, second, to establish on this continent a new political order that would allow for political change, that would respect human rights and human dignity; an order that would give freedom to all the citizens of East and West; an order that would grant to the peoples of the East the same rights of self-determination that we enjoy here in the West, and in a Europe that would be able ultimately to overcome its painful division.

We are now living through a time of breathtaking movement. There has not been such all-embracing and radical change since the end of the Second World War. The ever closer union of

Europe, the economic and ideological decline of Communism, Gorbachev's reform drive, the first disarmament agreement in human history, the growing importance of economic power - even overshadowing military power, the spreading influence of democratic ideas and free market forces, the revival in superpower relations - everywhere the dynamic of history is plain to see.

The East is turning to the West. Our political approach of co-operation instead of confrontation, as set out in the Harmel Report, is gaining increasing acceptance. Our ideas are on the advance. Democracy, human rights, pluralism. You need to read Gorbachev's speech to the United Nations to see how far concepts which we have fostered for two decades have penetrated the Soviet vocabulary. Our initiatives are determining the course of political events.

The conclusion of the Vienna follow-up meeting has been a new triumph for the CSCE process which the West first set in motion. In all areas of disarmament, the real impetus has come from the West. Just consider the zero option, the START negotiations, the talks on the elimination of chemical weapons or the concept of conventional disarmament from the Atlantic to the Urals.

More fundamentally, the competitive success of our free societies and market economies have given Mr. Gorbachev his main motive for reform. It is the freedom, the standard of living and the industrial success of the West which the Soviets fear, not our tanks. At the origin of Gorbachev's perestroïka is the need to reverse the decline of the Communist system if the Soviet Union is to remain a world power.

Thus it is not we who need to modernize our thinking. Our policy has never been guided by the spirit of confrontation. We have never been driven by the image of an enemy, and certainly are not today.

For all these reasons I passionately disagree with those who say that Mr. Gorbachev has the initiative. They confuse day-to-day politics with long-term strategy and the Soviets' "proposal of the week" firework display with true conceptual leadership. The latter lies with NATO, in spite of all the voices of doubt, and it will remain with us.

Our vision of the world in the year 2000 is clear in its fundamentals:
1. A global order founded on respect for the rights of peoples and individuals and characterized by the spirit of peaceful co-operation, in which the industrial nations of East and West can combine forces with the peoples of the Third World to resolve the great problems of humanity.
2. A new pattern of East-West relations bringing co-operation and peaceful competition in the place of confrontation and ideological

and military antagonism, reducing military potentials, opening borders and ultimately ending the division of Europe and Germany. The aim is a peaceful European system which guarantees individual freedom and the right of national self-determination.

3. Further development of the Western community of shared values and destiny embodied by the Atlantic Alliance, working towards a mature partnership in which a united Western Europe plays a role in accordance with its strength, bears a fair share of the common burden and of global responsibilities. Without the strength and stability of a continuing Atlantic security system neither these long-term visions nor the goals of the immediate future can be achieved. In the coming decade the Atlantic Alliance and the dynamic of the European unification will remain the driving forces of world political developments.

There will be better prospects for peace and freedom in the last decade of the 20th century than ever before. Twenty-five years ago Hannah Arendt wrote that wars and revolutions had up to then given the 20th century its distinct shape. Today, in 1989, there are encouraging signs of hope.

The guns have fallen silent in the Iran-Iraq war. Soviet troops have begun to leave Afghanistan, and we expect and demand that they will pull out completely according to plan. Cuban troops are now leaving Angola. In Indo-China the occupying forces of Vietnam are being reduced. The tensions between the United States and the Soviet Union, and between the Soviet Union and China, are easing. North and South Korea have begun a dialogue. Diplomacy has made progress in the attempt to resolve the Western Sahara conflict, and the PLO has unreservedly accepted United Nations' Resolutions 242 and 338.

Of course there are still many question marks, and setbacks cannot be excluded. But, in general, the historical lesson that times of radical change are also times of opportunity is proving to be true. By the same token, these times offer those with a clear vision and the strength of will the chance to shape the future. NATO is set on doing so. We willed the change. We made a crucial contribution to bringing it about. We do not fear it, but are determined to seize every opportunity and not to remain suspicious and passive.

Our hand is outstretched. We are prepared for a decisive improvement in East-West relations and for extensive disarmament. We want dynamism and not statics, unity and not division, open doors and not walls.

With Mr. Gorbachev and his perestroïka policy the chances of reshaping East-West relations have improved substantially. There is no doubt about that. There is also no doubt that we have an interest in success in so far as he is opening up Soviet society and politics.

Our readiness to co-operate depends on progress in three areas:
1. human rights and free exchanges;
2. responsible behaviour in foreign policy, involving a contribution to removing tensions in world crisis areas;
3. reduction of military potential.

It is on this basis that we will support Mr. Gorbachev's economic reforms. What we should encourage are economic relations on their own merits: normal business transactions, not subsidized government loans; joint ventures based on sound economic criteria, not politics; enterprise and normal commercial risk, not feather-bedding of inefficient industries. You will all be familiar with that old Chinese proverb: "Give a man a fish and you feed him for a day. Teach a man to fish and you feed him for life". Let us open our universities and business schools to Soviet managers; let our economic planners share their experiences with their Soviet counterparts; let our entrepreneurs tell Soviet industrialists what motivates human endeavour. I believe firmly that the application of modern Western business culture to the Soviet system would in the long run speed the process of genuine reform more than any number of soft loans.

Finally, we are looking for a more constructive Soviet attitude towards world affairs. The Soviet Union must act responsibly in the international arena. After all, the East-West confrontation, however central it may be to those of us who live in this part of the world, is not the only issue affecting humanity.

There is no lack of burning issues in which our common interests are at stake, and where East-West co-operation could be beneficial. Countering terrorism, tackling environmental and energy problems, stopping the international drug trade, relieving the chronic underdevelopment of so much of the world, to name but a few. Also we shall engage the Soviet Union in discussions regarding those stubborn political problems that make some of the world's trouble spots so explosive, and where, once again, it is in the interest of both East and West that we seek a solution to these problems.

It is clear from our political goals that the Alliance challenges the present *status quo*. This *status quo* not only denies freedom and justice to the peoples of Eastern Europe; it also, and despite forty years of peace, still does not guarantee Western Europeans security on their own territory. Weapons are the reflection and not the cause of the East-West confrontation. This is beyond doubt. But it is also true that our political goals cannot be realized until the military instability that threatens peace in Europe is removed. Here too we have a clear vision of the direction in which we wish to go.

We are striving for a European continent where military forces exist only to prevent war and to ensure self-defence, not for the purpose of initiating aggression or for political and military intimidation. Our goal is a Europe in which recourse to the use of force is no longer an option.

Our NATO forces are already structured to reflect these peaceful principles. The major threat to stability comes as a result from the preponderance of forces on the Eastern side. And Soviet forces, in particular, are concentrated in such a way that we cannot but doubt their strategic intention and their rôle in maintaining the division of Europe.

Indeed, the Soviet Union possesses more tanks and artillery than all the other members of the Warsaw Pact and the Alliance combined. It is these weapons, together with armoured troop carriers, that are ideally suited to large-scale offensive operations with little or no warning time. They can also be used to seize and hold territory. In their current configuration, Soviet forces have the capacity to launch a surprise attack, and to conduct offensive operations against NATO. Military stability thus requires that this dangerous imbalance be corrected. For this reason, we have proposed negotiations on conventional armed forces in Europe. The Soviet Union and its allies have recently agreed to a mandate based almost entirely on NATO's concept.

We have suggested that these talks cover the whole of Europe, from the Atlantic to the Urals, as it is only in this extended zone that reductions and constraints can really make a decisive contribution to stability. When the new talks open next month in Vienna, the Alliance will strive for conventional parity at a substantially lower overall level of forces. This will imply asymmetrical reductions by the side with superior numbers in the force categories under discussion. As reduced numbers in themselves do not necessarily produce greater security, we will also be seeking restrictions on the location, nationality and state of readiness of those forces that will be allowed to remain in Europe once an agreement has been concluded. Above all, we will be seeking to restrict active units.

Aggression cannot be launched without the prior concentration of offensive equipment. Therefore, we will seek overall limits on the total holdings of equipment. Let us, for example, look at tanks. We propose to cut the number of tanks in Europe roughly in half. Even after Mr. Gorbachev's announced unilateral reductions are completed, the Warsaw Pact will still have 41,000 tanks in active units in Europe - most of which will be Soviet - compared to only 16,000 in active units for the Alliance. In other words, an advantage of 2.5 to 1. As tanks are designed for standing-start and fast-moving operations, this disparity is the one that gives us most cause for concern. Therefore the Alliance has proposed an overall limit of about 40,000 tanks in Europe, of which no one country will be allowed to have more than one-third, or about 12,000 tanks.

But tanks, although a major concern, are not the only items we are looking to restrict. We are seeking similar reductions on other offensive military systems, such as artillery and armoured troop vehicles.

Finally, we shall require a rigorous and reliable régime for verifying future agreements. This must include the periodic exchange of detailed data about forces and deployments and the right to conduct on-site inspections.

It should be clear from my comments so far that the Alliance whole-heartedly welcomes these forthcoming negotiations. The continuation of the present security imbalance in Europe can only bring the seeds of military instability.

The Allies have devoted two years of painstaking work to formulating our concept of conventional stability in Europe, and to developing our proposals. We are convinced that our approach is not only practical, but indeed the **only** concept that will achieve this objective. Our task now is to persuade the Soviet Union to agree to our concept, and to restructure its forces along the lines we have suggested.

Although we are accustomed to disappointment, there are indications from the Soviet Union that this may not be a forlorn hope. In recent weeks, leaders of Warsaw Pact states have announced unilateral reductions, and an intention to begin soon withdrawing certain units from Eastern Europe. These unilateral reductions are obviously welcome.

We have been pointing out for years that the Soviet Union has such an overwhelming superiority in conventional forces that it can afford to reduce without endangering its security. We can thus take some hope from the fact that the Soviet Union is now talking of the principle of asymmetrical reductions to parity; that it will withdraw at least some of its offensive military equipment from Eastern Europe; and that it now suggests restructuring its forces for defensive purposes only. But at the same time we do not yet have enough information regarding long-term Soviet intentions to evaluate with any confidence the significance of these unilateral reductions.

Furthermore, it is a fact that the Soviet Union will have, even after the reductions are complete, a substantial offensive capability against the West. Unilateral concessions can be unilaterally cancelled. In the absence of agreed verification measures, we will have no means of knowing when or if this happens.

However, we can also hope that, in announcing these reductions, the Soviet Union genuinely desires to improve East-West relations, and sees its initiative as a first step in renouncing an offensive force posture.

Is the glass half full or half empty? On the basis of the available evidence, we cannot say which view is more justified. The unilateral reductions suggest a new Soviet policy, but they do not confirm it. There are questions that must be asked.

First, we must learn what will happen to the other items of offensive equipment - such as armoured troop carriers - that Mr. Gorbachev has not mentioned so far. We will need to focus on all the equipment that can be considered as invasion assets, and which the Soviet Union has integrated into its concept of combined arms operations.

Second, we will ask questions about the logistical supporting structure that the Soviet Union has established in Europe to sustain an offensive operation. I am thinking of forward supply depots, stockpiles of equipment and spare parts, and ammunition dumps. We cannot assume that Soviet divisions have been disbanded until these logistical facilities are disbanded too.

Third, we will need to find out more about Soviet plans for the Western military districts of the Soviet Union. These areas are sufficiently close to the West to be used as a jumping off point in a reinforced attack. It seems from recent Soviet reductions that some of the troop reductions will be from the Western military districts. But given the importance of this area, we must ask the Soviet Union for more details.

Fourth, the Soviets recently announced a modest reduction in Soviet military production. But we must remember the high level from which they start. Even if carried out, this in itself will not have much impact on the current enormous output of Soviet tanks and artillery pieces. So how can we be sure that all the offensive equipment to be withdrawn will not be replaced by modernized versions in the near future, and which can always be introduced into Eastern Europe later on?

Fifth, our assessment of the announced reductions will also depend on the quality of the equipment to be eliminated. We want to see whether it includes the modern, operational materials, instead of outdated reserves.

Sixth, and finally, we will need more details on the Soviet conception of "defensive defence". What exactly does the Soviet leadership have in mind, and how can we verify these new "defensive" units to ensure that they no longer can attain strategic objectives on our territory?

While the West is pressing these considerations, the talks on conventional armed forces in Europe will be underway in Vienna. Our attention is now fully focussed on these negotiations, and rightly so. It is in Vienna that the real conditions for military stability in Europe will be discussed. We must insist on a comprehensive system of agreed restraints and limitations in which we can have total confidence, as it will be applied by all, in the interest of all. Unilateral measures are no substitute for the hard bargaining that lies ahead.

Therefore, although I am interested in learning more about the Soviet reductions, my most immmediate concern is to have the reaction of the Soviet Union to **our** proposals. Is the Soviet Union ready to accept the restrictions on tanks, artillery and armoured troop carriers that we will put forward? Is it ready to accept limits on the stationing of its forces outside its national territory? Will it agree to our ideas for stringent verification? In short, will it agree to these first essential steps on the way to achieving lasting conventional stability in Europe?

The period of historical flux which we are living through brings risks as well as opportunities.

Progress with nuclear arms control stands in contrast to the spread of chemical weapons and missile technology, against the background of the population explosion and structural poverty and hunger in the developing countries. Dangerous international imbalances and the excessive debts of some Third World countries are marking the transition to a global economic order. The democracies are still threatened by terrorism, the international drug trade and persistent military asymmetries.

Political, ethnic and religious conflicts in many trouble spots ensure that the world is still not at peace. Even the Soviet reform process is by no means irreversible. Mr. Gorbachev is indeed firmly ensconced at the helm but his problems have not gone away. The gap between increasing political and social openness and economic stagnation and failure is widening.

The reform process has unleashed forces among the different ethnic groupings and in the satellite countries which it will be difficult for the Soviet Union to manage. We cannot yet tell whether Mr. Gorbachev will win through. We can only hope so. There is no certainty. Nobody can say what policy would be followed were he to fail.

We should also not lose sight of the following facts:

1. The Soviet Union is continuing to modernize its weapons;
2. The Warsaw Pact still has military superiority in Europe;
3. Even after the cutbacks in the defence budget which have now been announced, the Soviet Union will still spend more than 13% of its gross national product on armaments;
4. We have no certainty about future production rates of weapons, for example, tanks. Even if production is reduced by 19.5%, as announced, the Soviet output of tanks will still be 2,600 a year.

This situation requires us to have not merely the courage to face change but also steadfastness and loyal adherence to the proven principles of our policy. The Harmel concept is not out of date, and our flexible response strategy cannot be called into question, if only because for decades it has perfectly fulfilled its purpose of preventing war. Above all, it would be a disastrous mistake to neglect our defence precisely at a time of radical historical change, and thus to tear down that wall which protects us from attempts to solve problems by force. We cannot entrust our security to one person alone or to intentions. Both can change overnight. What counts is the other side's potential. That is what must guide our efforts for defence. Any Soviet politician - whether he be Mr. Gorbachev's successor or rival - must know that, whatever happens in the Soviet Union, the option of a military solution to Moscow's problems remains barred, so that there is no alternative to a policy of peaceful internal reform.

So there are three conditions for our future success.

First, we must maintain an effective defence. It is vital that we maintain the combat strength and readiness of our Allied military forces, particularly in view of the forthcoming disarmament negotiations. Any unilateral reduction on the side of the clearly weaker party must further restrict our negotiating room, making multilateral disarmament less probable.

Second, we must remain united. Alliance solidarity, arrived at through extensive negotiations and adhered to steadfastly at the conference table, has forged the new opening in East-West relations. Concertation of the political approaches of the sixteen Allies is the life-blood of NATO.

If we are to preserve Allied unity, we must be serious about equitable burden-sharing. We must tackle it energetically and ultimately find the right solution. It is also vital that we maintain a spirit of Atlantic solidarity to help us to resolve the points of economic conflict between Americans and Europeans which spring partly from the prospect of 1992. We must not allow economic rivalry to have a prejudicial effect on Alliance solidarity in the field of security policy. Therefore we must do everything to resist moves towards protection-ism on either side of the Atlantic. We can afford neither a "fortress Europe" nor a "USA in splendid isolation".

Last but not least, we need the continuing support of our publics. We know from opinion polls that the Alliance is considered to be essential by the large majority of our citizens. But support for our objectives does not equally mean support for the burdens of our daily defence. This situation calls for strong leadership if we are to keep public expectations within hopeful but realistic bounds.

The three challenges that I have described are serious ones; but they are the problems of our success, and we can meet them if we continue to have the courage of our convictions. On the other hand, Mr. Gorbachev faces challenges of a totally different dimension, for the problems of the Soviet Union are the problems of decline and misguided policies. They cannot be solved by economic reform alone but only by a transformation of the political system. We wish Mr. Gorbachev well with this herculean task. But let us not base our policy on the assumption that, because we hope for the best, the best will automatically happen. This is not the time to lower our guard.

With change finally coming to the East, the Allies will face issues that are more complex than anything we have known in the past. At the same time, the potential for success is greater than what we had come to expect. The Alliance is the essential medium through which a more humane, just and secure peace can be achieved in Europe.

The opportunities that we face today are proof of the wisdom - and the vision - of those Western statesmen who came together in Washington forty years ago. They did not know how long it would take us to complete our task, and I cannot today make a prediction either; but at least they mapped out for us a path that history has shown to be the right one. Let us pursue this path with confidence and vigour.

I am optimistic as I look towards the future. Our societies are more flexible and creative. Our economic structures are more successful. Our social systems are more just and our thinking is more attuned to humanity's concerns.

The future Tasks of the Alliance

SPEECH TO
THE QUADRANGULAR
FORUM

Brussels
1 April
1989

I am experiencing the fortieth anniversary of NATO rather like the manager of a successful football team which has just won the league title. His initial instinct is to celebrate the season's glories. But instead his mind is inevitably on the team's promotion to the higher division. How will the team cope with the new, more demanding environment where not only the rewards, but also the challenges, are so much greater? Such is life. The more successful we are; the more new tasks we find ourselves taking on.

At least our football manager knows that in the new division, the rules of the game will be the same. But this familiar reference point is denied us. In our case, the goalposts of East-West relations have clearly moved. The suppositions on which our Alliance policy has been based for the past four decades have not so much disappeared, as become blurred. As a result we can confidently state that the old, post-war European order is on its way out; but not so fast that we can yet distinguish the contours of the new as it appears in the distance.

Let us take, for instance, the two factors that were uppermost in the minds of our founding fathers forty years ago: the Communist challenge to Western liberalism and the threat of Soviet national power politics based on military strength.

The ideological attraction of communism is now at its lowest ebb since the publication of the Communist Manifesto nearly 150 years ago: on all fronts, the Western world, the developing world, Eastern Europe and the Soviet Union. The issue we face now is not the irrepressible advance of communism but its irrepressible retreat. It was our economic recovery in the

1950s that caused the demise of communism in the West; paradoxically it is the absence of such an economic recovery in the East which is today discrediting this socio-economic model.

Regimes that once based their political legitimacy on the denunciation of Western values now seek their salvation in them. While the leaders hope to rescue the Communist system through well-controlled reform, they are caught up in a dynamic of change that makes the outcome of their efforts highly unpredictable. Once the process of political evolution is under way, it may well be impossible for those leaders to stop at half-way measures. More open and pluralistic Communist parties subject to elections and parliamentary control will help reform. Yet this may well make it more manifest that only genuine pluralism and real choice will release the creative energies that moral and economic regeneration demands. Like Christopher Columbus, the Communist leaders may well be setting sail for a destination in the East only to end up in the West.

Yet we can be relatively optimistic about this current bout of Communist soul-searching. In its quest for growth, the East will need to import our values as much as our technology. It must also find ways to integrate its economies into the international trading system through participation in our Western economic and financial institutions. We will therefore have more influence over the domestic evolution of these societies than we have enjoyed in the past. The only useful type of revolution is the revolution in mentalities, and this is what we see beginning today among many decision-makers in the ruling Communist élites. It bodes well for political as well as economic change in the East, and for reform based on consensus rather than diktat.

The shift in the other goalpost, that of Soviet power politics based on military strength, is more difficult to evaluate. Mr. Gorbachev has now been in power for more than four years but we are really none the wiser regarding long-term Soviet plans. The leadership would now appear to accept what we have been telling them for years: that to attempt to achieve security through superior military means and political intimidation only produces more insecurity - for the Soviet Union as well as for everyone else. The unilateral reductions announced so far, together with a constructive approach to the negotiations on conventional forces in Europe - for instance in acknowledging the asymmetries in their favour - give us grounds for hope. But there are no sufficient indications that the Soviet Union is preparing to give up its favourable "correlation of forces", let alone reduce to a point where it would no longer threaten its European neighbours. Soviet forces out of Eastern Europe and back within Soviet borders will enhance our security; but as long as they exceed the minimal levels needed for national defence and the preservation of sovereignty, they will still be a major factor in East-West relations which we will have to match. So on this topic, I am cautious. The road to Vienna has been a long and arduous one, but the road leading from it to true military stability in Europe will be even more so.

These moving goalposts have led some observers to say that the *raison d'être* of the Alliance is being called into question, and to predict all kinds of trouble for the Alliance in a situation of change. I have never believed that it was either possible or desirable for us to cling to the *status quo*. Equally, I do not believe that the opportunities we have today are the result of a fortunate historical accident. We have these opportunities because of the dynamics of European unification and Western co-operation in an Alliance of free societies that believes in common security, economic prosperity and social progress. Perhaps the ultimate collapse of communism would be inevitable because of its internal contradictions. But this process has certainly been accelerated because of the rate of change in the West in the past decade. Recognizing the virtues of freedom and creativity, we have liberalized our economies and embraced new technologies and working practices. We have striven to remove barriers to free trade, as in the agreement between the United States and Canada and in the European Community's programme for the internal market of 1992. Our flexible and innovative societies not only cope with change but welcome it. Our peoples adapt because they know the result will be more prosperity, and thus more opportunity for individual self-fulfilment. Communist societies, on the other hand, not only see the West pull ahead, but discover that their own rigid structures make it virtually impossible for them to catch up.

Whatever the distortions of nostalgia, I do not accept that the old world of Cold War diplomacy was as safe and predictable as is assumed now, when we are fascinated with the new. Nor is order, as such, a goal to be pursued at all costs, especially when it is at the price of repression and injustice. The military stand-off of the past may have preserved the peace, but it did not - and indeed could not - remove the sources of tension and instability. Nor could political dialogue do so if it remained premissed on an eternally divided Europe. There can be no lasting peace which is not founded on justice; and for this our liberal values must be universally recognized. The mission of the Alliance is not inward-looking - only to safeguard its own security; it is outward-looking - to spread freedom, justice and security to the wider world. Only in this way can our own security genuinely be preserved over time.

Thus I see the present juncture as a great opportunity for us to move beyond the qualified and untidy peace of the past towards a new order of peace based on sturdier and more durable foundations. This can come about only as the result of a new pattern of East-West relations where co-operation and peaceful competition overtake confrontation, and ideological and military antagonism. We strive to reduce military potentials, open borders and ultimately end the division of Europe and Germany.

Conscious and deliberate change - as opposed to the spontaneous, chaotic sort - is the hardest of all human tasks. How can we establish the framework to encourage further this long overdue process of change, while channelling it towards constructive objectives?

Clearly NATO will have to perform two functions more or less simultaneously: to act as a magnetic pole of stability and reassurance on which the new forces of change can anchor themselves; and to promote change by encouraging, supporting and actively co-operating with those forces in the East working for a transformation of their societies towards our objectives. In this process we must distinguish between what we can reasonably contribute and what is, for the time being at least, beyond our power to control. Let me discuss each of these functions in turn.

NATO has always been a stabilizing force in East-West relations. We have transformed a potentially explosive situation in Europe, based on an ideological threat and a stark imbalance of conventional military power, into the most rationally-conceived and accident-free security system that the world has ever known. Over the years we have defused many crises and prevented untold others. Yet we have never done this in the name of upholding the *status quo*. And we have never seen change purely in terms of accommodating ourselves to the inevitable while hoping to preserve the old East-West balance in its essential features.

The crucial role of the Alliance is to preserve what has already proved a triumphant success: to provide the conditions of confident security in which change in Western Europe and a wider Europe can take place at its own rhythm. Of course: we need a vision of the future Europe which includes Eastern Europe: a Europe in which all citizens enjoy individual freedom and all peoples self-determination, one which would be embedded in a new security framework in which the democracies of North America would still play an essential role, and to which the Soviet Union would be committed. I am reluctant however to believe that we need some institutional master plan. I tend to think of the example of a medieval cathedral. Only very few were designed by a single architect. Most were designed over centuries, molded to the sensibilities and realities of changing times. These are often the most impressive.

We can and should try to influence events and lead the mainstream of history in our direction. I very much understand and am sympathetic with imaginative efforts and designs for the future. And, of course, we have to discuss the future of Eastern Europe with the Soviet Union. We will continue to respect legitimate Soviet security interests. But we cannot, and should not, try to patronise developments in the East. We can open ways and create opportunities, and encourage these countries to make the hard choices which they and they alone must make for themselves. We wish evolution not revolution, diversification not destabilization. But it is not our task, nor within our possibilities, to control the course of events there; neither by ourselves, nor with the USSR in a new Yalta-type settlement based on fixed zones of influence. The concessions we could expect from such an agreement would not solve the deep-rooted problems of Eastern Europe, nor those of East-West relations more broadly. Change, on the basis of our values and goals, is already under way and accelerating. While the West and East may try to harmonize views on this, neither we - nor they - could have faith in an agreement which might control the pace of change in the short term, only to see magnified turmoil return to haunt us later. Stability is necessary to create the conditions for peaceful change, not frustrate it.

To function optimally, **our** stabilizing role must be based on an adequate defence. This can only have a deterrent function if it includes a nuclear component. Forty years ago the nuclear weapon was the ultimate war-fighting weapon. NATO has transformed it into the ultimate peace-keeping instrument. Our security concept extends its protection to all the members of our Alliance whether they are nuclear powers or not. Nuclear deterrence is the bedrock of our security. In preserving peace it also serves Soviet interests. It is incumbent on the Soviet Union to recognize this fact and to accept the concept of stable nuclear deterrence, and to restructure its own nuclear forces, down to minimal levels.

I strongly dispute recent claims by Soviet leaders that NATO's nuclear weapons in Europe are a gesture of hostility and an obstacle to the Vienna negotiations. Such considerations, after all, have not prevented the Soviet Union from completing its own modernization of a far greater number of such weapons in recent years.

Yet a robust defence is not required only for abstract deterrence. We have to consider the possibility - however much we wish otherwise - that reform in the East will go wrong, and that the Soviet leadership, present or future, will come under intense pressure. It will remain for some time to come a small leadership, in absolute control, and thus liable to change course unpredictably. Should we allow our defences to rust away, a stressed Soviet leadership might be tempted to abandon an approach that we have finally persuaded them to take, and to return to political intimidation. This failed to work in the past, but we must never give the Kremlin the impression that it could yet work in the future.

Moreover, we can only exercise a stabilizing function if we are ourselves stable. We must remain united and not allow a diminishing Soviet military threat to make us inward-looking or exaggerate our intra-Alliance economic problems. We are a role model for the East; by maintaining the momentum of Western European unification and transatlantic partnership we are forcing the pace of change and bringing closer the day when the division of Europe can be overcome. So let us not snatch defeat from the jaws of victory by allowing such issues as burden-sharing, protectionism or fiscal policy to divide us.

Certainly we will also need to adapt ourselves to our new tasks. A stronger Western Europe that can play its full part in the defence of this Alliance, as well as in our common Western global responsibilities, is a necessity. We are already taking a fresh look at how we can best use our precious resources and share our respective roles and burdens equitably. But let us not exaggerate these challenges; they are no greater than those we have faced successfully in the past. Indeed they are the consequence of the success of this Alliance.

On this foundation we can enhance East-West co-operation and move change along. There are many aspects, but the East's economic difficulties cry out for priority attention. The question of how the West can and should co-operate with the East is a complex one; but at least let me suggest here, and simply by way of example, some possibilities that we can consider.

Obviously only the East can solve its own economic problems by introducing reforms - political as well as economic - that tackle the roots and not just the symptoms of its current malaise. Yet provided the current momentum of reform is maintained, the East will find in us a constructive partner. For instance, the East as a trading bloc has so far been only weakly connected with the world economy. Thus there is potential for integrating it more into our trading system. We can consider expanding joint ventures. A number of these have been established in East European countries and they already exceed one hundred and sixty in the Soviet Union. To be successful, Eastern structures must be changed, and market forces engaged. This will be even more painful and difficult than in the West.

We also have a common interest in closer co-operation in the domain of environmental protection and anti-pollution policies. Subject to the necessary safeguards, the West can perhaps assist its Eastern neighbours with developing pollution-control equipment and practices that will enable them to make their production techniques cleaner and safer.

Another promising area of economic co-operation concerns the whole domain of energy saving and corresponding investment policies.

What is certainly very important is to help the East in offering formation programmes for managers, bankers or post-graduates so that they can acquire Western-type entrepreneurial skills. This could be done bilaterally or on a multilateral basis with the help of international organizations.

Yet there is a sticking point in this improving picture of East-West co-operation: human rights. I do not contest that there have been significant gains - in emigration, freedom of expression, the rehabilitation of the past. We have seen the East agree to significant new undertakings in the final document to the latest round of the CSCE in Vienna; the Soviet Union decide to abide by the rulings of the International Court of Justice as regards a number of humanitarian treaties; and even East criticize East in the United Nations Commission on Human Rights in Geneva. But the glass which is half full all too frequently reminds me of the other, empty half. Young men shot on a not so porous Berlin Wall; a playwright of international renown jailed for taking part in a demonstration; villages systematically bulldozed into the ground to solve minority dissent.

Observance of human rights is not just a moral imperative; it is also a practical one. The states of Eastern Europe cannot extricate themselves from their current morass by measures from the top down that have little or no popular support. Reform must be based on a true social dialogue and the willingness of the populations to do what is necessary to rebuild their societies. Yet no response will be forthcoming if basic human rights and freedoms continue to be denied or granted only at the discretion of governments; instead they must be anchored in law and institutions.

The future is an open book. Into it we write our hopes for what the world will look like in the year 2000, but also our more realistic expectations. There is no contradiction here. Unless we seek the best, we will undoubtedly never come close to achieving it. And if there is one lesson from the past forty years of this Alliance, it is that with courage and conviction visions can indeed be turned into realities. In 1949 there was nothing inevitable about Western European recovery, the permanent involvement of the United States in world affairs and the Soviet Union seeking accommodation with the West. Yet a group of leaders saw the situation less in terms of obstacles than of possibilities. It was their vision that allowed them to shape events and turn around a situation that at one stage looked very bleak.

Today we are operating in much more favourable historical circumstances, but the same human qualities will still prove decisive. Our task, to function both as an anchor of stability and an instrument of change, will not be easy. We will have to cope with the inevitable setbacks we will encounter on our path, and adjust course. But I am and will remain optimistic. I count on you. You all have proven wisdom and priceless experience. So many of you have already played a major role in the success story that I have described. As we now progress from the league of peace-keeping to the league of peace-building, let us all recall the dogged perseverance and the team spirit that won us our victories, and that make us firm favourites for the future.

□

40th Anniversary of NATO

ADDRESS TO THE NORTH ATLANTIC COUNCIL [1]

Brussels
4 April
1989

With our Atlantic Alliance being 40 years old today we celebrate not only an institution but much more a vision: that of peace in freedom. This is what NATO has given us: the longest period of general peace that Europe has enjoyed since the days of the Roman Empire. Our citizens have experienced these years not only as ones of security but also of prosperity and social progress. Protected by this Alliance - the most successful in history - they face the future not with fear but with confidence.

So assured does our peace today seem that it is hard for us to imagine that it could once have been otherwise. Yet if we look back for just one moment to the year of the signing of the Washington Treaty, 1949, we can measure how much has been achieved, and how quickly. Then our continent lay in ruins. Economic recovery proceeded at a snail's pace. The prevalent mood was one of exhaustion and discouragement. With democracy struggling to recover from the traumas of war and occupation, the field was open to political extremism of all kinds. The future looked bleak. The Soviet Union cast the shadow of its military power across the whole of Europe. Even the most optimistic observer could not guarantee that in such conditions Western Europe would not also become the same victim of Soviet expansionism and intimidation as its Eastern counterpart.

More than any other instance of post-war Western co-operation, NATO was responsible for Western Europe's moral and economic resurrection. Within ten years an apparently hopeless situation was transformed. The United States, emerging from World War II as a superpower, known before that period for its isolationism, had committed its destiny to the defence of our common freedoms. *Pax Atlantica* was born. Under

1. Address delivered partly in English and partly in French. Discours bilingue en anglais et en français.

43

its roof former European enemies were beginning a bold experiment in political and economic co-operation. Democracy had been revived. The Federal Republic of Germany had found a framework whereby it could anchor itself in the West. The threat of an alien ideology had receded from both within and without our borders. Marshall aid found a politically stable context where it could be used to full advantage. Pessimism turned to optimism as our citizens once more began to invest in their future.

Without NATO none of these things - let alone all of them - would have happened. The Alliance was from the outset more than just a security pact. It became the expression of a common purpose and a political vision, a community of values and destiny. Within its transatlantic framework of order, the West could carry out its two historic missions. First, to ensure the cohesion and solidarity of our liberal democracies, and second, to function beyond our borders as a stabilizing force in the wider world, providing for security and peaceful change in the interactions of states.

NATO does not lead by military force or by a messianic ideology, but by the attractiveness of its ideas and the force of its example. We know that our security depends ultimately on freedom, prosperity and social justice. This, in turn, is dependent on the maintenance of Alliance solidarity. We form the largest and most prosperous community that the world has ever seen. Our Third Dimension of co-operation in the fields of science and the environment helps us to lay the basis for future prosperity. Not only does this Third Dimension push the frontiers of science outwards, it ensures that new scientific knowledge and methods are shared among all the Allies. We recognize that only freedom and democracy release the creative energies that are inherent in mankind and which are the locomotive of all social progress. Being trading nations we need to compete as well as co-operate with each other. The resulting dynamism is the vehicle of progress, but its innovative force must be properly managed. The organizational genius of the Alliance ensures that this dynamism does not undermine, but reinforces, the system on which we all depend. As a result, the Atlantic has become the vital and unifying space across which advanced societies articulate their common interests and values.

Yet if our vitality comes from within, we must protect it from the threats from without, from challenges to our security from other systems which find our free and democratic way of life and living standards, and not our tanks, a threat to their own survival. For forty years we have faced such a challenge from the Soviet Union, notwithstanding the fact that our Alliance is purely defensive. Moreover our military forces have not and will not exceed the minimal level needed to ensure deterrence and guarantee our sovereignty.

The Alliance has done more, however, than keep the Soviet military threat at bay. We have succeeded in transforming a potentially explosive situation, based on an ideological hostility and a stark imbalance of conventional military power, into the most fail-safe security system that the world has ever seen. Our strategy proves our collective determination to resist aggression. We seek to share the risks as well as the benefits of deterrence as equitably as possible. No member of our Alliance is denied the protection afforded to the strongest. Above all, we have transformed the ultimate war-fighting weapon into the ultimate instrument of peace-keeping. Nuclear deterrence has not merely contained the risk of nuclear war; it has also contained the risk of all war. For this reason it is the bedrock of our security.

Our secure defence has been the key stabilizing force in East-West relations. It has enabled us to defuse all those tensions that in any earlier age could have quite easily led to war. Defence is not a brake on détente. It is the prerequisite of all productive East-West development.

Tout au long de ces quarante dernières années, l'OTAN a suivi avec vigilance ce qu'elle a créé, havre de paix et de prospérité dans un monde troublé et divisé. Nous n'avons cependant jamais eu pour vocation de nous replier sur nous-mêmes, dans l'espoir fallacieux de nous protéger de l'injustice et de l'oppression environnantes. La stabilité a pour but de fournir le cadre d'une évolution pacifique. Nos "pères fondateurs" nous ont fait la promesse que notre persévérance à combiner la défense et le dialogue dans nos relations avec l'Est serait finalement payée de retour, que le régime totalitaire communiste finirait par s'adoucir. En de très nombreuses occasions, l'armement soviétique a été la seule réponse à nos invitations au dialogue, mais nous n'avons jamais perdu courage.

Le changement que nous avons toujours recherché vient enfin de s'amorcer. Nos valeurs et nos idées ont toujours constitué un défi sérieux pour l'Est, or, maintenant, nous les voyons aussi déterminer le rythme et le cours des événements. L'Est se tourne vers l'Ouest. L'Histoire est de notre côté, quelles que soient les affirmations de ceux qui disent incarner les lois de l'Histoire. Les régimes communistes qui, naguère, fondaient leur légitimité sur la dénonciation de nos valeurs occidentales, cherchent maintenant à y adhérer.

L'OTAN entre aujourd'hui dans sa cinquième décennie. Nous savons ce qu'a été l'Alliance dans le passé. Mais que sera-t-elle à l'avenir? Certains disent qu'avec l'affaiblissement de la menace soviétique, l'Alliance a rempli sa mission historique et qu'il lui faut, soit changer, soit disparaître de la scène. Laissez-moi vous dire qu'ils ont tort. Dans un monde en mouvement, notre Alliance n'est pas devenue soudain moins importante : elle a, au contraire, gagné en importance. L'évolution pacifique de l'Ouest comme de l'Est dépend aujourd'hui, plus que jamais, de l'aptitude de l'OTAN à agir comme un pôle magnétique de stabilité et de tranquillité sur lequel les forces nouvelles de changement peuvent venir s'ancrer; mais aussi comme l'instigatrice du changement, en encourageant, appuyant et aidant activement les forces qui, à l'Est, travaillent à la transformation de la société dans le sens de nos objectifs.

Dans le monde de demain, l'OTAN sera de plus en plus un instrument de changement. Notre but est d'obtenir pour tous les Etats de l'Europe un ordre politique juste, qui garantira la paix et le droit des peuples à décider de leur propre évolution politique et sociale. Nous nous efforcerons de bâtir une Europe nouvelle, enracinée dans la communauté de démocraties libres : une Europe où la liberté et le pluralisme politique s'épanouiront, où les forces militaires n'auront pas d'autres rôles que celui de garantir la souveraineté des Etats, permettant ainsi à tous les pays - grands ou petits - de jouir d'une même sécurité. Une Europe, enfin, qui sur la base de l'autodétermination de tous ses peuples sera capable de dépasser les divisions artificielles et celle de l'Allemagne.

Les racines du déclin du communisme sont morales et spirituelles, aussi bien qu'économiques. Dans le vide laissé à l'Est par l'échec historique du communisme, nous pouvons et nous voulons insérer notre propre programme pour l'avenir. Nous avons une occasion exceptionnelle de remodeler les relations Est-Ouest et de favoriser et d'influencer pacifiquement le changement en Europe de l'Est et en Union soviétique par une coopération active. Nous devons exploiter les nouvelles énergies historiques et les mobiliser pour atteindre des objectifs précis, qui feront d'une paix plus juste et durable en Europe un processus irréversible. Enfin, nous devons amener l'Est à s'engager dans des voies nouvelles communes pour aborder les grandes questions du monde.

Sans l'Alliance, cette vision ne serait rien d'autre qu'un rêve coupé de toute réalité. Mais avec l'Alliance, c'est un objectif tout à fait à notre portée. Au cours de cette cinquième décennie, l'OTAN restera l'instrument essentiel pour promouvoir les intérêts occidentaux dans une phase de transition historique. Elle est le catalyseur de la volonté politique du plus grand nombre de démocraties occidentales. Elle seule permet de réunir l'Amérique du Nord et l'Europe occidentale dans l'association transatlantique dont dépend tout progrès substantiel. En effet, ni l'Amérique du Nord ni l'Europe occidentale ne pourraient, isolément, espérer accomplir cette tâche historique. Ce n'est que par le biais de cette Alliance que chacun de nos Etats membres peut espérer apporter sa pleine contribution à ce processus de changement pacifique. Et ce n'est que grâce à cette Alliance que chacun peut se garantir contre les revers ou les échecs éventuels que l'on ne saurait exclure en période de bouleversement historique.

En exploitant toutes les occasions de changement pacifique, l'Alliance restera un garant de la sécurité, un fondement de la stabilité mondiale et une forme d'assurance contre les risques de troubles, de crise et de guerre : l'OTAN demeurera irremplaçable à l'avenir. Prévenir les guerres et sauvegarder la paix, protéger et défendre la liberté resteront ses tâches les plus nobles et les plus importantes. Mais les périodes de changement rapide sont également des périodes de grande incertitude. Il nous a fallu quarante ans pour convaincre l'Est que l'intimidation politique ne peut réussir. Ne donnons pas aux dirigeants soviétiques soumis à diverses tensions l'impression que cela pourrait encore réussir, car nous avons baissé notre garde. Quelle que soit l'équipe au pouvoir en Union soviétique et quelles que soient ses intentions, nous aurons besoin d'un dispositif de défense crédible, qui ne laisse aucune place à l'aventurisme militaire. Là encore, cet objectif ne pourra être atteint que par une alliance transatlantique.

Even if we succeed in transforming the East-West confrontation into peaceful competition, the Soviet Union will remain a huge power, a mighty military force and an important factor in Europe. So we need NATO as a framework to organize and maintain the transatlantic commitment to our collective security on which so much depends.

And I see yet another function of NATO which will be as important in the future as today and as it was in the past: to serve as a forum to balance and reconcile different European and American interests, be it in the political or economic fields. In particular, we will need our Atlantic Alliance to protect the emergence of a Western European identity and to serve as a platform for the redefinition of the respective responsibilities and burdens of Europe and the United States in the global environment of the next decades.

So, without this Alliance, there will be neither stability nor peaceful change. NATO remains the backbone and lighthouse of mankind's future in freedom and peace.

Today the future looks more promising than ever before. The opportunities now outweigh the risks. We have these opportunities because we willed them, and we are not afraid to take advantage of them. But even if the wind of history is blowing in our favour, progress will not be automatic; there will be setbacks and disappointments. So as we look to shape the future, let us remember the five lessons of our past that have served us so well.

That we must adapt our policies to new tasks. Our political strategy of defence and détente and our military strategy both remain valid. But the means we use to implement them will require readjustment from time to time. We will be working towards a stronger Western Europe that can play its full part in the defence of this Alliance as well as in our common Western global responsibilities. We are already taking a fresh look at how we can best use our precious resources and share our respective rôles and burdens equitably. But let us not exaggerate these challenges; they are no greater than those we have faced successfully in the past. Indeed they are the consequence of the success of this Alliance.

That we maintain our political solidarity and cohesion. As long as we stand together, there is no force in this world stronger than this Alliance. United we will remain masters of our destiny. Divided we shall become victims of historical developments decided by others.

That we must maintain a credible deterrent. For the foreseeable future this will require both a nuclear and conventional component. We only want the minimum number of weapons necessary for purely defensive purposes, but this minimum has to be kept up to date.

That we must continue to have the active support of our publics. Like all democratic institutions the Alliance is ultimately for their benefit. Our publics overwhelmingly wish NATO to continue; that much is certain. But voters in parliamentary democracies all too frequently support the ends of policy while being reluctant to provide the necessary means. It is our task to convince them that in reality they are asked to pay only the smallest price for the greatest of all human benefits - peace in freedom.

That we maintain principled, conceptual leadership. It is not for us to match the unilateral reductions of the Warsaw Pact, which enjoys the fruits of overarming for decades. But we are providing the conceptual leadership in disarmament negotiations aiming at greater military stability and, in particular, more equal ceilings and at lower levels than we both have today. We are the moving force behind progress in human rights. We have the one valid vision for a just and lasting peace in Europe. And we have the concepts to make that vision possible.

Our security seems so natural that we sometimes fail to realise just how many men and women in all of our sixteen countries are involved in upholding it. Whether soldiers, airmen and sailors maintaining their permanent vigil or civilians ensuring that our Alliance functions efficiently: there is a whole NATO family of people, past and present, who have selflessly dedicated themselves to our cause. They are the architects of peace in freedom and all of them deserve our thanks and gratitude, as does also the government and people of Belgium for providing such a welcoming home to our Alliance institutions for more than two decades now.

All of us who are associated with this great vision today have a necessary part to play in achieving it in the future. Forty years ago our founding fathers demonstrated that with courage and conviction visions can indeed become realities. Today, in much more favourable historical circumstances, let us also have a similar vision and purpose. It is we who are privileged to have this task - and this opportunity - to achieve a just and lasting peace in a Europe freed forever from the harness of dogma and the shadow of the gun.

☐

*O*pening address to the North Atlantic Council Meeting at the level of Heads of State and Government

Brussels
29 May
1989

It is my honour and privilege to open this meeting of the North Atlantic Council at the level of Heads of State and Government. Allow me to extend a warm welcome to all participants.

We are meeting in fascinating times of change. We are confronted with the challenges of our success. This is even more obvious today than at the last NATO Summit, fifteen months ago. We can take particular pride in our accomplishments since that time, including the successful conclusion of the Vienna CSCE meeting, and the promising start of the important talks on conventional arms control in Vienna.

In recent weeks our fortieth anniversary celebrations have given us the opportunity to look back. Today is the time for us to look forward; not only to evaluate the significance of the change we see all around us, but to further define a future course for this Alliance.

This is a time that bears the hallmark of our success. NATO has given us peace - the longest European peace since Roman times. It has also opened prospects for change. The East is turning to the West. One hundred and fifty years after the Communist Manifesto, communism has manifestly failed. Outdated ideology and inefficiency stand in stark contrast to our values and concepts, and the responsiveness of our system to human aspirations. Events follow our conceptual leadership and will continue to do so if we maintain our initiative.

We are living through a time of great opportunity, but one accompanied also by considerable potential risk. Historical turning points always combine both elements - and both require equal skill in management. Without prejudging the future, I think we can say that the post-war world, as we have known it, is coming to an end. Now is the time to combine the lessons we have learned and our success with the possibilities we see opening up to advance our ambitious agenda.

Our opportunity is to bring the world closer to our vision: open borders, more freedom, less weapons and the rule of law. A Europe undivided in which all citizens enjoy their human rights and all peoples can exercise their right of self-determination. A global order not of confrontation, but of co-operation between West and East to solve the pressing problems of mankind. This Alliance has never been static. It was always dynamic, its objective remains to overcome the *status quo*, while preserving our hard-won peace and freedom.

The risk we have to guard against is complacency. Historic periods of deep change, such as we are living through, inevitably produce uncertainty, fragility and instability. We need to maintain the base of our stability, a secure defence. Above all we cannot, at the moment when long-sought achievements seem to be coming within our grasp, afford to lower our guard.

Let us keep both opportunity and risk in balanced perspective, and not make the mistake of focusing only on the one or the other. For it is the dual nature of our historical challenge that clearly defines the future role and tasks of the Alliance.

On the one hand, our task is actively to shape events. We not only welcome change in the Soviet Union and Eastern Europe, we will encourage and make full use of it. We will offer the East our co-operation and continuing impetus and incentives to reform. Our model shows them the way to greater prosperity and security, over time. We will reward those who have the courage to make hard choices. But in return we challenge the Eastern leaders on the political ground and across the whole range of our common concerns - from human rights and open societies to less weapons. With our policies and concepts now bearing fruit, the political role of this Alliance will come into its full dimension as never before.

On the other hand, it would be foolhardy of us to abandon the only safe and secure ground on which we can stand: the proven record of success and the invaluable experience of common effort within this Alliance. It is the strongest community - morally, politically, economically, militarily - that the West in all its long history has ever known.

To this end we must maintain a strong defence and a firm, reliable posture of deterrence. Even with the most optimistic outcome of developments in East-West relations, we will face, for many years to come, a formidable and unpredictable military power as our neighbour. We do not need permanently to suspect his intentions; but intentions cannot be a durable basis for our relationship. We cannot build our own security on the assumption of his permanent goodwill. Indeed, we owe it to our peoples, and to history, to sustain our effort to make the recourse to military strength, to preserve stability and deterrence.

We need to provide conventional and nuclear weapons at a level which supports the indivisibility of our Alliance security. Nuclear weapons are the ultimate guarantor of a war prevention strategy. Conventional weapons have a bad historical record in this respect. Certainly we want to reduce weapons - both nuclear and conventional - in East and West, to the minimum which the legitimate security interest of East and West requires. Time and again, we have demonstrated this in deeds. Both our defence plans and our approach to arms control are predicted on this fundamental principle. And the minimal levels which we need must be kept up-to-date.

A healthy transatlantic relationship is today, as it has always been, the cornerstone of both our security and a model for human aspirations. Thus we must reinforce it still further; develop it into the most equal and balanced form of transatlantic partnership. We must continue to look afresh at the distribution of roles, risks and responsibilities within our Alliance and encourage the European pillar to evolve in line with Western Europe's emerging political and economic strength.

The key to successful management of East-West relations is the successful management of West-West relations. Only if we remain united will we determine events; divided, even with all our success and dynamism, we will be the victims of events determined by others - all of us, without exception.

I look to your wisdom, courage and statesmanship in leading our Alliance into a fifth decade of even greater achievements. I know that you will not allow us to squander our unique historic opportunity. And how indeed could we fail? For it is our societies that are the most open and dynamic, our economies that are the most prosperous, our peoples the most creative, and our values that inspire the cry of freedom throughout the non-Western world. So there is good reason to look toward our fiftieth anniversary with optimism and confidence.

□

Discours d'ouverture à la Réunion du Conseil de l'Atlantique Nord au niveau des Chefs d'Etat et de Gouvernement

Bruxelles
29 mai
1989

C'est pour moi un honneur et un privilège que d'ouvrir cette réunion du Conseil de l'Atlantique Nord au niveau des Chefs d'Etat et de gouvernement. Qu'il me soit d'abord permis de souhaiter chaleureusement la bienvenue à tous les participants.

Notre réunion se situe dans une période de changement tout à fait passionnante. Nous sommes confrontés aux défis nés de notre propre succès. C'est là une réalité encore plus évidente aujourd'hui qu'au dernier Sommet de l'OTAN, il y a quinze mois. Nous pouvons être particulièrement fiers de ce que nous avons accompli depuis cette époque, notamment de l'heureuse conclusion de la conférence de Vienne sur la CSCE et des débuts prometteurs des importants pourparlers de Vienne sur la maîtrise des armements conventionnels.

Ces dernières semaines, la célébration de notre quarantième anniversaire a été pour nous l'occasion de jeter un regard sur le passé. Aujourd'hui, le moment est venu de nous tourner vers l'avenir, non seulement pour évaluer la portée du changement que nous observons tout autour de nous, mais aussi pour définir plus avant la voie que notre Alliance va devoir suivre.

Nous vivons des temps qui portent la marque de notre succès. L'OTAN nous a donné la paix - la plus longue paix en Europe depuis l'époque des Romains. Elle a aussi ouvert des perspectives de changement. L'Est se tourne vers l'Ouest. Cent cinquante ans après le Manifeste communiste, le communisme a manisfestement échoué. Son idéologie d'un autre âge et son inefficacité contrastent de façon saisissante avec nos valeurs et nos conceptions, de même qu'avec notre système, qui permet de répondre aux aspirations des hommes. Les événements suivent

53

la direction que nous avons conçue, et ils la suivront encore si nous maintenons notre initiative.

Nous traversons une période qui présente de grandes possibilités, mais aussi des risques potentiels considérables. Ces deux éléments se retrouvent à tous les tournants de l'Histoire, et tous deux exigent une gestion d'une égale habileté. Sans préjuger de l'avenir, je crois que nous pouvons dire que le monde de l'après-guerre, tel que nous l'avons connu, touche à sa fin. Le moment est venu de combiner les enseignements du passé et notre succès avec les possibilités que nous voyons apparaître pour faire avancer notre ambitieux programme.

L'occasion nous est donnée de rapprocher le monde de la vision que nous en avons : des frontières ouvertes, plus de liberté, moins d'armes et le règne du droit. Une Europe sans division, où tous les citoyens jouissent des droits de l'homme et où tous les peuples puissent exercer leur droit à l'auto-détermination. Un ordre mondial caractérisé, non pas par la confrontation, mais par la coopération entre l'Est et l'Ouest pour résoudre les problèmes pressants qui se posent à l'humanité. Notre Alliance n'a jamais été statique. Elle a toujours été dynamique, et son objectif demeure de surmonter le statu quo, tout en préservant la paix et la liberté que nous avons durement gagnées.

Le risque que nous devons éviter est celui de l'autosatisfaction. Les périodes historiques de profondes mutations, comme celle que nous traversons, suscitent inévitablement l'incertitude, la fragilité et l'instabilité. Il nous faut maintenir la base de notre stabilité : une défense solide. Et surtout, nous ne pouvons pas, au moment où des résultats longtemps recherchés semblent arriver à notre portée, nous permettre de baisser notre garde.

Plaçons toujours à la fois les possibilités et les risques dans une perspective équilibrée, et ne commettons pas l'erreur de nous attacher uniquement aux unes ou aux autres. Car c'est la dualité de notre défi historique qui, à l'évidence, définit le rôle et les tâches futurs de l'Alliance.

D'un côté, notre tâche est d'influer activement sur le cours des événements. Non seulement nous nous félicitons du changement qui se produit en Union soviétique et en Europe de l'Est, mais nous allons l'encourager et en tirer pleinement parti. Nous allons offrir à l'Est notre coopération et le maintien de l'impulsion et des encouragements donnés à la réforme. Notre modèle montre à l'Est le chemin d'une prospérité et d'une sécurité plus grandes au fil du temps. Nous récompenserons ceux qui auront eu le courage de faire des choix difficiles. Mais en retour, nous lançons un défi aux dirigeants de l'Est sur le terrain politique et dans toute la gamme de nos préoccupations communes - des droits de l'homme et des sociétés ouvertes à la réduction des armements. Maintenant que nos politiques et nos concepts portent leurs fruits, le rôle politique de notre Alliance va prendre toute sa dimension, comme jamais auparavant.

D'un autre côté, il serait téméraire d'abandonner ce qui est pour nous le seul terrain sûr et solide : la réussite incontestable et l'expérience inestimable de l'effort commun au sein de notre Alliance. C'est la communauté la plus forte - moralement, politiquement, économiquement, militairement - que l'Occident ait jamais connue au cours de sa longue histoire.

Dans cette optique, nous devons garder une défense forte et un dispositif de dissuasion ferme, digne de confiance. Même si les relations Est-Ouest évoluent dans le sens le plus favorable que nous puissions imaginer, nous aurons à nos portes, pendant de nombreuses années encore, une puissance militaire redoutable et imprévisible. Nous n'avons pas à suspecter en permanence les intentions de ce puissant voisin; mais les intentions ne peuvent pas constituer une base durable pour nos relations. Nous ne pouvons pas bâtir notre propre sécurité sur l'hypothèse de sa bonne volonté constante. Nous nous devons en fait, devant nos peuples et devant l'histoire, de soutenir l'effort que nous faisons pour que le recours à la force des armes demeure superflu dans la conduite de nos affaires. Un potentiel militaire suffisant est donc nécessaire, pour préserver la stabilité et la dissuasion.

Il nous faut maintenir nos armes conventionnelles et nucléaires à un niveau qui atteste bien le caractère indivisible de la sécurité de notre Alliance. Les armes nucléaires sont l'ultime garantie d'une stratégie de prévention de la guerre. Les armes conventionnelles ont, comme le prouve l'histoire, fort mal rempli ce rôle. Il est bien certain que nous voulons ramener les armes - tant nucléaires que conventionnelles - à l'Est et à l'Ouest au niveau minimum que requiert l'intérêt légitime de la sécurité de l'Est et de l'Ouest. Maintes et maintes fois nous avons démontré cette volonté par nos actes. Nos plans de défense aussi bien que notre approche de la maîtrise des armements reposent sur ce principe fondamental. Et les quantités minima qui nous sont nécessaires doivent être maintenues à niveau.

Une relation transatlantique saine est aujourd'hui, comme elle l'a toujours été, la pierre angulaire de notre sécurité et un modèle pour les aspirations des hommes. C'est pourquoi nous devons encore la renforcer, lui donner la forme de l'association transatlantique la plus égale et la plus équilibrée. Nous devons continuer à réexaminer la répartition des rôles, des risques et des responsabilités au sein de notre Alliance et aider, par nos encouragements, son pilier européen à évoluer de la même façon que la force politique et économique que nous voyons actuellement apparaître en Europe occidentale.

La clé de la bonne gestion des relations Est-Ouest est la bonne gestion des relations Ouest-Ouest. C'est seulement en restant unis que nous pourrons déterminer le cours des événements; divisés, et même forts de nos succès et de notre dynamisme, nous ne pourrons tous, sans exception, que subir des événements que d'autres auront déterminés.

Je m'en remets à votre sagesse, à votre courage et à vos qualités de dirigeant pour faire guider notre Alliance, à l'entrée de sa cinquième décennie, vers des succès plus grands encore. Je sais que vous ne voudrez pas laisser passer cette occasion pour nous historique. Comment d'ailleurs pourrions-nous échouer? Car ce sont nos sociétés qui sont les plus ouvertes et les plus dynamiques, nos économies qui sont les plus prospères, nos peuples qui sont les plus novateurs et nos valeurs qui inspirent l'appel à la liberté que nous entendons résonner partout autour du monde occidental. Ainsi, nous avons tout lieu de regarder vers l'horizon notre cinquantième anniversaire avec confiance et optimisme.

Address to the Eighth NATO Maritime Symposium-Sealink

Annapolis
13 June
1989

I am sure that you all know that speech-making is the staple diet of a NATO Secretary General. But when the invitation came from Admiral Kelso to be the keynote speaker 'at this Eighth SEALINK Symposium I responded with more than my usual alacrity. For one thing I love a varied audience. It is indeed remarkable for one event to bring together some 300 eminent personalities from all walks of life - military, political, educational, industrial and commercial. Moreover, land-locked in Brussels and so near to SHAPE, I welcome this opportunity to salute another great expression of our Alliance solidarity, namely SACLANT and with it the maritime side of our Atlantic Alliance. The fact that this symposium is taking place in the ennobling environment of the US Naval Academy provided the winning touch.

Before you judge my naval expertise, however, I am certain that you will want to hear me address an area where my authority rests on sounder foundations: namely the state of our Alliance.

Our Alliance is strong and cohesive. We have just finished a highly successful summit meeting. It gave us the opportunity to turn towards the future. From all participants there was a strong common will:
- to meet the challenges ahead of us;
- to define our common policy towards the East;
- to determine the future rôle of our Alliance.

In all three areas we succeeded. It was a triumph for each of us; but much more importantly, for the Alliance as a whole. And as I stand on American soil today, it is wholly appropriate that I mention President Bush. His leadership set the tone for the whole meeting. It was positive, imaginative and farsighted.

Our Alliance is actively shaping events. We are not sitting back waiting for others. We are setting the agenda in East-West relations. We are striving hard to overcome the *status quo* and end the division of Europe. It is only in the military sphere that this is a defensive alliance. When it comes to our Western vision of the world tomorrow, to our values, ideas and concepts, we are on the political offensive. We know from our stable democracies, from our prosperity that our values appeal because they work. So we offer them to all peoples with energy and conviction.

This Alliance is turning towards the future. I regret that our Summit Declaration has not received the attention which it deserves, but I am sure that it will play a major rôle in our future work. It contains the outline of our active, forward-looking strategy towards the East. We are determined to seize our historic opportunity not just to improve, but to fundamentally reshape East-West relations, stamping our imprint on the process of change. Our opportunity is to bring the world closer to our vision: open borders, more freedom, less weapons and the rule of law. A Europe undivided in which all citizens enjoy their human rights and all peoples can exercise their right of self-determination. A global order not of confrontation, but of co-operation between West and East to solve the pressing problems of mankind.

After 40, sometimes frustrating years, the historic change in the East brings the realization of this vision finally within our grasp. Our forward-looking strategy will help us move ever closer to it, overcoming the *status quo* in successive stages, while preserving our hard-won peace and freedom. We can have both stability and political progress because our strategy is a balanced one. It contains offers, but also reasonable challenges. Our Declaration reminds us that East-West relations are not only about arms control. This Alliance intends to make progress across the entire gamut of our common East-West preoccupations.

The other result of our summit meeting is a resounding reaffirmation of one clear fact: this Alliance has the initiative - in whatever area of the East-West relationship you care to choose.

- Take human rights and individual freedoms: look at how our Western initiatives were taken up by the East in Vienna last year at the end of the CSCE follow-up meeting.

- Take East-West co-operation: we have been calling on the Soviet leaders for a long time to engage with us on international problems, such as environment, drugs and terrorism, and now they have started taking up these themes in their speeches.

- Or arms control and security: in every East-West negotiation it is our proposals and negotiating objectives that lead the way, whether we think of a 50% cut in strategic nuclear weapons, a worldwide ban on chemical weapons or the aim of eliminating surprise attack and major offensive capabilities in the Vienna CSCE talks.

So, our 40th anniversary NATO Summit confirms that the Alliance has fully responded to the time of historic change in which we live today. Clearly the post-war world is coming to an end. Everywhere you look change is not only in the air. It is also visible on the ground. The East is turning to the West. One hundred and fifty years after the Communist Manifesto, communism has manifestly failed. Outdated ideology and inefficiency stand in stark contrast to our values and concepts, and the responsiveness of our system to human aspirations. Events follow our conceptual leadership. But they will continue to do so only if we have the dynamic policies to shape them. So it is essential that the political dimension of our great Alliance now comes into its own as never before.

First in the field of arms control. The Comprehensive Concept which we also produced at our summit is precisely that: a comprehensive analysis of all areas of arms control that makes it clear that we have ambitious goals across the entire spectrum of negotiations. We are determined to fully exploit the greater potential for fruitful arms control today - provided that it remains compatible with our security. In each negotiation we seek security at the lowest possible levels for both sides. We seek greater openness and transparency, as demonstrated recently with the "open skies" initiative. And President Bush has now come forward with a bold new initiative to reduce both American and Soviet manpower in Europe, together with equipment, by 1993. It is an ambitious schedule but this Alliance is fully prepared to meet it.

For we are serious about conventional arms control. Indeed it is an Alliance priority. It is the conventional imbalance that gives expression to, and supports, the division of Europe; that limits the sovereignty of six Eastern European countries; that casts its shadow of intimidation over Western Europe. These are the forces that are used to seize and hold territory and to conduct short-warning and major offensive operations. So we cannot have military stability in Europe until this heavy shadow of Soviet military power is removed once and for all.

The second area of our political activity will be overcoming the division of Europe. Arms control is the agenda of stability through radical change. The same is true of our overall political agenda. We will challenge the Soviet leadership to see how serious they are about a new relationship with us - one based on real reform and political change. Our challenges are not only addressed to arms control. They focus on all those political topics which our

Western values lead us to care deeply about - and from which alone real, irreversible improvements in the daily lives of Eastern Europeans can come.

Thus I ask the questions. Will Mr. Gorbachev formally renounce the Brezhnev Doctrine? Will he open borders still further: irrevocably allow free travel and emigration, permit his people to enjoy all those freedoms that the Soviet constitution and Soviet international agreements have always promised them? Will he agree to military stability in Europe? - because there is no co-operation that can take place in the shadow of the gun, or when one side has an enormous military superiority over the other. This will be the test: Soviet willingness to join with us as partners in building a new political architecture in Europe; one based on democracy and the rule of law, not the permanent monopoly of arbitrary power; one based on human rights and freedom, not oppression and mistrust; one in which military forces lose their threatening character.

It is now up to Mr. Gorbachev to respond to our offers and meet our challenges. This is not only in our interest. It is even more so in his. For how can he hope to make his country prosperous, stable and productive if he does not integrate it into the international trading system? And on which basis can such an integration be feasible, except with the full recognition of liberal values? They generate the dynamism and innovation on which all progress - social, economic, technological - depends. And they alone ensure real and lasting peace on which that social progress also, ultimately, depends.

The message of our Alliance Summit is that we will leave no avenue of fruitful East-West dialogue unexplored. We are indeed living through a time of great opportunity. But we must also recognize that it is a time accompanied by considerable potential risk. Historical turning points also combine both elements - and both require equal skill in management.

Mr. Gorbachev is the very incarnation of this duality. I am convinced he is serious. We encourage and support his reform efforts. He offers us hope and raises our expectations. Yet at the same time he certainly has no intention of presiding over the decline of the Soviet Union. He will pursue his nation's interests as he sees them. He is and wants to remain a Communist. He still exercises dictatorial powers. He is neither democrat nor pacifist. So a firm and durable security posture is an essential precondition for the pursuit of our political agenda. In the security field we see encouraging signs of progress although Soviet military potential is still overwhelming. The Soviets obviously still pursue the objective of the total removal of American nuclear weapons from Europe. Their long-term goal remains clearly to decouple North America from Western Europe. Mr. Gorbachev should understand the true meaning of military stability in Europe which must include a substantial American presence and a nuclear deterrent, at minimum levels.

So although East-West relations are moving our way, let us guard against complacency. Historic periods of deep change, such as we are living through, inevitably produce uncertainty, fragility and instability. Reversals and setbacks cannot be discounted - the tragic events we have witnessed in China in the last few days should remind all of us of this reality of life. We need to maintain the base of our stability, a secure defence. And it is up to us, the opinion leaders of this Alliance, to convince our publics that structural disarmament through neglect is not an alternative form of arms control. If we are to convince the Soviet Union that there is no military alternative to the long and difficult process of internal reform, we need to maintain a credible deterrent - and that means an adequate mix of conventional and nuclear weapons that are kept up to date.

This is true of the naval domain as of all the others. NATO, as its very name suggests, is a maritime alliance *par excellence*. There is more water in the NATO area than land. Proximity to the sea has made us into outward-looking dynamic trading societies. We carry 95% of imports and the exports on which our prosperity depends by sea. The defence of both the central front and the flanks lacks the advantage of depth. In times of tension, crisis and war, we are totally dependent on our ability to reinforce Europe over great expanses of water. Our sea lines of communication are the equivalent of the Warsaw Pact's roads and railways. Take one example. Seventy-five per cent of the Warsaw Pact's reinforcement equipment is moved by rail (the rest goes by road or by Black Sea and Baltic ferries). Yet NATO moves 90% of all its reinforcement equipment by sea.

I only have to remind you of the two World Wars this century to drive my point home. Military historians may disagree as to the precise cause of victory or defeat, but one thing is certain: control of the sea, and in particular anti-submarine warfare, played a crucial rôle. In the first six months of World War Two the Allies lost 100 merchant ships per month. It was not until May 1943 that they managed to organize effective convoy systems. Failure to do so would have been to court disaster.

Today we face 200 operational Soviet submarines, with a further 100 in reserve: by far the largest underwater force in the world. And yet the problem of the reinforcement of Europe from the United States and Canada remains as it has always been. We can only dispatch a limited number of troops by air; most, together with all their heavy equipment and supplies, must come by sea. Indeed to come to grips with this problem, we are currently carrying out a "Study on the Supply and Demand for Merchant Shipping in Times of Crisis and War". This is being jointly financed by NATO Headquarters and SACLANT. Looking towards the year 2000, the study will give us a clearer idea of how much we actually need to transport, and if our NATO merchant fleet is up to the job. It has, as you all know, declined severely in recent years and we may already be dependent on neutral and flag-of-convenience shipping.

What is clear, however, is that whatever ships we have to use, we need Allied naval forces to defend them, and to keep open the sea lines of communication. These naval forces have other vital tasks to perform too: in times of peace in forming an essential part of deterrence by their presence on the world's oceans; in times of war by their ability to bottle up the powerful Soviet navy, which might otherwise be used to assist a Soviet offensive against our flank countries while its submarines attempted to choke NATO into surrender. Our naval forces also play a key rôle in protecting vital out-of-area Western interests. I need only to refer to recent Western success in the Gulf to stress how powerless we would have been had we not had first-class naval forces.

For these reasons the Alliance rejects demands by the Warsaw Pact to include naval forces in the Vienna Conventional Forces. The use of the sea is not an option for NATO; it is a necessity. Because of the multiple functions our navies carry out, NATO ships cannot be directly compared to Soviet ships whose rôles are more circumscribed. I would not for one moment deny Soviet claims that we have more frigates, destroyers and aircraft carriers - some 500 to their 300. But our ships perform an essential rôle in compensating for our severe geographical disadvantages. They fulfil multiple rôles simultaneously. Without them we could not organize a credible defence of Western Europe, beyond a few days. We therefore resist the concept of reductions, limited zones or other constraints that would impair the operational flexibility of our navies. Why should this worry the Soviet Union? Our ships cannot seize and hold territory like tanks, artillery and armoured fighting vehicles. So they do not form part of the offensive equipment that we are focussing on in Vienna.

There is another reason too: if we are successful in the years ahead in negotiating a new régime of conventional stability in Europe, we will have smaller forces in place in Central Europe and our flank countries. As a result, our common defence will become increasingly dependent on reserve and reinforcement forces; on their availability, their readiness and, above all, on our ability to transport them rapidly and safely to our forward lines in a crisis.

Does this mean that NATO is not interested in greater military stability on the seas? Of course not. Many naval confidence- and security-building measures already exist. Indeed our naval colleagues can take justifiable pride in having often been ahead of their army and air force counterparts in this domain. There are bilateral agreements for Eastern and Western navies to observe each other at close quarters and to avoid incidents at sea. Our Alliance member states will no doubt be exploring other such transparency measures in the future. They give us a valuable opportunity to underscore our purely defensive intentions.

Our senior service forms an intrinsic part of the lifeblood of our Alliance. I am thus perturbed that in recent years many of our nations have been forced by budgetary constraints to cut back on their naval forces. We need to face realities and look for better ways of using our scarce resources - through armaments co-operation as in, for instance, the NATO Frigate for the 1990s project and task specialization. But there are limits to what we can live with if we are to protect our citizens, given our maritime requirements. Our governments must know that to maintain effective maritime forces is the best investment in our security and in the maintenance of peace.

In the meantime, in this 40th anniversary year of our great Alliance, let us thank our NATO navies - their officers, their crews and their shore-based personnel - for protecting us so well for so long. They bind the defence of North America to Western Europe. To our NATO airmen the Atlantic may today be no more than "the Pond". But to our navies it is 12 million square miles - or 20 times the land mass of Europe - of lonely and potentially hostile sea. SACLANT has to defend it all. We are indebted to you for being there and for maintaining over it your constant vigil.

Address to The Konrad Adenauer Stiftung

Brussels
7 July
1989

As the 1980s draw to a close, the Alliance is already rising to the challenge of the 21st century. Our recent summit meeting proves two things: that we fully grasp the dimensions of this challenge; and that this Alliance has the vitality, the unity and the forward-looking policies to faithfully serve our Western interests.

We are dealing not with inevitabilities, but with choices. What type of continent, based on which foundations, do we want to emerge from this dynamic of change? And how can we impose our preferences on those of others? This was the theme of our summit; but it concerns not just Heads of State and Government. It is the collective responsibility of all Western policy-makers to think long and hard about our options and to formulate our goals. Thus I am glad to see the Konrad Adenauer Stiftung prove by this meeting that it too is responding to the challenge.

All of us are aware that we are living in a time of historic transition. The post-war world is coming to an end. Nobody regrets this. It was the Cold War world, characterised by oppression, injustice and lack of freedom in Eastern Europe. However, in the current phase of transition and uncertainty, history is like the Roman god, Janus, with his two faces: on the one hand, there are opportunities, new possibilities to create a more peaceful and stable Europe, to bring greater democracy, freedom and economic prosperity to Eastern Europe, and in doing so to make a substantial contribution to world peace and development. Yet on the other hand, the very scope of change means that there are risks and dangers. We must not over-estimate the risks, but at the same time we cannot afford to ignore them.

This fundamental duality determines the future rôle and tasks of our Alliance. We must help peaceful change to move along at its natural speed while preserving a framework of stability. Indeed the two aspects are interrelated: without stability there can be no real progress; without real progress no stability. This is one of those rare junctures in history when we can actively shape events. To succeed, we will need vision, courage and inspired political leadership; just like that displayed by the Atlantic Alliance's founding fathers 40 years ago when they responded to the need, hunger and despair that dominated post-war Europe. In a similar period of great historic change, they had a clear purpose that turned the situation around, replacing fear with hope, pessimism with optimism. Western Europe recovered, and we regained our security, prosperity and freedom.

We have reaped the fruit planted by our predecessors. It is the success of this Alliance in keeping the peace in Europe for the longest period since Roman times, in containing Soviet expansionism, and in giving the West the cohesion to re-emerge as the driving force of democracy and social progress that explains the pressure for change in the Communist world today.

We owe it to ourselves to complete the task that they began: to create the basis of a permanent peace in Europe and of democratic political change in the East. With our ideas of pluralism, freedom and economic liberalism in the ascendancy, not only in Europe but throughout the world, we have never had a better opportunity. For everywhere you care to look, these ideas race across borders. The desires of some Eastern leaders to keep their walls, barbed wire and border guards, or even introduce them anew, remind me of King Canute's attempt to roll back the waves.

The Alliance is the reason why we are at this hopeful juncture today. We must therefore remember that it is only with firm cohesion that we can manage the process of change successfully. If we forget this all-important lesson of our past - and allow our opportunity to slip away - we will have only ourselves to blame.

I have outlined the challenge. It brings me to my essential point. The Alliance is fully capable of meeting it. NATO is no prisoner of its past, nor victim of its own success. It is geared to the future. Better East-West relations or reform in parts of the East do not mean that our agenda is exhausted. On the contrary, they give us a fuller agenda and many new tasks. Our Alliance has always been indispensable as a framework of stability and war prevention. In addition, it is just as indispensable as an instrument of peaceful political change. The two go together. No other framework brings the combined weight of Western Europe and North America to bear on this great challenge of promoting and managing change; and without both continents working together, we cannot hope to succeed.

We will use this time of change to our full advantage. Already we are actively shaping events. Each day brings the achievement of our goals closer. It is only in the military sphere that this is a defensive alliance. When it comes to our vision of the world in the year 2000, to our values, ideas and concepts, we are on the political offensive.

Our ultimate aim is nothing less than to overcome the division of Europe, including that of Germany. A bold ambition, but finally after forty years of NATO, it is now within our grasp. Today the Communist countries are no longer able to sustain indefinitely the artificial barriers which sheltered them. They cannot operate in isolation from the international community or world economic system. If they now persevere with the past, their crisis becomes only worse. If some leaders are turning finally to our values, it is not simply because they find no answers within the traditional reference points of their ideology; nor simply because they see their peoples attracted overwhelmingly to these values. It is first and foremost because Western notions - human rights, the rule of law, market forces - are the only ones that experience has shown to work in practice. There is no alternative.

As a consequence, the political rôle and function of NATO is increasing in importance. Something that was occasionally lost sight of during the Cold War is acknowledged again: NATO is a political Alliance, a community of the destinies and values of the free world.

In our Summit Declaration you will find our vision of Europe in the year 2000 and beyond. It is not a vague concept. It indicates clear foundations and an architecture for the future Europe:
- open borders, civil freedoms and human rights, the rule of law;
- a Europe in which all peoples can exercise their right of self-determination;
- a Europe in which vastly reduced military forces lose their threatening character.

The message of the summit is that we are for movement, for dynamic change of the *status quo*, to overcome confrontation and end the Cold War, sweeping away its most offensive symbols such as walls and barbed wire, and we are for doing so quickly, in a manner which builds on the security and stability we have created over the years. We know that the worst enemies of security are not weapons, even if they are nuclear weapons. It is not missiles which prevent lasting peace, but political confrontation, the division of Europe and the suppression of human rights. Weapons and soldiers are not the cause of tension and conflict - they are rather the consequence.

This is why we must concentrate on the political future of Europe. It is time to free the political debate from its fixation with weapons, strategy and disarmament and turn it towards the decisive questions of the political reshaping of Europe. We cannot finally resolve the problem of security by military means. What we must achieve is a Europe in which armed might becomes unimportant. The shining example for this is the Franco-German rapprochement.

We have an interest in Gorbachev's success. We are not standing passively aside. We support his reform policies as well as we can when they enhance openness, human rights and pluralism. However, we will not let ourselves be deceived by illusions. The Soviet Union is not democratic. It is still - and will be for a long time - a great military power, and thus dangerous. And of course the actions of its leader are determined by the national superpower interests of the Soviet Union, and not by consideration for us. Reform policies could still fail, and of course people and aims could change.

Therefore we must remain on our guard and not neglect our security. It would be foolish to remain passive and suspicious, but equally we cannot entrust security and freedom to the goodwill of a Soviet leader alone. We can and must do both things: encourage détente and maintain a credible defence. Then we are ready for anything.

That is our Alliance's policy as it is set out in the Summit Declaration. Unfortunately this important and even visionary document has not yet received the attention it deserves. I am confident that it will.

Our Declaration makes clear: we will reward those Eastern countries determined to move forward and to embrace our values irreversibly. On the other hand, we will withold our assistance to those other countries that still seem intent on resisting the winds of change and on clinging desperately to a discredited, outmoded system.

We will redouble our efforts and use all possibilities for co-operation and dialogue. Some examples are:
- increased economic and trade relations with the East;
- technological and management exchanges, the setting up of co-operative training programmes;
- common strategies in the fields of the environment, terrorism, drugs, etc.;
- scholarship programmes for study and research.

At the same time, we must make sure that our support leads to more democracy and freedom in the East. We therefore expect actions such as:
- formal renunciation of the Brezhnev doctrine;
- guarantees of free travel and emigration;
- progress in making the protection of human rights a reality in the law

and legal practice of the Eastern nations;
- the removal of the Berlin wall;
- co-operation in preventing regional conflicts.

In particular, the statement on the right to self-determination of all peoples contained in the German-Soviet Declaration of 13 June 1989 must now be reflected in practice. This will be a measure of the progress in our relations.

Attention has tended to focus on arms control and strategic nuclear forces. And indeed disarmament and arms control are important factors for increasing stability in Europe. The comprehensive concept of disarmament and arms control, which the Heads of State and Government approved at the Summit, shows that our governments have developed clear and extensive foundations for negotiations. In all areas we seek security at the lowest possible level of armament.

Indeed, in the field of disarmament the decisive initiatives have also come from the West. For example:
- the zero option for intermediate range missiles;
- the 50% reduction in strategic weapons;
- the total prohibition of chemical weapons;
- the security and confidence-building measures;
- the conference on conventional arms control in Vienna.

Yet at the same time disarmament and arms control cannot be substitutes for political solutions. And they are only possible if our security remains guaranteed. Détente and defence do not contradict each other. I must warn against attempts to set up these two goals against each other as if the Alliance and its defensive strategy stood in the way of an understanding between East and West.

In the field of conventional weapons we have set ourselves particularly ambitious goals, as the new initiative of US President Bush makes clear. Obviously for this Alliance the Vienna negotiations have overriding importance. For it is there that our security interests intersect most closely with our political goals. Major Soviet force reductions and withdrawals will not only allow but also accelerate the political changes we wish to encourage. So I invite all of you to watch Vienna as the reliable barometer of the real Soviet intentions for Europe.

The new proposal confirms once again that the true initiative in East-West relations lies with the West. It is true of ideas and conceptual leadership, of the dynamic energy to change history and of the proposals in the disarmament process. The East is turning to the West. Communism has proved incapable of solving the problems of modern industrial societies. Its attraction is faded and its leaders know it. So we are right to be optimistic - history is on the side of freedom. The wind is against the dictatorships.

So, for me at least, the answer to the question you have set me this morning is clear. The West does not need a new strategy for its security.

Indeed, I am convinced that the principles of our political and military strategy, which have guaranteed our peace for decades, are today as valid as ever. This strategy has contributed decisively to protecting Europe from war, while all about us there have been 150 conflicts since the Second World War. There is no other currently conceivable strategy which could so successfully protect us. And when I say "us", I mean all 16 Allies, not simply the nations on or near the East-West border in Central Europe. A NATO strategy must give equal protection to all, despite immense geographical disparities and problems of reinforcement and resupply. Of course: no strategy is for eternity. And every strategy has to be adapted to changing circumstances. A conventional balance in Europe at minimum levels would have consequences for our strategy - without eliminating the need for a minimum nuclear deterrent.

Nuclear weapons have prevented not merely atomic conflicts, but also conventional wars between states which possess nuclear weapons. They have achieved something which conventional weapons could not through the milleniums of our history: they have prevented the use of military force. The complete elimination of nuclear weapons would not make the world safer. In any case it would not be possible, because the knowledge of how to make them could not be removed from human minds. A Europe free of nuclear weapons would not bring more but less security against military conflicts. Nuclear deterrence has proven to be superior to previous methods in displacing war as a political option.

Thus, it is false to see a contradiction between the existence of nuclear weapons and the construction of a peaceful European order. Our strategy of deterrence and our weapons are no barrier to political progress. They cannot conceivably be used for any other purpose but self-defence. Our goal remains a militarily stable situation with an agreed minimum of conventional and nuclear weapons on both sides to exclude any thought of war.

It is equally nonsensical to imagine a contradiction between the Alliance strategy and German interests, as has been done in recent months in connection with the discussion on short-range nuclear weapons. A special threat to Germany has mistakenly been raised. This culminated in the specially foolish slogan "the shorter the range the deader the Germans". Those who argue like this have thoroughly misunderstood our strategy. It is not a strategy of war, but of war prevention, and that is how it has worked in practice. Germans have had the greatest benefit from the peace which it has maintained - the security, freedom and well-being of our country has rested on this foundation for four decades. It is first and foremost in the German interest that the strategy of flexible response and forward defence remains credible in the future.

Thinking in war scenarios will thus certainly lead us astray. There is no special threat to Germany except that inherent in its geographical situation on the dividing line between East and West. From that situation we can see that there is only one real German interest: to prevent all wars whether nuclear or conventional, for any war in Europe would destroy our country.

The Soviet Union would do well to give up its attempts to denuclearise Europe. Together with us it should create a security structure for Europe including an agreed minimum of nuclear weapons which would guarantee military stability and plainly show any war or even the threat of military force to be senseless and useless. Such a mutually agreed security order in Europe and between the global powers would maintain deterrence as a safeguard in a security system which is governed by stability, legitimacy and confidence in the displacement of war as an instrument of politics.

The two outstanding tasks of the Alliance in the next decade are mapped out. The first is the political guidance of historical change towards a new, more just and lasting order of peace and freedom. The second is maintenance of a stable basis for preventing war and guaranteeing peace. "Change in security" should be our motto.

Courage and leadership are now more necessary than ever. On the one hand to boldly point the way ahead in East-West relations; on the other hand to persuade our publics that success has its conditions: without a robust defence, their hopes for a brighter tomorrow could fade even more rapidly than they arose.

The recent Summit of Heads of State and Government was a triumph for the understanding that we can only approach our political goals together. We are ready to take up the challenge of history. Our vision of an undivided and free Europe is a great one which it is worth striving for. And this Atlantic Alliance, provided we keep it strong and united, gives us the opportunity to make it a reality in our lifetime.

□

The Future of the Alliance

ADDRESS GIVEN
AT ISTANBUL UNIVERSITY

Istanbul
18 September
1989

When I was a student, East-West relations were dominated by ideology. Throughout much of my political career, they have been dominated by weapons and military balances. But now that I am Secretary General of NATO, I have the impression that they are more and more dominated by economics; which means that you, the young but accomplished representatives of our Western business community, are now in the front line of East-West relations.

You are being appealed to from East and from West to use your resources and enterprise culture to aid the Eastern reform programmes; to set up joint ventures, invest in Eastern countries, re-schedule debt, establish private enterprise trusts and the like. When you contemplate the changes underway in the East, I imagine that your thoughts are not all that different from those of our Western political leaders. After all, the situation is a confusing patchwork of different circumstances in different countries. Some Eastern European countries are relatively static - but only at the price of loading greater problems on to the future. Others are going through great upheavals - but at least they seem to be finally grappling with their political and economic short-comings.

So how should you in the business community, and we in the political community, respond to these changes? What do they imply for us in the West, for our political goals, our business interests? Clearly we can see considerable opportunities, yet they seem to be long-term; and we can see considerable risks, which are all only too immediately apparent. We need an approach that can lead us safely to the long term opportunites across the minefield of short term risks. For the businessman, as for the political leader, an investment or policy can only bear fruit in a context which is stable and predictable. So how can we have the necessary changes to make Western involvement in the East bear fruit, while having the necessary stability to give our actions time to work? This is the fundamental question.

And it is not an academic one. You only need to look at what is happening in Eastern Europe today to see that Communism has failed. Its leaders no longer have answers to their problems. Their systems are falling further and further behind the West, like dinosaurs caught out by climatic change. Its citizens are no longer prepared to tolerate its inadequacies - the mounting industrial and ethnic unrest in Eastern Europe proves that. And many do not believe it can be reformed - as we can see from the increasing numbers who will take any opportunity to flee to the West. Marxism provides no guidance on the problems of modern industrial and high technology societies. So the East is turning to the West for help, inspiration and expertise. We cannot sit passively on the sidelines and watch a human tragedy unfold. It is our humanitarian duty to help all peoples who aspire to our values. For they know as we have learned that only democracy and market forces provide prosperity, dynamism, creativity and human happiness. But it is also in our interest to help. More failure, more despair would produce shockwaves that could well engulf us. Thus it is urgent that we tackle these questions today, while we still have the time to evaluate our options and boldly define our course.

Today also our challenge is still our opportunity. If we are wise, we can use the failure of communism to build a new Europe, more just, more open, more humane, more peaceful; a Europe in which no one would be forced to accept second-class status. For freedom, self-determination and prosperity would be available to all peoples. In such a Europe our Western values must apply throughout, not come to an arbitrary halt in the middle of my country, Germany. It is not sufficient for Mr. Gorbachev to speak of a Common European Home as if it were only a matter of physical architecture. What counts is the rules that apply inside this construction, the spirit, the values. Only they, not its external form, can make it inhabitable. Which is why I prefer the term a "European order of peace and justice". This would be in all our interests. Universal democracy, human rights and market forces would give a tremendous boost to our goals - whether they be in business, culture, education or communications. Change and movement are necessary to build this new Europe but they alone cannot bring it about. So I come back to my fundamental questions. How do we make of necessity virtue, of challenge opportunity, of confrontation co-operation?

The answer is not an easy one; but all of you who observed our NATO Summit meeting last May will know that this Alliance is now fully grappling with the question and that we are giving the West the conceptual leadership it needs. Our answer is:

- an offer of economic co-operation;
- a policy to fundamentally restructure East-West political relations;
- a security framework that will stabilize the East-West military balance at a much lower balance of forces.

Let us take each in turn. First, our offer of economic co-operation. We have offered the forces of reform in the East the fruits of our productive societies. Help such as debt rescheduling and food aid to solve their immediate problems; and proposals to deal with their long term structural problems - greater access to Western technology that cannot be exploited for military purposes; training of managers and scientists, scholarships for the study of democratic institutions; technical exchanges, help with environmental pollution. We have stated clearly that we will leave no stone of beneficial co-operation unturned.

Our framework for the Western strategy *vis-à-vis* Eastern Europe is clear and solid. In the months since our meeting, its ideas are already being implemented by Alliance governments and other Western institutions. Take for instance:
- The German-Soviet Declaration of June 1989 which provides for places at German universities and business schools for Soviet managers and post-graduates, for cultural and scientific exchanges;
- The actions that Western governments are now taking to look anew at the debt burdens on Poland and Hungary;
- United States and EC countries' assistance to Poland and Hungary in the creation of private enterprise trusts and to help with pollution;
- The initiative of the Paris Economic Summit to bring the Western nations together, under the co-ordination of the European Community, to provide emergency food relief for Poland.

Yet, the Alliance also has made it clear that there are stringent conditions attached to such assistance programmes. The Communist forces that still cling to power in Eastern Europe must, at the very least, not impede the natural development of democracy. Indeed it is in their interest to encourage such a process. They must decisively choose between guns and butter; they must create the conditions which will attract Western investment. For no private investment (I am certain all of you here today will confirm this) will go into economies that show only limited prospects for growth, innovation and free enterprise; and no Western government will pour resources into centrally-planned bureaucratic and inefficient systems. The aim of Western help to perestroïka is not to rescue Communism, but to enable it to transform itself peacefully into a more pluralist, more creative and dynamic system - to achieve what you call in the business world "a soft landing". Yet on this point I must also sound a note of caution. Western goodwill and finance will not be enough to make the East prosperous. Nor can significant improvements be achieved overnight. Our success depends on the ability of the Eastern leaders to make their reforms work. And here - even with all our readiness to help - we have to face facts. After four years of perestroïka, the Soviet economy is still stagnating - our NATO studies show only a small increase in production, mounting supply bottlenecks, accelerating inflation and growing budget deficits. Large question marks also hang over the economic futures of Poland and Hungary. So let us be optimistic, but also realistic. And, above all, let us have a sober eye for results.

All the same, the Alliance will help those countries that sincerely wish to move in our direction and embrace our values. We are not seeking a *quid pro quo*. We are pointing out that it is in the régimes' own interest to promote political and market reform. Government to government assistance can provide immediate relief; but only the opening up of these societies, the separation of the executive, legislative and judicial branches of government, the abolition of central planning mechanisms and receptivity to outside ideas and influence will provide the stimulus that Eastern Europe needs to narrow the gap with the West.

Yet our policy is not predicated on economic changes alone. We have seen recently in China what happens when economic reform is attempted within a rigid one-party system, and when the aspirations of peoples are not quite the same thing as the intentions of leaders. This Alliance will, in particular, not tolerate human right abuses. The liberalisation that has occurred in Hungary, Poland and the Soviet Union is welcome; it must continue, but it must not obscure the dark practices elsewhere in Eastern Europe - over three hundred thousand ethnic Turks forced to leave Bulgaria; villages bulldozed in Romania; peaceful demonstrations brutally repressed in Czechoslovakia, and the pressure East Germany has placed on Hungary to dissuade the Hungarian government from allowing thousands of East German refugees to travel to the Federal Republic. These East Germans wish to leave not because they lack food or jobs or housing, but because these things mean nothing without freedom and hope. Human rights are not only morally correct: they are the basis of all social progress. Régimes that repress them have ultimately more to fear from their own peoples than the West.

The Alliance strategy towards Eastern Europe is thus predicated on a simple formula: the more they reform and liberalise, the more we will be willing - and able - to do. Yet this Alliance is not seeking only a rescue formula for Eastern Europe. I come here to the second track of our Alliance strategy for the nineteen nineties: restructuring East-West political relations - fundamentally and permanently. The old ideological antagonisms of the past must give way to peaceful competition; confrontation must give way to co-operation. And if there is much that we could do economically to help the Soviet Union and its Allies, there is much that they must do politically:
    - they must reduce their military forces to a level that eliminates all threat

to the Alliance countries - and they should conclude arms control agreements with us that will make this restructuring permanent;
- they should tear down the Berlin Wall, and implement to the full all their human rights obligations under the Helsinki Final Act;
- they should not interfere with the desires of neutral countries, such as Austria, to move closer to the West;
- they should join us in combating international terrorism, the drugs trade, environmental pollution;
- they should help us prevent the spread of dangerous weaponry - such as nuclear or chemical weapons to the world's trouble spots;
- they should help us to solve the regional disputes that threaten to involve East and West directly.

The economic rescue of Eastern Europe will take a long time. But this new form of East-West global co-operation can begin today and produce results tomorrow. Again it is in the interest of both sides - for much of this agenda is a common one. I am indeed hopeful for this new form of East-West relations. President Gorbachev has referred to it too in his speeches. And the Soviet Union has moved recently to solve some regional disputes, to play a more constructive rôle at the United Nations, to accept international legal standards and to condemn recent instances of terrorism directed against the West. We will be engaging the Soviets directly to strengthen this global co-operation - out of it will come the trust and reliability to facilitate our economic relations.

And finally, we must address the third track of our Alliance strategy: building in Europe a security framework with less weapons; one which will be more stable; one which will make future wars on our continent a virtual impossibility. For forty years, for far too long, we have lived with a situation of military imbalance. Soviet forces have overshadowed Europe; they have maintained its division, limiting the sovereignty of the nations of Eastern and Central Europe, giving us legitimate anxieties regarding Soviet intentions towards the West.

The Alliance will not rest until it has transformed this situation. We have a proposal on the negotiating table in Vienna that, if accepted, will start to reduce and then in time eliminate the Eastern capability for surprise attack and large-scale offensive operations. Our proposal is designed to achieve parity in numbers of key items of military equipment: tanks, armoured carriers, artillery, aircraft and helicopters. While reductions in numbers in themselves will be necessary for a more secure balance, they will not in themselves ensure the stability we seek. Changes in force structure and military behaviour are needed also to achieve that. So the Alliance is now hard at work on a related proposal that will bring about these changes. In particular, we will be seeking:
- limitations on equipment in active units - more equipment in storage;
- limitations on exercises and out of garrison activities;

- exchanges of information;
- intrusive and round-the-clock verification.

Above all, our objective of greater military stability is not a distant dream. The Alliance has proposed reaching agreement on these proposals in one year. And if recent Soviet flexibility in meeting our positions is anything to go by, we believe that we can.

NATO is on the move. We are not a military coalition wedded to the *status quo*. We are a political Alliance striving to transform the *status quo*. For forty bitter years we were forced to accept it, but we never wanted to accept it. If weapons do not cause wars, it is equally true that peace is not simply less or no weapons. Peace can be built only on freedom, equality of opportunity, social justice in a Europe where all peoples enjoy the benefits and the responsibilities of the democratic citizen. You are young entrepreneurs. You believe in the value of free markets. You have the dynamism and confidence to plan boldly for the future. This is the spirit that resurrected Western Europe from the rubble and ashes of World War II. It is the same spirit that will play a decisive rôle in bringing prosperity to Eastern Europe. Our political strategy of stimulating change while managing its consequences can prepare the way for your future efforts. Its policy of offers and challenges is a bold but sensible way forward. NATO alone brings the combined weight of Western Europe and North America to bear on this awesome question of Europe's future. Neither continent, whatever its strength, has the resources, the political power or the ability to maintain international security which are the key to success. United, others will move in our direction. Divided we will move in theirs.

And there is another equally important contribution that NATO makes to the success of this venture. It can maintain stability in a period of international turbulence. For real change is never calm, always stormy. Forty years ago, Western Europe could not begin its economic recovery until political circumstances both at home and abroad were more settled. The Alliance provided the protective shield behind which confidence was restored and people began once more to plan and invest in their future. The Alliance's framework of stability now extends across the whole of Europe, embracing ally and neutral alike. Such a framework will be needed more than ever in a period when our Eastern partners are less predictable, more disturbed. We will continue to live next door to an unruly and over-armed superpower. Certainly we do not need to permanently suspect his intentions or base our planning on worst case scenarios. But we cannot wish away basic facts either:
- even if we can achieve all our immediate arms control objectives, the Soviet Union will still possess enormous military power. To date, we have no indications that it is spending less on defence or producing fewer new weapons;
- we have no evidence that the Soviet Union is going to withdraw from

Eastern Europe. Even with unilateral reductions and a positive result at the Vienna negotiations on conventional forces in Europe, its military presence in Eastern Europe will still be considerable;
- the Soviet Union is still ruled by very few men; their actions are not yet subject to democratic control; they do not wish to renounce Communism and they are not pacifists; their intentions can change.

Mr. Gorbachev speaks of a future Europe in which "a balance of interests" will replace the balance of power. It is an alluring prospect; but it all hinges on how the Soviet Union defines its interests in Europe; if they are compatible with our security; if they can allow the inherent right of self-determination of the peoples of Central and Eastern Europe; if they can facilitate and not stand in the way of fruitful East-West co-operation.

We must maintain a secure defence. It will convince the Soviet leaders that there is no easy return to Cold War diplomacy, no realistic alternative to internal reform and external accommodation. On the other hand, our secure defence, because it is minimal and non-provocative, cannot impede political change in the East, nor be an obstacle to the eventual reunification of Europe.

So vigilance is still required, not inflated expectations nor complacency. We must oppose the structural, unilateral disarmament that these can engender. It is the enemy of real arms control. It is a false economy. And arms control too is not about saving money; it is about having more security. Protection is never cheap, but it is a tiny investment when one thinks of the risks and dangers we face without it. Every businessman knows that he or she needs insurance against unlikely but potentially dangerous risks, and he or she knows that a percentage of the profits have to be re-invested to ensure future growth and success. It is no different for us in the Alliance. If we allow our secure defence to rust away, we will be relying on two hazardous assumptions: that Soviet intentions will always be benevolent, and that perfect arms control agreements will solve all of our security problems. Just as seriously, we will undermine our political strategy towards Eastern Europe by taking away the scaffolding from around the building before the cement has set.

But I am confident that we in the West have the wisdom to recognise these pitfalls and avoid them; and I know that we have the courage and dynamism to seize our great opportunities. Within the protective framework of the Atlantic Alliance our peoples are more creative, our economies more prosperous, our societies more open and productive.

□

L'avenir de l'Alliance

DISCOURS PRONONCE
A L'UNIVERSITE D'ISTANBUL

Istanbul
18 septembre
1989

Quand j'étais étudiant, les relations Est-Ouest étaient dominées par l'idéologie. Pendant une grande partie de ma carrière politique, elles l'ont été par les armements et les équilibres militaires. A présent que je suis secrétaire général de l'OTAN, j'ai l'impression qu'elles sont de plus en plus dominées par l'économie, ce qui signifie que c'est vous, les jeunes mais talentueux représentants du monde des affaires occidental, qui êtes aujourd'hui aux avant-postes des relations Est-Ouest.

On fait appel à vous, à l'Est comme à l'Ouest, pour que vous usiez de vos ressources et de votre connaissance de l'entreprise afin de contribuer à la réussite des programmes de réformes lancés à l'Ouest, de créer des sociétés mixtes, d'investir dans les pays de l'Est, de rééchelonner leur dette, de constituer des trusts privés, et caetera. Lorsque vous observez les changements en cours à l'Est, j'imagine que vos réflexions ne sont pas si différentes que cela de celles des dirigeants politiques occidentaux. Pour vous aussi, après tout, la situation est une étonnante mosaïque faite d'éléments qui diffèrent d'un pays à l'autre. Certains Etats d'Europe de l'Est ne tolèrent pratiquement aucune évolution, ne faisant ainsi qu'aggraver les problèmes qui surgiront demain. D'autres connaissent de grands bouleversements, mais ils semblent au moins vouloir enfin affronter résolument leurs difficultés politiques et économiques.

Alors, de quelle manière devons-nous réagir à ces changements, nous, les hommes politiques, et vous qui appartenez au monde des affaires ? Quelles peuvent être les conséquences de ces changements pour les pays occidentaux, pour leurs objectifs politiques et pour leurs intérêts commerciaux ? Certes, nous constatons que les avantages sont très nombreux, même s'ils

81

semblent n'exister qu'à long terme, mais nous constatons que les risques sont très nombreux, eux aussi, et qu'ils ne se dessinent déjà que trop nettement. Nous devons adopter une démarche qui puisse nous faire profiter des avantages à long terme, tout en nous permettant d'éviter les risques qui apparaissent dans l'immédiat. Pour l'homme d'affaires ou le dirigeant politique, un investissement ou le choix d'une ligne d'action ne peut être fructueux que dans une situation stable et prévisible. Dès lors, comment pouvons-nous faire en sorte que se produisent les changements nécessaires pour que l'action menée à l'Est par les pays occidentaux porte ses fruits, tout en pouvant compter sur la stabilité indispensable pour que cette action ait le temps de faire sentir ses effets ? C'est la question fondamentale.

Et ce n'est pas une question purement théorique! Vous n'avez qu'à regarder ce qui se passe aujourd'hui en Europe de l'Est pour voir que le communisme a échoué. Les dirigeants est-européens n'ont plus de solutions à leurs problèmes. Leurs régimes, pareils aux dinosaures surpris par les variations climatiques, sont de plus en plus à la traîne des pays occidentaux. Les citoyens d'Europe de l'Est ne sont plus disposés à tolérer les carences du système - la montée des troubles sociaux et ethniques le prouve. Et nombreux sont ceux qui pensent que ce système ne peut pas être réformé, comme en témoigne le nombre sans cesse croissant de ceux qui font tout pour fuir à l'Ouest. Le marxisme ne permet pas de résoudre les problèmes des sociétés industrielles modernes, tournées vers les technologies de pointe. Si les pays de l'Est frappent aujourd'hui à notre porte, c'est qu'ils ont besoin d'aide, d'inspiration et de compétences. Nous ne pouvons rester dans la coulisse et assister, sans rien faire, à une tragédie humaine. Nous avons le devoir humanitaire d'aider tous les peuples qui aspirent à partager nos valeurs. Ils savent en effet, comme nous l'avons appris, que seules la démocratie et les forces du marché apportent la prospérité, le dynamisme, la créativité, et le bonheur tout simplement. Mais nous avons également intérêt à aider tous ces peuples. La multiplication des échecs et l'accumulation du désespoir provoqueraient des raz-de-marée qui pourraient bien nous engloutir. Il importe donc que nous traitions ces questions dès maintenant, ce qui nous laisse encore le temps d'évaluer les diverses possibilités qui s'offrent à nous et de définir résolument notre ligne de conduite.

Le défi que nous avons à relever aujourd'hui nous ouvre cependant de grandes possibilités. Si nous faisons preuve de sagesse, nous pourrons profiter de l'échec du communisme pour bâtir une Europe nouvelle, plus juste, plus ouverte, plus humaine, plus pacifique, une Europe où personne ne soit forcé d'accepter un statut de citoyen de deuxième rang, car tous les peuples jouiraient de la liberté, de l'autodétermination et de la prospérité. Dans cette Europe-là, nos valeurs occidentales devront être universelles, et non subir un coup d'arrêt arbitraire au beau milieu de mon pays, l'Allemagne. Il ne suffit pas que M. Gorbatchev parle d'une maison commune européenne comme si c'était une simple question d'architecture physique. Ce qui compte, ce sont les règles que l'on applique à l'intérieur de cette construction, l'esprit, les valeurs. Elles seules, et non la forme extérieure de la maison, peuvent rendre celle-ci habitable. C'est la raison pour laquelle je préfère parler d'un "ordre européen de paix et de justice". Celui-ci servirait nos intérêts à tous. L'universalité de la démocratie, des droits de l'homme et des principes de l'économie de marché donnerait une formidable impulsion à nos objectifs, aussi bien dans le domaine des affaires que dans ceux de la culture, de l'enseignement ou de la communication. Le changement et le progrès sont indispensables pour la construction de cette nouvelle Europe, mais ils ne sont pas suffisants. J'en reviens donc à ma question fondamentale : comment pouvons-nous faire de la nécessité une vertu, comment pouvons-nous faire d'un défi à relever une occasion à saisir, comment pouvons-nous transformer progressivement la confrontation en une coopération ?

La réponse n'est pas facile, mais tous ceux d'entre vous qui se sont intéressés au dernier sommet de l'OTAN, au mois de mai, savent que l'Alliance atlantique s'emploie sans relâche à répondre à cette question et que nous donnons à l'Ouest le leadership conceptuel dont il a besoin. Notre réponse consiste à :
- offrir une coopération économique;
- définir une ligne d'action propre à restructurer fondamentalement les relations politiques entre l'Est et l'Ouest;
- mettre en place un cadre de sécurité qui permettra de stabiliser le rapport des forces entre l'Est et l'Ouest, à un niveau beaucoup plus bas.

Examinons successivement chacun de ces éléments, en commençant par notre proposition de coopération économique. Nous avons offert aux réformateurs des pays de l'Est les fruits de nos sociétés axées sur la rentabilité. Nous avons proposé de procéder au rééchelonnement de leur dette et de leur fournir une aide alimentaire pour qu'ils puissent résoudre leurs problèmes immédiats et, s'agissant de leurs problèmes structurels à long terme, nous avons également formulé diverses propositions : accès plus facile aux technologies occidentales ne pouvant être exploitées à des fins militaires, formation de gestionnaires et de scientifiques, octroi de bourses pour l'étude d'institutions démocratiques, échanges techniques, ou encore contribution à la lutte contre la pollution. Nous avons clairement indiqué que nous ne négligerions aucune possibilité de coopération bénéfique.

Le cadre que nous offrons pour la stratégie occidentale vis-à-vis de l'Europe de l'Est est clair et solide. Les idées qui ont été avancées au sommet de l'OTAN sont déjà mises en pratique, depuis plusieurs mois, par les pays de l'Alliance et par d'autres institutions occidentales. Je peux donner comme exemples :
- la déclaration germano-soviétique de juin 1989, aux termes de laquelle des places seront réservées dans les universités et les écoles commerciales allemandes à des responsables d'entreprise et à de jeunes chercheurs

soviétiques, les deux pays étant convenus aussi de procéder à des échanges culturels et scientifiques;

- les initiatives que des pays occidentaux sont en train de prendre en vue de réexaminer le problème de la dette qui pèse sur la Pologne et sur la Hongrie;

- l'assistance que les Etats-Unis et les pays de la Communauté européenne ont apportée à la Pologne et à la Hongrie pour la création de trusts privés et pour la lutte contre la pollution;

- l'initiative qui a été prise au sommet des sept pays les plus industrialisés, à Paris, en vue d'amener les pays occidentaux à fournir tous ensemble, grâce à la coordination assurée par la CEE, une aide alimentaire d'urgence à la Pologne.

Toutefois, l'Alliance a bien précisé également que des conditions rigoureuses s'attacheraient à de tels programmes d'assistance. Les forces communistes qui s'accrochent encore au pouvoir en Europe de l'Est doivent, à tout le moins, se garder d'entraver le développement naturel de la démocratie. Elles ont même intérêt à favoriser ce processus. Elles doivent choisir une fois pour toutes entre le beurre et les canons, et créer les conditions propres à attirer les investissements occidentaux. En effet, aucun investisseur privé - je suis sûr que vous le confirmerez tous - ne se tournera vers des pays dont l'économie n'offre que des perspectives limitées en matière de croissance, d'innovation et de libre entreprise, et aucun gouvernement occidental ne dégagera d'importantes ressources au profit de systèmes économiques planifiés bureaucratiques et inefficaces. Le but de la contribution que les pays occidentaux apportent à la perestroïka n'est pas de sauver le communisme, mais de lui permettre de se transformer pacifiquement en un système plus pluraliste, plus créatif et plus dynamique - lui permettre de réussir ce que vous appelez, dans le monde des affaires, un "atterrissage en douceur". A ce sujet, je dois cependant lancer une mise en garde. La bonne volonté et l'argent des Occidentaux ne suffiront pas à donner la prospérité à l'Est. Et ce n'est pas du jour au lendemain que seront réalisées de très grandes améliorations. Notre réussite dépend de la capacité des dirigeants de l'Est de faire aboutir leurs réformes. Et là, si forte que soit notre détermination à les aider, nous devons regarder la réalité en face. Après quatre années de perestroïka, l'économie soviétique stagne toujours : les études de l'OTAN font apparaître une faible hausse seulement de la production, une multiplication des goulets d'étranglement au niveau de l'offre, une accélération de l'inflation et une augmentation des déficits budgétaires. De nombreuses incertitudes planent également sur l'avenir économique de la Pologne et de la Hongrie. Montrons-nous donc optimistes, mais soyons aussi réalistes. Et avant tout, tenons-nous en sagement aux résultats !

Quoi qu'il en soit, l'Alliance aidera les pays qui souhaitent sincèrement se rapprocher de nous et épouser nos valeurs. Nous n'essayons pas de créer un quiproquo. Nous insistons sur le fait qu'il est de l'intérêt des régimes eux-mêmes de promouvoir une réforme politique et économique. Une assistance de gouvernement à gouvernement peut apporter une amélioration dans l'immédiat, mais seule l'ouverture de ces sociétés, la séparation des pouvoirs exécutif, législatif et judiciaire, l'abolition des mécanismes de planification centrale et la réceptivité à l'égard des idées et des influences de l'extérieur donneront à l'Europe de l'Est le stimulant dont elle a besoin pour réduire l'écart avec l'Ouest.

Notre ligne d'action, néanmoins, ne s'articule pas uniquement autour des changements économiques. Récemment, nous avons vu, en Chine, ce qui se passe lorsqu'une réforme économique est entreprise au sein d'un système rigide à parti unique et que les aspirations du peuple ne correspondent pas vraiment aux intentions des dirigeants. En particulier, l'Alliance ne tolérera pas que les droits de l'homme soient bafoués. On ne peut que se féliciter de la libéralisation qui s'est opérée en Hongrie, en Pologne et en Union soviétique; il faut qu'elle se poursuive, mais elle ne doit pas masquer les sombres agissements dont se rendent coupables d'autres pays d'Europe de l'Est. Je veux parler des trois cent mille personnes - au moins - d'origine turque qui ont dû quitter la Bulgarie, des villages qui ont été rasés en Roumanie, des manifestations pacifiques qui ont été brutalement réprimées en Tchécoslovaquie, ou encore des pressions que l'Allemagne de l'Est a exercées sur les autorités hongroises pour les dissuader de laisser des milliers de réfugiés est-allemands passer en République fédérale. Ceux-ci veulent quitter leur pays non parce que les denrées alimentaires, les emplois et les logements font défaut, mais parce que ces choses ne sont rien sans la liberté et l'espoir. Le respect des droits de l'homme n'est pas seulement un devoir moral : c'est le fondement de tout progrès social. Les régimes qui violent ces droits ont, finalement, plus à craindre de leur peuple que des pays occidentaux.

La stratégie de l'Alliance vis-à-vis de l'Europe de l'Est repose donc sur un postulat très simple : plus loin les pays de l'Est iront sur la voie de la réforme et de la libéralisation, plus nous serons disposés - et aptes - à agir. Pourtant, nous ne voulons pas nous limiter à la recherche d'une formule de sauvetage pour l'Europe de l'Est. Et j'en arrive ainsi au deuxième volet de notre stratégie pour les années quatre-vingt-dix : la restructuration des relations politiques Est-Ouest - de façon fondamentale et permanente. Les vieux antagonismes idéologiques doivent céder le pas à la compétition pacifique; la confrontation doit céder le pas à la coopération. Et, s'il est vrai que nous pouvons faire beaucoup, sur le plan économique, pour aider l'URSS et ses alliés, il est tout aussi vrai que l'une et les autres doivent faire beaucoup sur le plan politique :
- ramener la taille de leurs forces armées à un niveau qui exclue toute menace pour les pays de l'Alliance, et conclure avec nous des accords de maîtrise des armements qui rendent cette restructuration immuable;
- abattre le mur de Berlin et honorer dans leur intégralité les obligations qu'ils ont souscrites en matière de droits de l'homme aux termes de l'Acte final d'Helsinki;

- s'abstenir de contrecarrer les desseins des pays neutres - telle l'Autriche - qui souhaitent se rapprocher de l'Ouest;
- nous rejoindre dans la lutte contre le terrorisme international, le trafic des stupéfiants et la pollution;
- nous aider à prévenir une prolifération des armements particulièrement dangereux - comme les armes nucléaires ou chimiques - jusque dans les foyers de tension de notre planète;
- enfin, oeuvrer avec nous au règlement des litiges régionaux dans lesquels l'Est et l'Ouest risquent de se voir entraîner directement.

Le sauvetage économique de l'Europe de l'Est prendra du temps. Mais, ce nouveau type de coopération Est-Ouest à l'échelle du globe peut démarrer dès aujourd'hui et porter ses fruits demain. Une fois de plus, il y va de l'intérêt des deux camps, car bon nombre des problèmes inscrits à cet ordre du jour leur sont communs. Je fonde, quant à moi, de grandes espérances sur cette nouvelle forme de relation entre l'Est et l'Ouest, à laquelle le président Gorbatchev a fait, lui aussi, allusion. Ces derniers temps, l'Union soviétique s'est montrée disposée à exercer une médiation dans certains conflits régionaux, à jouer un rôle plus constructif aux Nations Unies, à se soumettre aux normes juridiques internationales et à condamner divers actes de terrorisme dirigés contre l'Ouest. Nous engagerons directement les Soviétiques à consolider cette coopération mondiale, qui donnera naissance à la confiance et à la stabilité propres à promouvoir nos relations économiques.

Enfin, il nous faut parler du troisième volet de la stratégie de l'Alliance, à savoir, la construction d'un cadre de sécurité avec un moindre niveau d'armements, un cadre qui soit plus stable, un cadre qui rende pratiquement impossible une guerre future sur notre continent. Depuis trop longtemps, quarante ans!, nous vivons une situation marquée par le déséquilibre militaire. Les forces soviétiques projettent leur ombre sur l'Europe; elles qui ont perpétué la division de notre continent, en restreignant la souveraineté des nations d'Europe de l'Est et d'Europe centrale, elles qui nous donnent toutes les raisons de nous méfier des intentions de l'URSS à l'égard de l'Ouest.

L'Alliance n'aura de cesse qu'elle n'ait transformé cette situation. Aux négociations de Vienne, nous avons avancé une proposition qui, si elle est acceptée, se traduira par la réduction, puis, avec le temps, par l'élimination des moyens sur lesquels l'Est peut compter pour lancer des attaques par surprise ou des opérations offensives de grande envergure. Notre proposition vise à établir une parité numérique, s'agissant des grandes catégories de matériels militaires : chars, véhicules blindés de transport de troupes, artillerie, avions et hélicoptères. Certes, l'instauration d'un équilibre plus sûr exige que l'on opère des réductions dans les arsenaux eux-mêmes, mais celles-ci ne suffiront pas à garantir la stabilité que nous recherchons : elles doivent être accompagnées d'une modification des structures et des comportements militaires. C'est pourquoi l'Alliance travaille dur à une proposition connexe qui est de nature à amener de tels changements. Nous demanderons notamment :

- une limitation des dotations en équipements des unités d'active (de telle sorte qu'il y ait davantage de matériels dans les dépôts);
- des restrictions touchant aux exercices et aux activités hors garnison;
- des échanges d'informations;
- des vérifications "poussées" et continues.

Je veux souligner que notre quête d'une stabilité militaire accrue n'a rien d'utopique. L'Alliance a demandé qu'un accord sanctionne ses propositions d'ici un an, et, à en juger par la souplesse avec laquelle les Soviétiques ont récemment accueilli nos positions, ce délai semble pouvoir être tenu.

L'OTAN avance. Il ne faut pas voir en elle une coalition militaire acharnée au maintien du statu quo, mais bien une alliance politique qui s'efforce de le transformer. Ce statu quo, nous avons été contraints de l'accepter durant quarante longues et pénibles années, mais nous ne nous y sommes jamais résignés. Bien sûr, ce ne sont pas les armes qui déclenchent les guerres, mais il ne suffit pas d'en diminuer le nombre ou de les faire disparaître à jamais pour que règne la paix. La paix, on ne peut la construire que sur la liberté, l'égalité des chances, la justice sociale, dans une Europe dont tous les citoyens bénéficient des avantages et exercent les responsabilités inhérents à la démocratie. Vous êtes de jeunes entrepreneurs. Vous croyez dans le marché libre. Votre dynamisme et votre confiance vous autorisent à dresser les plans les plus audacieux. Tel est l'état d'esprit qui a permis à l'Europe occidentale de renaître des ruines et des cendres de la deuxième guerre mondiale. Il est désormais appelé à jouer un rôle décisif dans le retour de la prospérité en Europe de l'Est. Notre stratégie politique, qui consiste à provoquer le changement et à en assumer les conséquences, peut préparer le terrain sur lequel vous vous engagerez. Notre démarche, qui fait alterner ouvertures et défis, constitue une façon d'aller de l'avant tout à la fois hardie et raisonnable. Combinant le poids de l'Europe occidentale et celui de l'Amérique du Nord, l'OTAN peut, à elle seule, influer sur le dénouement de l'angoissante question posée par le futur de l'Europe. Quelle que soit sa puissance, aucun des deux continents, pris isolément, ne détient les ressources matérielles, le pouvoir politique ou l'aptitude nécessaires à la sauvegarde de la sécurité internationale, clé du succès. Si nous demeurons unis, nous verrons les autres se rapprocher de nous. Si nous sommes divisés, ce sera le contraire.

L'OTAN contribue d'une autre manière - toute aussi importante - à l'aboutissement de cette entreprise : elle peut préserver la stabilité au milieu des turbulences internationales. Car, le changement véritable n'intervient jamais dans le calme plat, sinon dans la tempête. Il y a quarante ans de cela, l'Europe occidentale n'a pu entamer son redressement économique avant que la situation politique, à l'intérieur de ses frontières comme à l'étranger, se fût apaisée.

C'est l'Alliance qui a brandi le bouclier à l'abri duquel les peuples ont pu, dans un climat de confiance enfin rétablie, recommencer à faire des projets et à investir dans leur avenir. L'espace de stabilité créé par l'Alliance s'étend désormais à travers toute l'Europe et s'ouvre à tous, alliés et pays neutres confondus. Il sera d'autant plus nécessaire que nos partenaires de l'Est entrent dans une période plus troublée qui rendra leurs réactions moins prévisibles. Nous continuons d'habiter à deux pas d'une superpuissance indisciplinée et surarmée. Loin de nous l'idée de la soupçonner en permanence, ou de fonder nos plans sur les pires scénarios. Pourtant, les faits sont là, et nous ne pouvons les effacer d'un simple coup de baguette magique :

- même si nous atteignons nos objectifs immédiats en matière de maîtrise des armements, l'URSS conservera une puissance militaire énorme. A ce jour, rien n'indique que ce pays consacre moins d'argent à sa défense ou produise moins d'armes nouvelles;

- nous n'avons pas non plus de preuve que les Soviétiques comptent se retirer d'Europe de l'Est. Leur présence militaire dans cette partie du monde restera impressionnante, en dépit des réductions unilatérales auxquelles ils peuvent procéder, et quand bien même les négociations de Vienne sur les forces conventionnelles en Europe déboucheraient sur des résultats positifs;

- l'URSS reste aux mains d'une oligarchie dont l'action échappe encore à tout contrôle démocratique; les maîtres du Kremlin, qui ne veulent pas renoncer au communisme, ne sont pas des pacifistes, et ils peuvent changer d'avis.

M. Gorbatchev parle d'une Europe où l'équilibre des forces cédera la place à "un équilibre d'intérêts". Perspective séduisante qui, toutefois, repose entièrement sur la définition que l'Union soviétique donne de ses propres intérêts en Europe : sont-ils compatibles avec notre sécurité ? Respectent-ils le droit naturel des populations d'Europe centrale et d'Europe de l'Est à l'autodétermination ? Peuvent-ils favoriser - et non entraver - une coopération Est-Ouest fructueuse ?

Nous devons maintenir une défense sûre. Elle convaincra les dirigeants soviétiques qu'il ne serait pas aisé d'en revenir à la diplomatie de la guerre froide, et que la seule solution réaliste consiste à procéder à une réforme intérieure et à s'adapter aux conditions extérieures. Mais, parce qu'elle est réduite à son niveau minimal et qu'elle est dépourvue de tout caractère provocateur, cette défense ne peut empêcher le changement politique à l'Est, ni la réunification de l'Europe, qui aura lieu tôt ou tard.

C'est donc de vigilance que nous avons encore besoin. Foin des espérances démesurées et des attitudes suffisantes, qui risquent d'engendrer un désarmement structurel et unilatéral auquel nous devons nous opposer. Les unes et les autres sont les ennemies d'une véritable maîtrise des armements et nourrissent le sentiment trompeur qu'il est possible de faire des économies. Or, la maîtrise des armements n'est pas destinée à faire faire des économies; elle est destinée à accroître la sécurité. Il n'y a pas de protection bon marché, mais les sacrifices financiers à consentir sont bien minces, si l'on songe aux risques auxquels nous nous verrions confrontés sans une telle protection. Tout homme - ou femme - d'affaires sait qu'il faut se prémunir contre n'importe quelle menace, aussi improbable qu'elle puisse paraître, et qu'il y a lieu de réinvestir une partie des bénéfices pour garantir la croissance et le succès de l'entreprise. Il en va de même pour l'Alliance. Si nous laissons se rouiller notre solide outil de défense, nous ferons deux paris hasardeux : que les Soviétiques seront toujours bien intentionnés, et que des accords parfaits de maîtrise des armements apporteront une solution à tous nos problèmes de sécurité. Mais nous compromettrons - ce qui est tout aussi grave - notre stratégie politique vis-à-vis de l'Europe de l'Est en enlevant l'échafaudage autour de la maison avant que le ciment n'ait pris.

J'ai confiance dans la perspicacité des Occidentaux : ils sauront reconnaître ces pièges et les éviter. De même, je suis persuadé que nous aurons le courage et le dynamisme voulus pour saisir les grandes occasions qui s'offrent à nous. Protégés par l'Alliance atlantique, nos peuples sont plus créatifs, nos économies plus prospères, et nos sociétés plus ouvertes et plus productives.

40 years of the Federal Republic of Germany 40 years of NATO

SPEECH GIVEN
ON THE OCCASION
OF THE 40TH ANNIVERSARY
OF THE FEDERAL REPUBLIC
OF GERMANY

Stuttgart
6 October
1989

The fact that both dates coincide is no accident. The efforts for Germany's revival in a democratic form after the devastation of the Second World War and the uniting of the Western world are part and parcel of the endeavour to re-establish our system of states after the war under the aegis of freedom and democracy - although the Federal Republic of Germany was able to join the Alliance only in 1955.

Today I should like to take an integral look at these two events both dating back to 1949, with the intent of coming nearer to answering a simple question: what will NATO signify in future for the security and freedom of our country and for our political fate? What has the Alliance given us, what is it going to give us? What can it achieve?

First of all: hardly any other date stands as much for the return of the Federal Republic of Germany to the community of equal democratic states as its accession to NATO. Ten years after Hitler's war erupted, the former war allies entered into the NATO Alliance - ten years after the end of the devastating military adventure of the Third Reich, a free German state has been received into the circle of these former war adversaries. The Federal Republic of Germany thus became a partner of the West in the key area of political existence, i.e. security policy. It is not accidental that the foundation of the Bundeswehr, the accession to the Western Alliance and the new German state regaining full sovereignty came to pass at the same time.

Equal rights, hence, in spite of the remaining responsibility of the Four Powers which is so essential to the option of a unitary German state, and apart from equal rights, the Alliance brought us security and protected us from war in the longest peace period in European history since the fall of the Roman Empire. At the same time, it elevated our security policy, with its enormous intellectual and political achievement of military integration, to a new political height. The establishment of an integrated military system is unparalleled in history. If NATO is founded on common values, on the joint will for freedom, then this collective confirmation of the will for defence of free peoples possibly constitutes the paramount expression of this community of values. On this will for defence, the Soviet expansionist aspirations foundered. This will has preserved freedom and made peace secure.

Above and beyond that, the Alliance's major achievement in the past lies in creating stability. Co-operation within the Alliance has provided us with the firm framework within which the liberal system of the Federal Republic of Germany could come into its own in economic prosperity and intellectual liberty, within which the path towards Europe could be constantly and consistently pursued. The crucial difference between the endeavours to re-establish the system of states after the First and the Second World Wars lies in the inclusion of the United States. The fact that America, which already in 1919 was the dominant economic power of the West and of the world, did not stand aloof any longer, but coupled its fate conventionally and factually to the fate of the European Continent for better or for worse, is the historical achievement of the founding generation of our Alliance. Without the Alliance and the lasting commitment of the United States to Europe's fate, Western Europe would at best have become a fragmented adjunct to the Soviet Union, and if there had been no Western European unification process, no pressure to democratize would have come to bear upon the Soviet Union. A security community of freedom, including the superpower USA and Canada, extending from the Pacific coastline to the boundaries of Iran, creates stability by its mere existence. NATO is a community of values and of stability. In the past 40 years, it provided a protective shield for the modern system of states of the free world.

This achievement of stability made the Alliance also the firm anchor and security-affording point of departure also for the realization of the political vision of the North Atlantic Treaty. Above all for the other part of Germany, for Eastern Europe and, not least, for the peoples of the Soviet Union, the freedom, strength and consistency of Western political action provided the pillar of hope to which the will to overcome the domination by violence and to achieve self-determination could be made fast. The Alliance has furnished a factual guarantee for the survival of the German capital Berlin and thus became a guarantor also of the German national aspiration. In the Harmel Doctrine, the Alliance as early as 1967 formulated its basic tenet: credible defence posture as a basis for political dialogue with the East, combined with political co-operation, to make it possible to scale down the requirements for a military security potential. NATO has always been a political alliance, not only a military one.

Equal and active co-operation of our country in the Western system of states, security, stability, common political action for overcoming the calamitous division of our continent - those are the beneficial effects which arose from our accession to the Alliance and which endured over successive decades. During that epoch, the identity of interests of the Federal Republic and of the Alliance has never been called into question.

What will the Alliance give us in the future?

Are those right who today diagnose a dramatic recession of military threat and conclude therefrom that NATO as a military alliance has fulfilled its *raison-d'être* and might as well fade away? Is NATO a cold war relic, must it hence disappear along with it?

To find the answer to that, you only need to imagine the Atlantic Alliance did not exist. We are living through a phase of rapid transformation in the European Community of states. The historical landscape so familiar to us from the post-war years is altering at a hardly believable pace. Communism as an ideology as well as an economic system is done for. Its leaders are fully aware of that. Almost every day confronts us with new developments. Who would hold together the free world in such a situation? Can anyone imagine this might be possible without the active commitment of the United States? Who would keep Europe's fate tied to that of the United States? Who would co-ordinate our policy *vis-à-vis* the East? Who could warrant our stability in times of violent turbulences and thus risks? Where were we to find security? Where unity? Torn apart, the free nations would soon fall victim to history's progress. It is only the Atlantic Alliance that enables us to dominate that progress, to shape history as the strongest, grandest and most successful alliance of free nations in the history of mankind. As a community of fate of free nations the Alliance affords us influence, security and stability.

We need the Alliance first and foremost as an instrument of change. This has been reconfirmed by the Summit: overcoming the division of Europe is and remains our paramount goal. We are certainly not married to the *status quo*. We wish to overcome it. We do not long for the cold war, although at that time fronts were easier to survey and many a situation may have been clearer. We wish to pave the way for a new peace order. On the basis of reliable defence the Alliance can now vigorously realise its political vision:

1. An undivided Europe which is founded upon human rights, democracy, pluralism and free self-determination of nations. NATO's objective is not only to overcome the division of Europe, but also of Germany. A new order in Europe can and will not pass up the German question. The latest Summit Meeting of NATO made a clear and unambiguous commitment to German unity.

2. A global order of co-operation between East and West with the aim of resolving the urgent problems of mankind.

3. An equal partnership between the nations of North America and of Europe.

This vision determines our political action. This is why we support Gorbachev and the reform forces in Eastern Europe. Such a policy lies in our own interest, to the extent that it amplifies human rights, opens the closed systems of the East, clears the way for freedom and democratization and benefits the free encounter among nations. We shall not miss the historical chance of change.

We know: change always entails a goodly measure of unrest, unpredictability, insecurity and instability. But this can be no reason for maintaining the obsolete post-war landscape. It cannot be maintained - should even the one or other wish to do that - as has been proved by the events of these days and the flight of tens of thousands of our countrymen. Stability is not tantamount to fearful preservation of the *status quo* but the farthest possible assurance of an organic, evolutionary change avoiding all dangers of a violent upheaval.

All peoples of Eastern and Central Europe must be given the right to self-determination. How they are going to decide is up to them. We have no intention of tutoring them in the exercise of their right. The Soviet Union should concede a free choice to these peoples. Not only in theory, but also in actual practice; that would be in its very own interest. Only in this manner will fruitful neighbourship, peaceful partnership and economic stability be imaginable in the long run.

We also need our Atlantic Alliance as an instrument of stability. Change must take place in security.

It is not us who triggered this process. And least of all, it is revanchism which is at work here, as the Soviet Foreign Minister Shevardnadze wanted to make the world believe by his speech at the United Nations. One dares hope that he himself does not truly think so. It is, after all, the natural urge for freedom of individuals and nations which is spontaneously coming to the fore.

Truly, chances for disarmament, for a further regression of threat and for comprehensive co-operative East-West relations have increased manifold. Our population is right if it is not afraid of war at the present time. We would be foolish if we were to forego the chance of breaking the centuries old, long-term cycle of war and peace.

This, however, will be a time-consuming process. Success in the arms control negotiations, too, will depend on our cohesion and defence posture in this phase of transition. It is not the immediate danger of war in the East-West relationship that we must keep an eye on; it is the long-term risks of instability and insecurity against which we must provide.

Nobody knows what can happen and how rapidly. Historical experience proves that times of change are always times of risk. The reform processes in the East and the relaxation of Soviet control over Eastern and Central Europe cause long-suppressed ethnic and national currents to erupt.

The historical process of re-orientation can only be mastered in conditions of stability ensured by a well-functioning alliance. The transatlantic connection provides the firm back-up by means of which we can derive historical advantages from the enormous restructuring process in the East.

The vigour of our defence efforts within the Atlantic Alliance makes it clear to every Soviet politician that there is but one way to resolve his country's problems: the peaceful one. Our defence efforts do not hinder détente. On the contrary: they afford us a firm foundation for dialogue and co-operation.

It is for yet another reason that undiminished defence efforts are essential. At present, the Soviet potential is nearly undiminished. We cannot be guided by the present intentions of the Soviet leadership which are certainly not focussed on war. But intentions may change, politicians can be replaced; we can found security only on our own efforts. This is why the Bundeswehr and the Allied forces remain so important; their strength and operational readiness must not be reduced before mutually agreed disarmament becomes reality.

The future vital interests of the Germans - freedom, unity, security and transformation - can also only be safeguarded by the Atlantic Alliance; it remains essential.

Within its framework the free Germans are offered the chance of contributing to solving two major tasks of our time: a new security structure and, even more so, a new political order in Europe.

With our Comprehensive Concept we in the Alliance defined the objective of disarmament: security and stability with less weapons: an order of mutual security in which both sides are incapable of surprise attacks or large-scale operations. This restriction so far only applied to the Atlantic Alliance.

Especially in recent weeks and months it has become clear: the initiative for the disarmament process rests with the West.

Important though disarmament is, it is no substitute for a political new order. Soldiers and weapons are not the cause of political tensions, but rather their consequence. This is why the building of a new peace order must be given precedence. However, it must be founded upon freedom, democracy and human rights. Within such an order, armies lose their threatening character, as is borne out by the German-French example.

There can be no doubt: history is on our side. The dynamism of the historical process favours us. Our ideas are advancing. The future of the East lies in the West and not vice-versa.

We, therefore, have reason to be optimistic. Our economic system is far more productive, our social order more flexible and creative. Above all, our system of values corresponds to nature and the aspirations of the human being.

Nothing happens automatically, though. Everything depends on us, on our resolve, on our cohesion, on our capacity for leadership and creativeness.

This Alliance has a future, and only together with it do we have a future. Thus I see the decades ahead also under the sign of this strong and history-making association of states ensuring freedom and peace for us.

□

La République Fédérale d'Allemagne a 40 ans - L'OTAN a 40 ans

Stuttgart
6 octobre
1989

Simple coïncidence? Certainement pas. La reconstitution sous une forme démocratique de l'Allemagne, après les dévastations de la Deuxième Guerre Mondiale et le rassemblement du monde occidental proviennent de la même tentative de réorganiser notre système étatique après la guerre, sous le signe de la liberté et de la démocratie. La République fédérale d'Allemagne, elle, n'entrera qu'en 1955 dans cette Alliance d'ores et déjà mise en route.

Je voudrais à cette occasion mettre en perspective les deux événements historiques dont la date de 1949 est le dénominateur commun, afin d'approfondir cette question très simple : quelle importance l'OTAN aura-t-elle dans les années à venir pour la sécurité et la libeté de notre pays, pour notre destin politique? Que nous a apporté l'Alliance, que nous apportera-t-elle, et que pourra-t-elle nous apporter?

Notons tout d'abord qu'aucune autre date ne saurait mieux symboliser le retour de la République fédérale d'Allemagne dans la communauté des Etats démocratiques et égaux que celle qui marque notre entrée dans l'OTAN. Dix ans après le déclenchement de la guerre hitlérienne, les anciens Alliés se réunissent dans l'Alliance atlantique - dix ans après l'échec de la désastreuse aventure militaire du Troisième Reich, un Etat allemand libre est accueilli au sein même de l'alliance de ses anciens ennemis. La République fédérale d'Allemagne devient le partenaire des pays de l'Ouest dans un domaine essentiel de l'existence politique, celui de la sécurité. Ce n'est pas par hasard que coïncident la création de la Bundeswehr, l'entrée dans l'Alliance occidentale et la récupération, par la République fédérale d'Allemagne, de son entière souveraineté.

Egalité, donc. Mais la responsabilité des quatre puissances qui est fondamentale pour l'option allemande en faveur d'un seul Etat demeure inchangée. A l'égalité s'ajoute la sécurité. L'Alliance a su écarter la guerre et nous avons connu la période de paix la plus longue de l'histoire de l'Europe depuis la décadence de l'Empire romain. Elle a donné en même temps une dimension politique nouvelle à notre politique de sécurité du fait de cette exceptionnelle réussite intellectuelle et politique qu'est l'intégration militaire. La mise en place d'un système militaire intégré est sans précédent dans l'histoire. Cette volonté commune de défense des peuples libres est sans doute l'expression la plus marquante de notre communauté des valeurs et l'OTAN repose sur des valeurs communes et une volonté commune de la liberté. Cette volonté de défense a voué à l'échec le mouvement expansionniste soviétique et c'est à elle que nous devons la liberté et la paix.

Par ailleurs, l'Alliance a su avant tout assurer la **stabilité**. La coopération au sein de l'Alliance a été un facteur de stabilité qui a permis à la République fédérale d'Allemagne de se développer dans la liberté spirituelle et politique et dans la prospérité, lui permettant ainsi d'avancer avec assurance sur la voie de la construction européenne. La participation des Etats-Unis caractérise la réorganisation du système étatique après la Deuxième Guerre mondiale par rapport aux tentatives entreprises après 1914/18. Facteur économique déjà de première grandeur en 1919, les Etats-Unis ne restent plus à l'écart mais acceptent, concrètement et contractuellement, de s'associer au destin du Vieux Continent pour le meilleur et pour le pire : tel est le mérite historique des pères fondateurs de notre Alliance.

Sans l'Alliance, sans lien durable avec les Etats-Unis, l'Europe de l'Ouest n'aurait été qu'une excroissance disparate de l'Union soviétique. Nous n'aurions pas connu le processus d'unification européenne ni les pressions démocratiques en direction de l'Union soviétique. Une association de sécurité pour la liberté, sous l'influence de la superpuissance américaine et du Canada, qui s'étend des rivages du Pacifique aux frontières de l'Iran est stabilisatrice du fait de son existence même. L'OTAN, par conséquent, est une **communauté** non seulement de **valeurs** mais aussi de **stabilité**. Elle a été, pendant ces quarante dernières années, l'indispensable dispositif de protection pour les Etats du monde libre.

Grâce à son action stabilisatrice, l'OTAN a pu réaliser la **vision politique** du Traité de l'Atlantique Nord. La liberté, la force et la continuité qui déterminent l'action politique occidentale ont été une source d'espoir, notamment pour l'autre partie de l'Allemagne, pour l'Europe de l'Est, pour les peuples d'Union soviétique enfin, dans leur désir de surmonter les totalitarismes et de s'élever contre le refus de l'autodétermination. L'Alliance a fourni la garantie concrète de survie à la capitale allemande de Berlin et fut ainsi le garant de la cause nationale allemande. Dès 1967, la doctrine Harmel fut le crédo de l'Alliance : assurer une défense crédible comme point de départ du dialogue politique avec l'Europe de l'Est qui doit aller de pair avec la coopération politique, dans le but de réduire enfin le dispositif de sécurité militaire. L'OTAN a toujours été une alliance politique et non pas une alliance uniquement militaire.

Coopération à part entière de notre pays avec les autres pays de l'Ouest; sécurité et stabilité; action politique commune visant à surmonter la désastreuse division de notre continent, tel est l'actif de notre entrée dans l'Alliance. A aucun moment, dans les décennies passées, la convergence des intérêts de la République fédérale d'Allemagne et de l'Alliance n'a dû être mise en doute.

Que nous apportera l'Alliance dans l'avenir?

Ont-ils raison, ceux qui, constatant le très net recul de la menace militaire, en concluent que l'OTAN, alliance militaire, a rempli sa mission, a perdu sa raison d'être et peut finalement disparaître? L'OTAN est-elle une survivance de la guerre froide appelée à disparaître avec elle?

Supposons que l'Alliance atlantique n'existe pas. Nous vivons à une époque de mutations rapides dans la vie en communauté des Etats européens. Le rythme des changements dans le traditionnel paysage historique de l'après-guerre est sans précédent. Le communisme, en tant qu'idéologie et système politique et économique, a échoué. Ses dirigeants le savent. Chaque jour en apporte de nouvelles preuves. Comment, dans ces conditions, assurer la cohésion du monde libre? Comment y parvenir sans l'engagement concret des Etats-Unis? Comment lier autrement les destins de l'Europe à celui des Etats-Unis? Comment coordonner nos politiques envers l'Est? Comment assurer notre stabilité à une époque mouvementée et par conséquent pleine de risques. Où trouver la sécurité, l'union? Désunies, les nations libres seraient les victimes de l'évolution historique. Seule, l'Alliance atlantique nous permet de maîtriser l'événement, d'agir sur l'histoire. Elle est l'association la plus forte, la plus importante et la plus efficace de l'histoire de l'humanité. Communauté d'Etats libres, l'Alliance est pour nous source d'influence, de sécurité, de stabilité.

L'Alliance est indispensable, tout d'abord dans son rôle d'agent du changement. La réunion au sommet nous en a de nouveau apporté la preuve : notre principal objectif est toujours de surmonter la division de l'Europe. Nous ne sommes pas prisonniers d'un statu quo. Nous souhaitons le surmonter. Nous sommes loin de regretter la guerre froide bien que les choses aient été à certains égards plus claires, plus prévisibles. Nous souhaitons préparer un nouvel ordre de paix. C'est en partant d'une défense sûre que l'Alliance peut désormais s'engager vigoureusement dans la réalisation de ses aspirations politiques :
1. Celle d'une Europe non divisée qui repose sur les droits de l'homme, la démocratie, le pluralisme et la libre autodétermination des pays. L'objectif de l'OTAN est de surmonter non seulement la division de

l'Europe mais aussi celle de l'Allemagne. Le nouvel ordre européen ne saura faire abstraction de la question allemande. Le dernier sommet de l'OTAN a formulé très clairement son attachement à l'unité allemande.

2. Celle d'un ordre global de la coopération entre l'Est et l'Ouest qui nous permettra de résoudre les problèmes urgents de l'humanité.

3. Celle enfin d'une association dans laquelle les Etats d'Amérique du Nord et de l'Europe coopèrent en tant que partenaires égaux.

Telles sont les aspirations qui guident notre action politique. C'est pourquoi nous apportons notre soutien à Gorbatchev et aux forces réformatrices de l'Europe de l'Est. Cette politique est conforme à nos intérêts dans la mesure où elle permet de promouvoir les droits de l'homme, d'agrandir une ouverture dans les systèmes fermés de l'Est, de servir la cause de la liberté et de la démocratisation et de favoriser la rencontre des peuples dans la liberté. Nous allons saisir cette chance historique de changement.

Le changement c'est aussi - nous le savons - l'inquiétude, l'imprévisibilité, l'insécurité, l'instabilité. Mais ce n'est pas une raison pour conserver les structures périmées de l'après-guerre, comme certains peuvent encore le souhaiter. L'afflux des dizaines de milliers de nos compatriotes nous en donne la preuve. Assurer la stabilité n'est pas préserver frileusement et à tout prix le statu quo. C'est au contraire évoluer dans la sécurité, en cherchant à éviter les dangers d'une transformation violente.

Tous les peuples d'Europe de l'Est et d'Europe centrale doivent disposer du droit à l'autodétermination. A eux de faire leur choix. Nous ne cherchons pas à exercer une tutelle et l'Union soviétique devrait, de son côté, accorder à ces peuples la possibilité du libre choix, théoriquement et dans la pratique. Ce serait en effet dans son intérêt, car c'est seulement dans cette voie que nous pourrons créer des relations fructueuses de bon voisinage, une association pacifique et assurer la stabilité économique.

L'Alliance atlantique est indispensable aussi comme agent de la stabilité. Le changement doit avoir lieu dans la sécurité.

Nous ne sommes pas à l'origine de l'événement, et ce n'est pas, loin de là, le fait du revanchisme, comme l'a suggéré le ministre soviétique des Affaires étrangères, M. Chevardnadze dans son discours aux Nations Unies. Espérons que ce ne sont pas, ses propres convictions. Nous sommes témoins, par contre, de l'aspiration naturelle des hommes et des peuples à la liberté.

A l'heure actuelle, le dossier du désarmement, le recul de la menace, la coopération au niveau des rapports Est-Ouest se présentent sous un jour particulièrement favorable. Notre peuple ne se trompe pas : nous n'avons pas à présent de guerre à craindre. Ce serait donc une grave erreur de ne pas saisir cette chance pour rompre l'éternelle alternance de la paix et de la guerre.

Il s'agit cependant, d'une tâche à plus long terme. Le succès des négociations sur la maîtrise des armements par exemple dépendra largement, dans cette phase de transition, de notre cohésion et de notre potentiel de défense. Ce n'est pas actuellement le danger immédiat d'une guerre qui pose un problème dans les relations Est-Ouest. C'est celui, à plus long terme, de l'instabilité et de l'insécurité que nous devons éviter.

L'Histoire nous apprend que tout changement comporte un risque - tout peu arriver et très vite. Le processus de réforme à l'Est et le relâchement du contrôle soviétique en Europe de l'Est et en Europe centrale libèrent des tendances ethniques et nationales longtemps réprimées.

Le processus de mutation ne peut être maîtrisé que dans la stabilité assurée d'une alliance efficace. Le lien atlantique crée la stabilité qui nous permet d'utiliser à notre avantage historique la réorientation fondamentale à l'Est.

L'efficacité de notre effort de défense au sein de l'Alliance atlantique fait comprendre à tout homme politique soviétique que la voie pacifique seule apportera une solution. L'effort de défense ne fait pas obstacle à la détente mais jette les bases sûres du dialogue et de la coopération.

Autre raison de ne pas réduire notre défense : le potentiel soviétique n'a pratiquement pas changé. Les intentions actuelles de la direction soviétique, qui ne recherche assurément pas la guerre, ne peuvent servir de repère. Les intentions peuvent changer, tout comme les hommes politiques. Notre sécurité doit se fonder sur l'effort que nous sommes prêts à faire. C'est pourquoi la Bundeswehr et les forces alliées demeurent de première importance. Leur potentiel et leur degré de préparation ne doivent pas diminuer avant un accord effectif de désarmement.

Les intérêts vitaux des Allemands - liberté, unité, sécurité et changement - et de l'Alliance atlantique feront aussi bon ménage à l'avenir également. L'Alliance, pour nous, sera toujours de la plus haute importance. Dans cette enceinte, les Allemands qui vivent dans la liberté ont la possibilité de coopérer à la réalisation des aspirations majeures de notre temps : la mise en place d'un nouveau dispositif de sécurité et, plus particulièrement, d'un nouvel ordre politique en Europe.

Dans notre concept global, les membres de l'Alliance que nous sommes ont défini l'objectif du désarmement, à savoir la sécurité et la stabilité moyennant un arsenal réduit; la mise en place d'un nouvel ordre de sécurité mutuelle écartant de part et d'autre la possibilité d'une attaque surprise ou d'une opération de grande envergure. Jusqu'ici, seule l'Alliance atlantique y avait consenti.

Les dernières semaines l'ont clairement montré : l'initiative en matière de désarmement est du côté de l'Ouest.

Cependant, quelle que soit l'importance du désarmement, il ne saurait remplacer un nouvel ordre politique. Les armées, les armements ne sont pas à l'origine des tensions politiques mais leur conséquence. C'est pourquoi l'établissement d'un nouvel ordre de paix est prioritaire. Il doit se fonder sur la liberté, la démocratie et les droits de l'homme. C'est alors que les armées cessent d'être dangereuses, comme le montre bien l'exemple franco-allemand.

Il ne peut y avoir de doute : l'Histoire est de notre côté. La dynamique du processus historique joue en notre faveur. Nos idées progressent. L'avenir de l'Est est à l'Ouest et non pas le contraire. Soyons donc optimistes : la productivité de nos structures économiques est supérieure ; il en est de même de la souplesse et de la créativité de nos structures sociales. Plus important encore : nos valeurs reflètent la nature et les aspirations de l'homme.

Rien ne se produit spontanément. Tout dépend de nous, de notre cohésion, de notre aptitude à diriger et à stimuler la créativité.

L'avenir de cette Alliance est aussi la nôtre. Cette Alliance d'Etats, acteurs de l'Histoire, sera dans les prochaines décennies également, le garant de notre liberté et de la paix.

*A*ddress given at the 35th Annual Session of the North Atlantic Assembly

Rome
9 October
1989

The French writer, Albert Camus, once lamented that "man eventually becomes accustomed to everything". I have always believed that this is an unjustly pessimistic view of our human condition; and in recent weeks I have seen enough to convince me that Camus, on this point at least, was wrong:

- 30,000 East Germans abandoning home, friends, jobs, everything, to escape to a new life of opportunity but also uncertainty in the West;

- thousands of Soviet miners striking not for more pay, but for better supplies;

- the joy of Poles as they greet their first non-Communist Prime Minister in 40 years;

- over a million inhabitants of the Baltic states forming a human chain to protest against the forced annexation of their nations;

- demonstrators in Prague braving the security forces to mark the 21st anniversary of the Warsaw Pact invasion; or in Leipzig calling for freedom of speech.

Clearly the peoples of the East have not become accustomed to their lot. Totalitarian rule has not made people less attracted by freedom, democracy and self-determination. The opposite is true. Nor has it made them incapable of exercising these values through political organization and self-expression: look at the debates in the new Congress of the People's Deputies, the activities of the popular fronts, Solidarity in Poland or the opposition parties in Hungary. The demand for pluralism and reform can now be heard in every Eastern nation. Some régimes have responded with a promising beginning: they are experiencing the turbulence of change but at least they are finally grappling with the real problems that have held them back for so long.

103

Others have responded with repression, merely postponing the day of reckoning by loading their problems on to the future. In the meantime, their citizens flee, draining their economies of the precious skills and resources they will need most when ultimately they face up to the needs of tomorrow.

It is obvious: the division of Europe has become politically untenable: not because of Western "revanchism" to which Mr. Shevardnadze referred: not because of our interference in their domestic affairs. No. Simply for two reasons. First, because communism has failed as much in ideological as in economic and social terms. It is not able to solve the problems of modern industrialised societies in the age of global communication. And even more important: second, because you cannot suppress freedom forever. The natural aspiration of men to live and work freely is the driving force behind the historical process of change which we are witnessing. And no dictator or system - not even by using force - will be able to stop or prevent this dynamic change in the long-term. Of course, the Atlantic Alliance has played an historic rôle in creating the conditions for change:

> - by a strategy of deterrence and coalition defence that made it clear to the Soviet Union that it could never hope to solve its problems through intimidation or further expansion; only in co-operation with us could peaceful political change in Europe be secured;
> - by a policy of dialogue that also made it clear to the Soviet Union that we would be willing partners when the East was ready; on the basis of reciprocity and mutual trust, this Alliance would do its utmost to help the Soviet Union and its allies to become more peaceful, democratic and prosperous nations;
> - finally, by our cohesion, our readiness to accept the rôles, risks and responsibilities of the collective defence, our practice of working together for the good of all: these factors have created a dynamism and prosperity that have made clear, even now to its leaders, that old-style Communism has failed: the East cannot hope to catch up with the West on the basis of Marxist-Leninist ideology, but only through openness, pluralism, market forces, exposure to Western ideas and values.

And the windows having opened in the closed societies of Eastern Europe, the Allies do not intend to let them slam shut again. It is not possible to freeze political developments in the East in the name of stability. The *status quo* of the past was not stability; there can never be stability that leaves peoples unreconciled to their governments, or which is based on stagnation. The *status quo* served Soviet interests; the West has nothing to lose, and everything to gain by its passing. We set out our objectives during the recent NATO Summit. Our vision is threefold:

> - a Europe undivided in which all peoples would exercise their inherent

right of self-determination; in which all would enjoy the same freedoms and economic opportunities; and in which no nation need ever fear military intimidation or aggression from its neighbours;
- a new global order of cooperation in which East and West would work together to solve humanity's most pressing problems; drugs, terrorism, the environment, regional tensions;
- a more equal transatlantic partnership based on a strong North America and a united and cohesive Western Europe; one which would assume its full share of the common defence and of global responsibilities.

Yet when Mr. Gorbachev speaks of his vision, the "Common European Home", is he not striving to restore the *status quo* by other means? Certainly this concept, based on a "balance of interests", seems much more attractive than military confrontation, but it is still premissed on the ideological division of Europe; with the Eastern half wedded to Mr. Gorbachev's "socialism". This has little in common with the Alliance's vision of Europe; a vision that stresses freedom and self-determination. Nevertheless, we will use our limited influence to support change by supporting Gorbachev's and others' reforms towards more openness, pluralism, human rights and human contact. In doing so, we will serve the aspirations of our European neighbours. And we will also serve Western interests; for our future security and prosperity cannot be immunized from the turbulent forces at work in the East. We have everything to gain from the success of reform. We are interested in peaceful evolution, not in revolution or upheaval, but on the other hand, movement always means partial instability. There is no real alternative to change. History does not allow stagnation.

Communist values in Eastern Europe have been upheld only through the deliberate policy and military control of the Soviet Union. Western values, on the other hand, have triumphed in Eastern Europe through force of example. We have not needed to promote them; democracy, human dignity, openness, market forces, self-determination: these are the ideas that spread their influence from the inside. The East is turning to the West.

East and West will not be reconciled, as some once believed, by converging in the middle. The debate takes place wholly on our terms. Our values and systems hold the key to the political and economic future of the Soviet Union and its allies. This is the reality with which Communist leaders must deal. Before building new political and economic structures, they must find a safe method of dismantling the old. Finding one's way out of a labyrinth has always proved more difficult than becoming lost in one. It is a predicament well summarized by Soviet academician, Oleg Bogomolov: "It is easy to turn an aquarium into fish soup, but how do you turn fish soup back into an aquarium?".

The challenge of a long-term programme of fundamental economic and societal reform would be daunting in itself; but it is severely compounded by the immediate economic crisis in which most of Eastern Europe now finds itself. The report of your own Political Committee on Soviet foreign policy under Gorbachev is eloquent on this topic. It notes, for instance, that Soviet economic growth is dwindling at 1.5%, the announced budget deficit is some $160 billion, or 9% of GNP. The Soviet share of world trade is only 4%, and for 1989 total hard currency income is estimated at only $24 billion, of which $18 billion is allocated to servicing the $43 billion foreign debt. The supply situation is now chaotic. Of the 1,200 items in the Soviet housewife's official shopping basket, only 200 are widely available. There is no lack of money. Indeed, as your report also points out, about $500 billion worth of rubles is being hoarded because there is nothing to buy. Such shortages are largely responsible for the current unrest amongst Soviet workers.

Indeed the experts now take a sombre view of the success of perestroïka. One of our NATO studies, for instance, looks at the future prospects for the Soviet economy. It assumes three models: that Gorbachev's reforms will succeed; that they will partially succeed, or that they will fail. What is interesting is that the actual outcome would seem to make very little difference. The best scenario gives a growth rate of only 2.6% and the worst 1.6%. And these small rates of projected growth do not allow for the likely increase in the Soviet population which would make them even more modest. So even the most optimistic assumption does not provide sufficient growth to make a significant qualitative difference to either the Soviet economy or Soviet society.

Political reform is thus coupled with economic necessity - that much is clear. The same can also be said in the case of the two other Warsaw Pact reformers - Poland and Hungary. Both are crippled by foreign debt repayments; there is a glaring lack of managers and administrators skilled in Western industrial and business techniques; both are experiencing considerable problems in converting their industries to Western competitive standards. The Institute for Economic and Market Research in Budapest, for instance, has said that only one in three Hungarian companies would survive in free trade with the West. In Poland the economic situation borders on the catastrophic: this past summer, while 24 Western nations were discussing food aid for Poland in Brussels, a grocer's shop in Katowice became the sole source of supply for 120,000 people. Poland is not a Third World country even if its per capita GNP now approximates that of Indonesia. These nations are caught up in a race against time: will political reform be fast enough to head off the mounting economic difficulties? Or will these economic difficulties be so severe as to undermine political reform?

Behind the rhetoric of Mr. Gorbachev's Common European Home lies the reality of a widening gap between East and West; and the knowledge that the East does not possess the resources to avert by itself a major tragedy in the

106

short term, and begin to narrow this gap in the long term. The NATO Summit Declaration has given the West the overall conceptual architecture that it must have in its approach to the East. For NATO deals with East-West relations in a global sense; the Alliance integrates the economic factors with the other features of these relations: military security, political change, respect for human rights and basic freedoms. Helping the East to reform is not just an economic task; it is first and foremost a political challenge. We cannot divide our strategy into separate tracks - economic, political, military - and allow them to evolve in isolation. How much financial assistance, for example, should we give to a nation that still spends 15-17% of its GNP on weapons that are largely fielded against us? How can we persuade a Western banker to put his money into Hungary when he can invest in a country, like Czechoslovakia or the GDR, that has a far worse human rights record but a much better international credit rating?

The judgements that have to be made are highly political. Even if the Alliance does not have responsibility for specific aid programmes, only NATO can harmonise and co-ordinate the efforts of the member nations as a whole on these herculean tasks; only NATO brings the combined resources of North America and Western Europe to bear on them.

Our Alliance strategy **is** an integrated one. We offer the East co-operation; indeed following our NATO Summit, Alliance governments have already started on the practical implementation of such co-operation:
- food assistance to Poland - 24 Western nations are involved; the United States has doubled its amount;
- trade facilitation, such as the recent economic agreement between the EEC and Poland, or the decision of the United States to grant Hungary most favoured trading nation status;
- private enterprise trusts to be established in Poland and Hungary;
- funds for pollution control projects;
- joint ventures;
- training courses and facilities for Eastern managers;
- a review of the debt burden of Poland and Hungary;
- scholarships for the study of Western institutions.

We are concentrating the major part of our efforts on Poland and Hungary; the two countries that are taking the necessary political steps to move closer to democracy, and to create the political conditions that will give their reforms a fighting chance of success. Poland and Hungary are the two test cases for our Alliance strategy. If reform fails, the lessons will not be lost on the hardliners in Czechoslovakia and East Germany. But if reform succeeds, that success will generate irresistible pressures for similar change throughout Eastern Europe.

It is clear that the success of this Western programme depends on a total reshaping of East-West relations. That is our goal. NATO has thus issued the East a number of reasonable challenges:
- first and foremost, the Warsaw Pact must scale back its forces in Eastern Europe to a level where an attack is impossible; I call on them to accept our proposals to eliminate conventional disparities and provide for stringent stabilization and verification measures;
- economic reforms must not be designed merely to relieve immediate economic pressures, but to permanently introduce market mechanisms;
- democratic institutions must be allowed to take root;
- human rights and the undertakings of the Helsinki Final Act must be respected in full; only in this way will the Eastern governments persuade their populations to accept the sacrifices of reform, and to work to rebuild their nations;
- the Soviet Union and its allies must co-operate with us on global concerns: environmental pollution, terrorism, the proliferation of dangerous weapons, regional tensions.

The post-war period has come to an end. We are seeing the profound transformation of the European political and security structure. This offers us opportunities which we should and will not miss. We are not sitting back, nor are we passive. We are actively shaping events. This is primarily a political Alliance with eminently political tasks. Its rôle in the future clearly is twofold. To serve as an instrument of political change but also as this basis of military stability. Our motto is: "change in security".

It is clear the Alliance is on the political offensive. Yet a political strategy must have a secure foundation. That does not mean that our defences have to be at the same level as today. We have pushed hard for the CFE talks in Vienna and we have done, and continue to do, revolutionary conceptual work to initiate the more reassuring defence postures of the future. The Soviet response in Vienna has been extremely encouraging; and following the meeting in Wyoming between the US and Soviet Foreign Ministers, we may be on the verge of major breakthroughs in the Geneva START talks and the negotiations for a worldwide ban of chemical weapons. Our timetable of one year to reach a CFE agreement is ambitious but realistic. Yet let us not forget two things:

First: that soldiers and arms are not the main problem between East and West. They are not the cause of the division of Europe. The tensions can only be overcome by a new political order ending the suppression of freedom and self-determination. In such a new political order armies would become meaningless.
Second: that the objective of arms control is to make the East-West security system a more co-operative one; safer, more transparent with lower levels of armaments; it is not to do away with that security system. Our

weapons are not merely a reflection of the weapons on the other side; they are a response to the political instabilities that we have to live with. Whatever scenario you choose, our unruly neighbour to the East will remain the problem child of any European security structure; too large to be internally cohesive; too different to be just a normal member of a European Community of nations. And arms control and diplomacy, however important, cannot suffice for this task; they must be backed by a solid defence. Thus the weapons and operational concepts that we retain at the end of our multilateral build-down must be kept up-to-date and effective. Even in an age of dramatically improved East-West relations, there will not be a cut-price security package for this Alliance.

I will not hide my concern at a tendency that I observe today in most of our member nations which are starting to unilaterally reduce their defence efforts - thus pre-empting the future results of possible arms control agreements. That is what I call structural disarmament. It is wrong and dangerous. And we do not even get the credit for it with our public opinion.

Thus, as parliamentarians, there are two things that you can do to ensure the success of NATO in the great political tasks it faces. First, present the case convincingly against structural disarmament on ours, the weaker side. This is the enemy of true arms control for it will undermine our position in Vienna at the very moment when we have never had a more golden opportunity. Second, use your influence to contribute to greater East-West contact and exchanges and to make the Western reform programme a bold, imaginative one. The North Atlantic Assembly has always had two crucial rôles: bringing together Alliance parliamentarians to discuss matters of common concern, and to inform the public better about NATO's rôle and objectives. From your recent visits to Hungary, Czechoslovakia, Poland and the Soviet Union, you have added a third: building a parliamentary tradition in Eastern Europe. It is a noble cause. I support you, and count on you.

Discours prononcé à la 35ème session annuelle de l'Assemblée de l'Atlantique Nord

Rome
9 octobre
1989

Albert Camus a un jour déploré que l'homme finisse par s'habituer à tout. J'ai toujours pensé que c'était là une vue injustement pessimiste de notre condition humaine; et j'ai assisté ces dernières semaines à assez d'événements pour me convaincre que, sur ce point du moins, Camus avait tort :

- 30.000 Allemands de l'Est abandonnant tout - foyer, amis, emploi - pour chercher à l'Ouest une vie nouvelle pleine de possibilités, mais aussi d'incertitudes;
- des milliers de mineurs soviétiques en grève pour obtenir, non pas de meilleurs salaires, mais des magasins mieux approvisionnés;
- la joie des Polonais saluant la nomination d'un premier ministre non communiste pour la première fois depuis quarante ans;
- plus d'un million d'habitants des Etats baltes formant une chaîne humaine pour protester contre l'annexion forcée de leurs pays;
- des manifestants qui, à Prague, bravent les forces de sécurité pour marquer le 21ème anniversaire de l'invasion de leur pays par les troupes du Pacte de Varsovie, ou qui, à Leipzig, réclament la liberté de parole.

A l'évidence, les peuples de l'Est ne se sont pas habitués à leur sort. Le totalitarisme n'a en rien diminué l'attrait de la liberté, de la démocratie et de l'autodétermination aux yeux des citoyens. Bien au contraire. Il ne les a pas davantage empêchés de mettre ces valeurs en pratique en s'organisant politiquement et en exprimant leurs aspirations, ce dont témoignent les débats au nouveau Congrès des députés du peuple, les activités des fronts populaires, de Solidarité en Pologne ou des partis d'opposition en Hongrie. Des appels au pluralisme et à la réforme se font maintenant entendre dans tous les pays de l'Est. Certains régimes y ont répondu par une attitude qui ne laisse pas d'être prometteuse : s'ils traversent maintenant les turbulences du changement, ils sont du moins finalement aux prises avec les vrais problèmes qui bloquaient depuis si longtemps toute évolution. D'autres y ont répondu par la répression, ne faisant que retarder le jour du grand bilan, en éludant leurs problèmes et en obérant ainsi l'avenir. Pendant ce temps, les citoyens de ces pays prennent la fuite, privant l'économie nationale de compétences et de ressources précieuses, qui seront des plus nécessaires lorsque viendra le moment inéluctable de faire face aux besoins du lendemain.

Il est tout à fait manifeste que, politiquement, la division de l'Europe est devenue impossible à maintenir. Non pas à cause du "revanchisme" occidental dont a parlé M. Chevardnadze. Non pas à cause d'une ingérence de notre part dans les affaires intérieures d'autres pays. Mais simplement pour deux raisons. D'abord parce que le communisme a échoué, aussi bien sur le plan idéologique que sur le plan économique et sur le plan social. Il ne parvient pas à résoudre les problèmes des sociétés industrielles modernes à l'âge de la communication planétaire. Ensuite, et c'est là un point encore plus important, parce qu'on ne peut pas étouffer pour toujours le désir de liberté. L'aspiration naturelle des hommes à vivre et travailler librement est le moteur du processus historique de changement auquel nous assistons aujourd'hui. Et nul dictateur, nul système - pas même en recourant à la force - ne pourra, à terme, arrêter cette dynamique du changement. Il est bien certain que l'Alliance atlantique a joué un rôle historique dans la création des conditions de changement :
- par une stratégie de dissuasion et de défense collective qui a fait clairement comprendre à l'Union soviétique qu'elle ne pourrait jamais compter résoudre ses problèmes par l'intimidation ou par de nouvelles menées expansionnistes; c'est seulement en coopérant avec nous qu'il sera possible d'assurer un changement politique pacifique en Europe;
- par une politique de dialogue qui a aussi fait clairement comprendre à l'Union soviétique qu'elle trouverait en nous des partenaires ouverts dès que l'Est serait lui-même prêt; sur la base de la réciprocité et de la confiance mutuelle, notre Alliance mettra tout en oeuvre pour aider l'Union soviétique et ses alliés à devenir des nations plus pacifiques, plus démocratiques et plus prospères;
- enfin, par notre cohésion, notre acceptation des rôles, des risques et des responsabilités de la défense collective, par une coopération conçue pour le bien de tous, nous avons réuni les facteurs nécessaires pour créer un dynamisme et une prospérité qui ont fait clairement apparaître, même à ses chefs de file, la faillite du communisme à l'ancienne mode : l'Est ne peut espérer rattraper l'Ouest par la vertu de l'idéologie marxiste-léniniste, mais par la pratique de l'ouverture et du pluralisme, par le jeu des forces du marché et par la confrontation avec les idées et les valeurs occidentales.

Et maintenant que les fenêtres se sont ouvertes dans les sociétés fermées d'Europe de l'Est, les Alliés n'ont pas l'intention de les laisser se refermer brutalement. Il n'est pas possible de geler l'évolution politique à l'Est au nom de la stabilité. Le statu quo du passé n'était pas la stabilité; on ne saurait concevoir une stabilité qui laisse les peuples en désaccord avec leurs gouvernements, ou qui soit fondée sur la stagnation. Le statu quo servait les intérêts de l'Union soviétique; l'Ouest n'a rien à perdre et tout à gagner à sa disparition. Nous avons fixé nos objectifs lors du récent Sommet de l'OTAN. Notre vision est triple :

- une Europe non divisée dans laquelle tous les peuples exerceraient leur droit imprescriptible à l'autodétermination, dans laquelle tous jouiraient des mêmes libertés et des mêmes opportunités économiques, et dans laquelle aucun Etat n'aurait jamais à redouter une intimidation militaire ou une agression de la part de ses voisins;
- un nouvel ordre mondial de coopération dans lequel l'Est et l'Ouest oeuvreraient ensemble pour résoudre les problèmes les plus pressants de l'humanité : la drogue, le terrorisme, l'environnement, les tensions régionales;
- une association transatlantique plus égale entre une Amérique du Nord forte et une Europe occidentale unie et cohérente, celle-ci assumant pleinement sa part de la défense commune et des responsabilités à l'échelle mondiale.

Pourtant, quand M. Gorbatchev parle de sa vision, de la "Maison commune européenne", ne cherche-t-il pas à rétablir le statu quo par d'autres moyens? Certes, ce concept, fondé sur un "équilibre des intérêts", paraît beaucoup plus séduisant que la confrontation militaire, mais il reste fondé sur la prémisse de la division idéologique de l'Europe, la partie orientale du Vieux Continent demeurant attachée au "socialisme" de M. Gorbatchev. Cela n'a pas grand-chose de commun avec la vision qu'a l'alliance de l'Europe, une vision qui privilégie la liberté et l'autodétermination. Néanmoins, nous utiliserons l'influence limitée dont nous disposons pour soutenir le changement en soutenant les réformes de M. Gorbatchev et d'autres dans le sens d'un développement de l'ouverture, du pluralisme, des droits de l'homme et des contacts entre les personnes. En agissant ainsi, nous servirons les aspirations de nos voisins européens. Et nous servirons aussi les intérêts de l'Ouest car, pour l'avenir, notre sécurité et notre prospérité ne peuvent être immunisées contre les forces turbulentes qui s'exercent à l'Est. Nous avons tout à gagner au succès de la réforme. Nous voulons une évolution pacifique, non pas une révolution ni un bouleversement - mais, d'autre part, le mouvement implique toujours une instabilité partielle. Rien ne saurait vraiment se substituer au changement. L'histoire ne permet pas la stagnation.

Les valeurs communistes n'ont été maintenues en Europe de l'Est que par la volonté politique et le contrôle militaire délibérés de l'Union soviétique.

Les valeurs occidentales, en revanche, ont triomphé en Europe de l'Est grâce à la vertu de l'exemple. Nous n'avons pas eu besoin de les promouvoir : la démocratie, la dignité de la personne humaine, l'ouverture, les forces du marché, l'autodétermination sont autant d'idées dont l'influence se répand de l'intérieur. L'Est vient vers l'Ouest.

L'Est et l'Ouest ne se rapprocheront pas, comme certains l'ont cru à un moment, en allant chacun vers le milieu. Le débat a lieu entièrement à nos conditions. C'est dans nos valeurs et nos systèmes que réside la clé de l'avenir politique et économique de l'Union soviétique et de ses alliés. Telle est la réalité à laquelle les dirigeants communistes doivent faire face. Avant d'édifier de nouvelles structures politiques et économiques, ils doivent trouver un moyen sûr de démanteler les anciennes. Trouver la sortie d'un labyrinthe a toujours été plus difficile que de s'y perdre. C'est une situation qu'a bien résumée l'académicien soviétique Oleg Bogomolov : "Il est facile de transformer un aquarium en soupe de poisson, mais comment faire pour retransformer la soupe de poisson en aquarium?".

Le défi que représente un programme à long terme de réforme fondamentale de l'économie et de la société est déjà formidable en soi; mais il est sérieusement aggravé par la crise économique immédiate que connaissent aujourd'hui la plupart des pays d'Europe de l'Est. Le rapport de votre Commission politique sur la politique étrangère de l'Union soviétique à l'ère Gorbatchev est éloquent à ce sujet. Il note par exemple que la croissance économique de l'Union soviétique tombe à 1,5% et que le déficit budgétaire annoncé est d'environ 160 milliards de dollars, soit 9% du PNB. La part de l'Union soviétique dans le commerce mondial n'est que de 4% et, pour 1989, les recettes totales en devises fortes sont estimées à 24 milliards de dollars seulement, dont 18 milliards sont réservés au service d'une dette extérieure de 43 milliards de dollars. La situation des approvisionnements est aujourd'hui chaotique. Sur les 1.200 articles qui, officiellement remplissent le panier de la ménagère soviétique, 200 seulement sont largement disponibles. Ce n'est pas l'argent qui manque. Au contraire, comme votre rapport le souligne aussi, des sommes représentant environ 500 milliards de roubles sont thésaurisées parce qu'il n'y a rien à acheter. Ces pénuries sont en grande partie responsables de l'agitation actuelle des travailleurs soviétiques.

Les experts sont maintenant assez pessimistes quant au succès de la perestroïka. C'est ainsi qu'une de nos études de l'OTAN considère les perspectives de l'économie soviétique. Elle envisage trois hypothèses : les réformes de M. Gorbatchev réussiront, elles réussiront partiellement, ou elles échoueront. Ce qui est intéressant, c'est que le résultat final semblerait ne faire que très peu de différence. Le scénario le plus favorable prévoit un taux de croissance de 2,6% seulement et le plus défavorable de 1,6%. Or ces taux limités de croissance prévus ne prennent pas en compte l'accroissement probable de la population soviétique qui les rendrait encore plus modestes. Ainsi, même dans l'hypothèse la plus optimiste, on ne s'attend pas à une croissance suffisante pour permettre une différence qualitative sensible ni pour l'économie ni pour la société soviétique.

Donc, les réformes politiques vont de pair avec les nécessités économiques - cela, au moins, apparaît clairement. Et c'est aussi vrai dans le cas des deux autres pays du Pacte de Varsovie qui se sont engagés sur la voie des réformes - la Pologne et la Hongrie. Tous deux sont durement touchés par le remboursement de leur dette extérieure; ils manquent au plus haut point de gestionnaires et d'administrateurs rompus aux techniques industrielles et commerciales de l'Ouest; tous deux se heurtent à de graves problèmes pour amener leur industrie aux niveaux compétitifs occidentaux. A Budapest, l'Institut pour la recherche économique et les études de marchés, par exemple, a déclaré que seule une entreprise hongroise sur trois survivrait à l'instauration d'un système de libre-échange avec l'Ouest. En Pologne, la situation économique touche à la catastrophe : cet été, alors que 24 pays occidentaux discutaient, à Bruxelles, de l'aide alimentaire à la Pologne, une épicerie de Katowice était devenue l'unique source de ravitaillement de 120.000 personnes. La Pologne n'est pas un pays du Tiers monde, même si son PNB par habitant est maintenant voisin de celui de l'Indonésie. Ces pays se trouvent pris dans une course contre la montre : les réformes politiques seront-elles assez rapides pour leur permettre de parer à des difficultés économiques grandissantes ? Ou ces difficultés économiques en arriveront-elles à saper les réformes politiques ?

Derrière la rhétorique de M. Gorbatchev parlant d'une Maison commune européenne, il y a la réalité d'un écart qui s'élargit entre l'Est et l'Ouest, et aussi la conscience du fait que l'Est n'est pas en mesure d'éviter par ses propres moyens une véritable tragédie à court terme, ni de seulement commencer à faire diminuer cet écart à long terme. La Déclaration du Sommet de l'OTAN a fourni à l'Ouest l'architecture conceptuelle générale dont il avait besoin dans son approche de l'Est. Car l'OTAN traite les relations Est-Ouest d'une façon globale; l'Alliance intègre les facteurs économiques aux autres éléments de ces relations : la sécurité militaire, le changement politique, le respect des droits de l'homme et des libertés fondamentales. Aider l'Est à opérer des réformes n'est pas seulement une tâche d'ordre économique; c'est aussi, et avant tout, un défi politique. Nous ne pouvons pas diviser notre stratégie entre trois voies distinctes - économique, politique, militaire - et la laisser évoluer séparément dans chacune de ces voies. Dans quelles limites, par exemple, devrions-nous accorder une aide financière à un pays qui dépense toujours de 15 à 17 % de son PNB pour se doter d'armes en grande partie dirigées contre nous ? Comment pouvons-nous persuader un banquier occidental de placer son argent en Hongrie quand il peut investir dans un pays qui, comme la Tchécoslovaquie ou la RDA, a un comportement bien pire dans le domaine des droits de l'homme, mais une bien meilleure position de solvabilité internationale ?

Les jugements auxquels il faut arriver sont hautement politiques. Même si l'Alliance n'a pas la responsabilité de programmes d'aide spécifiques, seule l'OTAN peut harmoniser et coordonner les efforts déployés par l'ensemble des pays membres dans ces travaux d'Hercule; seule l'OTAN y fait jouer les ressources combinées de l'Amérique du Nord et de l'Europe occidentale.

La stratégie de notre Alliance est véritablement une stratégie intégrée. Nous offrons à l'Est une coopération; en fait, après le Sommet de l'OTAN, les gouvernements des pays alliés ont déjà commencé à mettre cette coopération en pratique :
- aide alimentaire à la Pologne - 24 pays occidentaux y participent; les Etats-Unis ont doublé leur aide;
- mesures destinées à faciliter les échanges commerciaux, comme l'accord économique récemment conclu entre la CEE et la Pologne, ou la décision des Etats-Unis d'accorder à la Hongrie le statut de partenaire commercial le plus favorisé;
- établissement prévu, en Pologne et en Hongrie, de sociétés fiduciaires dans le cadre d'entreprises privées;
- crédits destinés à des projets de lutte contre la pollution;
- entreprises conjointes;
- facilités et stages de formation à l'intention de gestionnaires de l'Est;
- réexamen de la dette de la Pologne et de la Hongrie;
- bourses pour l'étude des institutions occidentales.

Nous centrons la majeure partie de nos efforts sur la Pologne et la Hongrie, c'est-à-dire sur les deux pays qui prennent les mesures politiques nécessaires pour se rapprocher de la démocratie et pour créer les conditions politiques qui donneront à leurs réformes d'assez bonnes chances de succès. La Pologne et la Hongrie sont les deux cas-tests pour la stratégie de notre Alliance. Si les réformes échouent, les leçons n'en seront pas perdues pour les tenants de la ligne dure en Tchécoslovaquie et en Allemagne de l'Est. Mais si elles réussissent, cette réussite engendrera des pressions irrésistibles en faveur d'un changement analogue dans toute l'Europe de l'Est.

Il est clair que le succès de ce programme occidental dépend d'une refonte totale des relations Est-Ouest. Or, tel est bien notre objectif, et c'est ainsi que l'OTAN propose à l'Est un certain nombre de défis raisonnables :
- par-dessus tout, le Pacte de Varsovie doit ramener ses forces en Europe de l'Est à un niveau tel qu'une attaque en devienne impossible; j'appelle les pays du Pacte à accepter nos propositions visant à éliminer les disparités dans le domaine conventionnel, et à adopter des mesures énergiques de stabilisation et de vérification;
- les réformes économiques ne doivent pas être destinées uniquement à atténuer les pressions économiques immédiates, mais doivent tendre à mettre en place de façon durable les mécanismes du marché;

- il faut permettre à des institutions démocratiques de voir le jour;
- les droits de l'homme, de même que les engagements pris aux termes de l'Acte final d'Helsinki, doivent être intégralement respectés; c'est à cette seule condition que les gouvernements des pays de l'Est pourront persuader la population de ces pays d'accepter les sacrifices liés à la réforme, et d'oeuvrer à la reconstruction nationale;
- l'Union soviétique et ses alliés doivent coopérer avec nous sur les grands problèmes mondiaux - pollution de l'environnement, terrorisme, prolifération des armes dangereuses, tensions régionales.

L'époque de l'après-guerre est révolue. Nous assistons à une profonde transformation de la structure de l'Europe sur le plan politique comme sur celui de la sécurité. Cela nous offre des occasions que nous ne pouvons pas, et que nous ne voulons pas, laisser s'échapper. Et, en effet, nous ne nous accordons aucun répit : loin de rester passifs, nous nous employons à façonner l'avenir. Notre Alliance est avant tout une Alliance politique, aux tâches éminemment politiques. Son rôle futur est manifestement double. Elle sera un instrument du changement politique, mais aussi un gage de stabilité militaire. Notre devise est "le changement dans la sécurité".

Nul ne contestera que l'Alliance est en pleine offensive politique. Mais toute stratégie politique doit avoir une base solide. Cela ne signifie pas que nos moyens de défense doivent rester au même niveau qu'aujourd'hui. Nous avons tout fait pour que s'ouvrent les négociations de Vienne sur les FCE, et nous avons mené, et continuons de mener, une action qui bouleverse bien des concepts, pour permettre une évolution vers des appareils défensifs moins menaçants. La réponse des Soviétiques à Vienne a été extrêmement encourageante; et après la rencontre dans le Wyoming entre les ministres des Affaires étrangères des Etats-Unis et de l'Union soviétique, il se pourrait que l'on enregistre bientôt des progrès décisifs dans les conversations START de Genève et les négociations sur l'interdiction des armes chimiques à l'échelle mondiale. Le délai d'un an que nous nous sommes fixé pour parvenir à un accord sur les FCE est ambitieux mais réaliste. Cependant, il y a deux facteurs que nous ne pouvons pas perdre de vue :

Premièrement: le problème qui existe entre l'Est et l'Ouest n'est pas tant un problème d'armes et de soldats, car ce ne sont pas eux qui ont causé la division de l'Europe. Les tensions ne pourront être surmontées que par l'instauration d'un nouvel ordre politique supprimant toute entrave à la liberté et à l'autodétermination. Avec un tel ordre politique, les armées deviendraient inutiles.

Deuxièmement: l'objectif de la maîtrise des armements est d'introduire dans le système de sécurité Est-Ouest une plus grande coopération, et de le rendre plus sûr, plus transparent, à des niveaux d'armements moins élevés; il ne consiste pas à abolir ce système de sécurité. Nos armements ne sont pas le simple reflet des armements de l'autre camp; ils existent à cause des instabilités politiques auxquelles nous sommes confrontés. Quel que soit le scénario envisagé, notre turbulent voisin de l'Est restera l'enfant terrible de toute structure de sécurité européenne - trop grand pour parvenir à la cohésion interne, trop différent pour être membre d'une communauté de nations européennes exactement comme d'autres pays. Si importantes qu'elles soient, la maîtrise des armements et la diplomatie ne peuvent suffire à la réalisation de cet objectif; elles doivent s'appuyer sur une défense solide. Ainsi, les armes et les concepts opérationnels que nous conserverons au terme d'une réduction multilatérale des forces devront rester modernes et efficaces. Même avec l'amélioration spectaculaire des relations Est-Ouest, l'Alliance ne peut se permettre une sécurité au rabais.

Je ne vous cacherai pas ma préoccupation devant une tendance que j'observe aujourd'hui dans la plupart des pays membres, qui commencent à réduire unilatéralement leurs efforts de défense, compromettant ainsi les résultats futurs d'éventuels accords de maîtrise des armements. C'est ce que j'appelle le désarmement structurel. Une telle politique est à la fois erronée et dangereuse. Et notre opinion publique ne nous en fait même pas crédit.

Il y a donc pour vous, parlementaires, deux manières d'assurer la réalisation des grands desseins politiques de l'OTAN : premièrement, soyez assez convaincants pour faire apparaître qu'un désarmement structurel est pour nous, le camp le plus faible, inacceptable. Il va à l'encontre d'une véritable maîtrise des armements, car il ne peut que saper notre position à Vienne alors même que s'offre une occasion comme nous n'en avons jamais connue; deuxièmement, usez de votre influence pour promouvoir un développement des contacts et des échanges Est-Ouest et pour faire du programme de réformes occidental un programme original et audacieux. L'Assemblée de l'Atlantique Nord a toujours eu deux rôles clés : réunir des parlementaires de l'Alliance pour qu'ils discutent de questions d'intérêt commun, et mieux informer le public sur la mission et les objectifs de l'OTAN. Depuis vos visites récentes en Hongrie, en Tchécoslovaquie, en Pologne et en Union soviétique, un troisième s'y est ajouté - celui qui consiste à créer une tradition parlementaire en Europe de l'Est. Peut-on imaginer plus noble cause ? Sachez, en tout cas, que je vous soutiens, et que je compte sur vous.

Reshaping East-West Relations

Washington DC
12 October
1989

It is a well-known fact that historians do not like dates. It is not that they deny that celebrated events actually did take place in, say, 1066, 1492 or 1789; but they usually insist that these events are not as significant as we were taught to believe at school. We should see them instead as just convenient reference points in an ongoing historical process.

This is no doubt sound advice; but I am going to disregard it. For I firmly believe that 1989 will go down in history as a watershed in East-West relations, and as a decisive point in the evolution of the Atlantic Alliance.

In 1989, the Soviet bloc in Eastern Europe began to crumble. It is not the fact that its internal contradictions are breaking it apart which surprises. But there are many who held that this could be a very long drawn-out affair. Yet with the onset of internal crisis, the Communist system has begun to unravel faster than anyone would have thought possible, and faster change has brought with it greater unpredictability. Senator Nunn has hit the nail on the head in this respect when he says that "Communism has lost, but democracy has not yet won"; but we have witnessed developments sufficiently important to make a return to the Stalinist past well-nigh unthinkable:

- Poland has elected its first non-Communist government in forty years with a Prime Minister who is a Catholic and, we have every reason to believe, a true reforming democrat;
- Hungary has braved the wrath of its Eastern neighbours by opening its border with Austria; moreover it has repudiated a bilateral treaty with its Warsaw Pact ally, the GDR, in order to uphold its commitments under the

Helsinki Final Act. Hungarians are planning now for the first completely free election ever to be held in a communist country;
- the Soviet Union has held a partially free election and a new Supreme Soviet has been nominated. It is not yet a parliament that we would recognise in the Western sense, but compared with its predecessor it represents a minor revolution. It has already flexed its muscles in debating the Afghan War, corruption in the Communist nomenklatura, and the appointment of government ministers. Its main opposition movement has the nation's most renowned dissident as its co-leader;
- the Soviet Union, having announced unilateral force reductions last December, has begun to pull troops and equipment out of Eastern Europe; not as much as we would like, or need, but, again, a start.

Theorists of totalitarianism used to point to two essential features: it could not change internally, and it would not give up its military power. But those are two areas where the Soviet Union has begun to move in 1989. How far and to what purpose we cannot yet say. Most encouraging of all, perhaps, is that people living in totalitarian societies have not become passive and apolitical.

The people in Solidarity, the Hungarian opposition or the Soviet popular fronts would, I trust, agree that they are both the beneficiaries as well as the instigators of change. Communism has not failed, nor is the Soviet bloc imploding, by accident. When the Atlantic Alliance was established forty years ago, it had a dual purpose: to give the West military protection; and to contain Soviet power in such a way that the Communist system would be forced to mellow. The first mission was ensured from day one; the second has taken until 1989. How was it achieved?

- by denying the Soviet Union the possibility of further expansion, thereby forcing it to fall back on its internal resources and systemic contradictions;
- by offering the Soviet Union and its allies the hand of dialogue and co-operation, encouraging them to change by making it clear that the West would not seek to exploit their difficulties; on the contrary we would provide them with help and a stable international environment;
- by keeping our Alliance strong and cohesive; our internal political stability, our dynamism and prosperity have opened up a widening gap *vis-à-vis* the East; the Soviet Union can no longer compete on the basis of Marxist-Leninist ideology and practice; it is falling further - perhaps irretrievably - behind.

The 40th anniversary of NATO has made the past look all the more positive because of the hopeful future that lies before us. The lean, Cold War years of frustration and perseverance have finally borne fruit. The *status quo* is condemned; that much is clear. We are responsible for change; Gorbachev is as much the product of our system as of his own. Certainly the dramatic suddenness of the decline of Communism, the pent-up frustrations and pressures that have been released, have made some wonder whether the old *status quo* of division and confrontation is not somehow preferable to the uncertainties we now face. But the *status quo*, in its own way, was dangerous and explosive. It gave us a hazardous military stability, and, more importantly, even less political stability. We neither could, nor wanted to, sustain it.

No doubt change is producing turbulence and instability; but these are the inevitable by-products of necessary change. We have to mitigate their negative aspects, and use our limited influence to ensure a peaceful evolution towards freedom. The imprints of change are obvious:

> - more open borders; more flow of information; instant communications; increased human contacts;
> - decentralisation of political control, of economic mechanisms;
> - the emergence everywhere of organized opposition forces calling for reform;
> - not just populations, but also Communist élites turning to the West for guidance, inspiration and help; using our concepts and values.

So, in Eastern Europe, the lesson of 1989 is clear: the question is not if, but when, and to what degree, the Communist systems will transform themselves by absorbing pluralism, human rights and market mechanisms. Their dilemma is embodied both in Mr. Gorbachev's defensive assertions that he is not abandoning socialism, and in the definition by an Eastern joke of "Socialism" as the long and difficult path from Capitalism to Capitalism. And it is not true, as Mr. Shevardnadze and others have charged, that their dilemmas stem from Western efforts to destabilise the East, or forces of Revanchism. The fault is with them: the failure of their systems to meet human aspirations. I hope these people do not really mean what they say. For, if so, it means they have understood nothing about the reality they face.

Our Alliance has the political initiative. We must secure change, anchor it to a new stable and durable political structure in Europe. The NATO Summit reaffirmed the Alliance's political vocation; not only to preserve the integrity of its territory, but to build a new Europe in which security is preserved by common liberal values, not military straitjackets. Everyone now knows what our blueprint for the year 2000 is: a Europe undivided, based on self-determination, democracy and market forces. On the other hand, confusion still reigns supreme as to what Mr. Gorbachev means by a Common European Home. But from my reading of Mr. Gorbachev's speech in Strasbourg, it appears that his vision is essentially the preservation of the *status quo*, while ours is of a dynamic process of overcoming the division of Europe.

You have seen our Summit Declaration. It is a conceptual architecture for managing change in Eastern Europe; not only by the NATO countries but by the West overall. We are fully engaged in assisting Poland and Hungary with their reform effort. I do not need to describe in detail all the initiatives: food aid by the 24 "Brussels group" of Western nations; discussions on debt in the Paris Club; on fresh credits in the IMF; bilateral initiatives to set up private enterprise trusts, or train Eastern managers and civil servants. I am, of course, not claiming credit on behalf of NATO for all these actions. It is obvious that the Alliance does not have, and cannot have, institutional responsibility for such operational tasks. But they flow from the framework set by the Summit Declaration and they will be co-ordinated within the Alliance, where we can look at the **integrated** picture: economic, military, and political, and bring to bear the combined weight of North America and Western Europe. And the overall package does not simply add up to a short-term relief operation for Poland and Hungary: it is a long-term programme designed to fundamentally reshape East-West relations - and to allow Communism to phase itself out peacefully. If reform fails, the lessons will not be lost on the hardliners in Czechoslovakia and East Germany. But if reform succeeds, that success will generate irresistible pressures for similar change throughout Eastern Europe.

I like to emphasize that NATO is above all a political Alliance with an essential rôle as an instrument of peaceful political change. Less has been said about the future rôle of defence, as if it were suddenly less important.

But manifestly it is not. Our Summit meeting made clear that our ambitious political strategy will succeed only if it is backed up by a robust defence, based on both nuclear and conventional forces. Periods of great political change are also periods of greater risk. And the larger the risk, the more it has to be underwritten by a sound insurance policy. To guard against setbacks and disappointments; to provide a framework of stability that will maximise our control over the pace and scope of change; above all to convince an over-armed and disturbed Soviet Union that it has no military solution to its problems.

Now there is a paradox: for forty years, our military defence functioned on the whole well. It was our political strategy that seemed not to be able to break East-West relations out of the Cold War-détente-Cold War syndrome. Today as we move, to use President Bush's phrase, "beyond containment" into post-Communist Europe, we have a political strategy stimulating and rewarding reform. But it is our military defence that has become problematic. As we become more long-term minded in the political field, we are threatened with "short termism" in the military field, looking for the immediate gain instead of the longer-term investment.

Take, for instance, structural disarmament. Even before we have concluded an agreement in Vienna, conventional disarmament by stealth on our side - the weaker one - has already begun. And we cannot even take credit for it. Modernisation programmes that were agreed within the Alliance in the early 1980s are now being scaled back. Only three Alliance nations are currently increasing defence spending - but only modestly. Three others expect no real increases in their defence budgets for 1990, and the remainder are cutting back - in some cases dramatically. Such an evolution would be worrying at the best of times. And we now have to contend with a US congressional resolution linking the US troop level in Europe to the maintenance of European force commitments.

The reduction in spending is already beginning to bite: less training, lower readiness, reduced draft periods, undermanned and under-equipped divisions, reductions in forces stationed outside national territory. Those forces that we do have, find it more difficult to train for their mission, due to understandable public opposition to peacetime military activity: low-level flying, field exercises, the reception of reserve and reinforcement units.

What concerns me is that we avoid assuming that major East-West conventional force reductions are just round the corner, and that we can anticipate these by cutting back now. The East-West military balance has not yet changed and the Soviets continue to spend and to modernize. If we unilaterally cut into our strength, Mr. Gorbachev will know that he does not need to reach a conventional arms control agreement with the NATO Allies to do so. We cannot assume that he will unilaterally give up his true military capabilities for nothing in return.

So structural disarmament is the enemy of genuine arms control and of genuine security. And when we do reach an agreement in Vienna, we will still need to pay for the destruction of equipment and verification. Moreover, we are not giving up our Alliance security system. We are seeking greater security, at reduced numbers. We will need to fund what we have left over: indeed the quality of our defence effort, when our forces are thinned out, will become even more important. So arms control is first about more security, and only second about financial savings. If the CFE negotiations are successful, we will save money sooner or later, but that should be seen as a beneficial side-effect, not as the rationale of this process.

How do we address burden-sharing in this historic context? My very first speech as Secretary General, here in Washington one year ago, warned that "the burden-sharing debate must not be allowed to degenerate into a numbers game or a transatlantic slanging match". I can say the same today, with even greater conviction.

You are as aware as I that burden-sharing is not an Alliance issue like all the others; rather it is an integral part of the Alliance itself. It is anchored in the geographic, political and economic disparities that make up NATO. Thus, it will disappear only when the Alliance itself disappears - or at least emerges with a totally new structural form. In recent times, we have used all sorts of defence and economic indicators to de-politicise burden-sharing and assess it more objectively. Such an approach is valuable and necessary; but burden-sharing will always be a highly political subject, touching the most sensitive nerves.

At the present stage, I would posit three theses for your consideration. First, despite our inability to eliminate them, we do not accept inequalities in our society. Similarly, the lack of a firm solution to burden-sharing does not mean that we cannot improve on the present situation. Second, in the Alliance context, it is clear Western Europe must do more: politically, economically, militarily. Third, I believe that the burden-sharing will play an important rôle in the context of the CFE process.

On the first point, NATO is now moving ahead. You all know our report on the sharing of the rôles, risks and responsibilities of collective security. Improved burden-sharing is a major feature of our 1989 Ministerial Guidance, the basis of our defence planning for the next two years. This November, ministers will be receiving a comprehensive progress report. Despite the gloomy budget outlook, it will contain many positive features:

- the decision by the Netherlands to deploy a new Army Corps Command Unit in Germany this year;
- the Italian offer of an additional battalion for the ACE Mobile Force;
- logistics and training agreements between the United Kingdom and the Federal Republic;
- more stockpiling of ammunition in the CINCSOUTH region;
- the Italian offer to provide a base for the 401st Tactical Air Wing.

On the second point, hardly anyone seriously contests the disproportionately large contribution made by the United States to allied defence - although I am happy to say, there is today more public understanding here in Washington of three basic truths:

- in protecting Western Europe, America is protecting its own vital interests;
- the European contribution to the common defence is greater than used to be assumed;
- the gap between American and European performance levels has narrowed in the wake of the sharp decline in the US defence budget since 1985; I heard Dick Cheney the other day speak of an 11% drop. In 1987,

the US spent about 6% of its GNP on defence, and Europe, as an average, about 3%. Within five years, the US level will be about 4.8% if current plans hold, while the European level should remain relatively constant.

Thus, it is clear that the US has been shifting its resources from defence to other priorities. As the bearer of one of the heaviest defence burdens in recent years, this is, arguably, appropriate. But the fact is that in many terms normally cited, the transatlantic imbalance is not as dramatic as some would have us believe and is in fact righting itself. But we always come back to the key point: burden-sharing is not just a military or financial accounting exercise. It involves all types of burdens including political tasks that uphold Western interests globally. But we are still left with the bottom line: Western Europe must do more.

Today I am more optimistic that things may finally be starting to happen. In the first place, the European Internal Market of 1992 is not only a slogan. It will be a reality - on schedule. Economists are predicting a 5% increase in overall Community GNP as a consequence of 1992. With its emergence as a major world economic centre, moving towards an ever-closer political union, I can foresee an invigorated rôle for Western Europe within the Alliance, with a larger share of both military and political responsibilities - in and outside Europe. After all, a solid Atlantic bridge must rest on a strong pillar on both sides of the ocean. I firmly believe this to be in the interest of the Alliance as well as of Europe.

Regarding my third thesis, we clearly have to assess the impact of arms control agreements on our future security needs. An accord in Vienna means fewer US troops in Europe: the agreed CFE proposal calls for withdrawal of 30,000 US troops and no European troops: a cut of up to 20% of US active duty forces at a stroke, in addition to reductions of defence equipment throughout the Alliance.

The outcome of CFE negotiations will have profound political implications. The allocation of force reductions among the Allies, affecting how the Alliance redistributes burdens and rôles to maintain its defences, will be, I predict, a difficult and highly-charged process. We are already at work in NATO on ways to implement the reductions while preserving Alliance solidarity and a credible defence.

I do not want to be misunderstood: it would be a mistake to look at the conventional arms control process as a way simply to shed burdens and cut costs. This is both dangerous and illusory: dangerous, because our goal must be to improve security and stability; illusory, because the costs of disarming are likely to be considerable. We will not be in the business simply of removing assets from the field, and striking the corresponding costs from the ledger.

When I say that the CFE process offers an opportunity to find a more lasting improvement to burden-sharing, I mean that it is clear that there will be a proportionately greater reliance on European defence forces for the security of Europe. The Alliance will have to adapt to an evolving security arrangement which factors in a reduced - though still significant and essential - US presence. By the way, I think it would be a mistake to focus on manpower in the context of post-CFE and burden-sharing. The Allies will have to look again at the balance of capabilities, modernisation, flexibility and sustainability of our defence effort: across the Atlantic, and among Allies themselves. We will have opportunities to encourage tighter European defence co-operation, more intra-Alliance specialisation, and greater rationalisation. It is still too early to be precise, but we are well embarked on a historic road which, I believe, has an excellent chance of leading to the real stability and security we have long sought.

We will not solve the burden-sharing dilemma by devising ever more sophisticated measuring mechanisms. It is in overcoming the division of Europe and in creating a new more stable security structure that we will finally relieve burdens. We are at a historic watershed, with results uncertain. But at least we can finally imagine the realisation of our vision. It would be foolhardy in the extreme to allow ourselves to be distracted from our efforts. I remind you: democracy has not yet won. The success of our political strategy is the key to our military strategy. Certainly there is much that we can do in the meantime to achieve a more equitable arrangement; but statesmanship will be required on both sides of the Atlantic. More important than anything else, a shift in NATO towards a lesser American and a greater European contribution will have to be skilfully managed, so as not to weaken the US rôle in Europe, nor its political engagement, and so as not to feed the false impression that Europeans can preserve their security or deal with the Soviet Union alone.

I am confident that we will avoid these pitfalls. Our prosperous economies, our dynamic peoples, our solid democratic traditions: these are already the ingredients of success. As long as we are far-sighted, and as long as we keep our eye on the essential, the future will belong to our great transatlantic Alliance of destiny.

□

Address to the German American Roundtable of the Konrad Adenauer Stiftung

Bonn
25 October
1989

It is curious how the human mind adjusts to even extra-ordinary events and developments. As we move through these times of rapid, indeed breath-taking change, some of its astounding features seem to become almost routine events for many. We are becoming used to a steady flow of news that would have struck us as earth-shaking only a few years ago and that is changing East-West relations almost beyond recognition.

We thus become almost oblivious to the revolutionary importance of changes around us. In less than five years we have seen huge fissures in the edifice of the Soviet empire, have seen this same empire seized by an economic crisis of dramatic proportions, and may be witnessing the systemic collapse of the official structures of the entire Communist group of states. Five years are no longer than the design phase of a single modern automobile or aircraft. In our immediate political geographical vicinity, these five years have witnessed a whole political universe begin first to shake and then disintegrate and totally revamp the preconditions on which a new such universe could be predicated.

Let me use this recollection to make two points: about the way historical processes work, and about the historical logic that presides over the rise and fall of political structures.

History never stops, it moves, but we have seen over time that it does not move at constant velocity. There are phases of stagnation and slow, imperceptible change and there are others of fundamental redefinition and acceleration. The Cold War period that coincided with NATO's 40 years, was a period of deadlock and immobility; the post-World War II order, amid

Western efforts at containing Soviet expansion, had congealed, freezing the world in an uncomfortable, paradoxical form of stability. Now, witness the last five years, the momentum of historical change has increased. Revealing unstoppable dynamics, history has accelerated once again, this time in an unprecedented way, raising the question whether the globalisation of politics and the advent of an age of global communications have perhaps propelled us into a new era of a high-pitched evolution of history altogether.

This process of acceleration is not limited to the East-West power equation. New dynamic forces of contemporary history are at work worldwide. Freedom, democracy, market forces, a powerful human imperative aspiring towards free individual and collective choice, human creativity - all of these riding on the fast train of modern technology. They are manifestations of Western political philosophy and most of them derive from Western values.

One can conceptualise post-World War history in terms of a fierce systemic and ideological competition: between the articulations of the great Western liberal tradition and those of authoritarianism, central planning and collectively ordained choice, an ideology based on materialism and communism. In this systemic struggle, these latter forces are today losing out. Oppressive regimes are on the wane worldwide. In the East as elsewhere, the dialectics of power are resolved in a quest for more freedom. Communism is losing out, not only with its ideological connotations, but in its lack of ability to satisfy the individual and collective needs of large post-industrial societies. Communist regimes stand in the way of evolution, of growth, of the knowledge revolution, of the full realisation of human potential.

Change in the East thus follows an implacable historical logic. The *status quo* cannot be restored, nor can it be temporarily patched up. The logic of freedom is absolute. The dismantling of ideology creates uncertainties, a transitional stage. Communism has lost, but it is not clear what exact societal forms will replace it or whether the transition can be managed in a way that will facilitate and not impede the emergence of a more cooperative and peaceful Eastern European world, susceptible of being integrated into a more secure and stable system of European states.

The dismantling of ideology and the dismantling of empires are long and painful processes. Setbacks and reversals are possible. The road to victory for democratic values is strewn with the rocks of delays and potential crises. There are opportunities and risks. The challenge history has in store for us in the decades to come is to maximise the first and to harness and minimise the second.

NATO was created to preserve peace and the territorial integrity of the core group of Western states at a time of historical stagnation and the menace of the Cold War age. NATO's determination has stabilised the East-West power equation over 40 years and created the reassurance and permanence of peace that has allowed for the full realisation of our democratic potential and wealth-generating capability. NATO's success is almost total. Even the containment of Soviet expansionism now produces the long-foreseen mellowing of the Soviet system.

With the world rapidly changing, it is logical that the Alliance cannot continue now to do business as before. And, indeed, the face of our Alliance has changed considerably in the last few years and will continue to change. It has gained a new dimension - strengthening its political role. The Alliance is already acting as an instrument of peaceful adaptation, helping the emergence of a new European political order under the auspices of Western values: democracy, freedom, interdependence, self-determination. In the future, greater stability will lie increasingly in the active management of change, in overcoming the *status quo*. NATO's recent Summit has conceptualised the methods to employ in the fulfilment of such management tasks. While the secular endeavour of bringing about systemic change is essentially incumbent on the states of the East, the Allies can assist with constructive action. But as the Summit leaders said the Alliance can - and must - hold out the rewards of our freer and more performing system, encouraging the States of the East to avail themselves of the fruit of systemic change. We clearly set out a three-fold vision: a Europe undivided, a global order of co-operation and a more mature and equal partnership between North America and Europe.

NATO's role is that of a midwife of change. We are not satisfied with the *status quo*. We want to overcome it. The act of birth of a new system is autonomous. But it can best succeed with prudent and knowledgeable help. Such constructive assistance is not charity; it is role-playing in a performance of history. Reform is in the shared interest of all, East and West alike.

There can be no doubt: NATO supports Gorbachev and the forces of reform in their endeavours as long as they move towards more openness, freedom, democracy, market economics and self-determination. Not only verbally but by deeds. We will assist them politically, economically and by arms control agreements to our mutual benefit.

The bygone age of containment, of the Cold War, has afforded us the comforts of a paradoxical stability. The paradox of that age lay in the fact that this kind of stability was politically and morally untenable. It was not our intention to perpetuate it. In a longer term view that stability was an illusion. It was stability on borrowed time. Lasting stability requires that people live reconciled with their life styles, with their ability to realise values, with their governments. Clear analysis will prevent us from indulging in a false nostalgia for these times. It is not our task to save communism or to stabilize communist regimes against the will of their own peoples. Our goal is to assist the transformation of communism and its transition towards freedom, democracy and self-determination. Our interest is to see this happen in an evolutionary and peaceful way. Nobody can be interested to see the systemic change in the East result in violent crashes. The consequences might be disastrous.

I see current Soviet thinking on the future shape of Europe, ill-defined and ambiguous as it still is, as the disillusioned quest for the retention of a European *status quo*. However, Soviet thought is evolving, and it may evolve in time towards a more mature view. But the concept of a Common European House must not be used to freeze processes of structural change nor must it be used to create an artificial dividing line between the Europeans and their transatlantic partners.

Self-determination for all Europeans is the call of the future and the Germans must participate in it as much as anybody else. That principle is absolute - and contested by no one in the West. In refusing to recognise this historical reality the current East German government is exacerbating its internal problems.

There is no question of interference, provocation or even revanchism on our part. We share a common interest in limiting the explosiveness of events. But nobody will stop natural aspirations of human beings for freedom and dignity to pave their way through history. Suppression and dictatorship can and will not last for ever. The question is not if but when and how democracy will win.

A central component of our challenge will be to reshape the political and military architecture of Europe. So we are trying:

1. To devise the political structures which will allow for a continuation of the West European process of unification, while offering East European states a perspective of ever closer cooperation, and an increasing measure of economic participation;
2. To design a new security system of military stability on the basis of reduced levels of weapons and non-offensive force postures.

There are many options, there are many pitfalls. The key value to my view would appear to be the stability and strength of our own Western structures. However our own thoughts on the future of the European Community, the Western European Union, the Council of Europe, the CSCE framework will evolve - they will not square with Gorbachev's concept of a Common European Home in its present form.

Twice in this century, each time in a post-war environment, the attempt has been undertaken to create a stable order of states in Europe. The crucial

130

contribution to a stable future was made after the Second World War with the inclusion of the United States of America and the firm commitment of the USA to the destiny of Europe. Our stability and mutual reassurance stems from our transatlantic cohesion. This insight must preside over the present third-major effort of this century to remodel the European community of states. The Alliance must play an essential role in the management of a Western integrated strategy *vis-à-vis* the East, functioning increasingly as a conceptual focus for defining the Western role in the management of change in Eastern Europe. That is my interpretation of the course the NATO Summit charted with a view to overcoming Europe's division.

And what of our rationale for defence in response to comprehensive change? Why is defence still necessary in the age of perestroïka and glasnost? There is no need to cite here the whole list of valid reasons: the primary fact remains that the military potentials stacked up against the Alliance have not yet significantly decreased, whatever the prospects of Soviet unilateral reductions, and of dramatic progress in arms control. No doubt the Soviet military machine is being re-dimensioned in a major way, but the transition period will be long and difficult and the outcome uncertain. Our task will be to influence this process prudently, to be prepared for periods in which reversals occur and in which the feeling of reassurance and confidence in a less militarily marked future are shaken. However positively arms control and the general East-West relationship will develop, geo-strategic factors and the gigantic size of the Soviet Union will be immutable. This means that it cannot be handled without an effective coalition security structure in Western Europe. NATO remains the only way of providing this underpinning of stable security, as a predictable and cohesive negotiating partnership for difficult years to come. This is especially true in a time of historic transition full of instability, uncertainty and unpredictability.

There is a fine line to be drawn between our deliberate planning and forward thinking in anticipation of a successful conclusion in Vienna, and a premature one-sided restructuring of our own defence potential. If we build down our defence lightheartedly, we would only undermine our CFE negotiating position and the restructuring of our defences afterwards. And we would not even do the Eastern forces of political reform a favour. Their efforts to peacefully reform their countries can only be strengthened by the perception of their supporters and rivals that there is no military solution to their problems.

Our armed forces must be modern and effective at all times. Allowing them to age and decay, based on the mere hope of future reductions and restructuring would be a recipe for insecurity. Let us not forget that the Soviets, even under the auspices of economic crisis and with the prospect of having to relinquish huge, over-proportionate numbers of forces, continue to modernise their forces across the entire spread of their arsenals. Specifically we must be aware that their current reductions are coupled with the simultaneous modernisation and streamlining of residual forces.

The security gains from a successful CFE agreement will be enormous, and the promise of ongoing negotiations in the 1990s, aiming at a more defensive structure of the Eastern side at yet lower numbers, even more attractive. Now is the time to provide to our populations a rationale for the ineluctable fact that a nuclear posture will nevertheless remain essential for the Alliance. But the role of nuclear weapons, as the ultimate guarantor of peace will be unaffected by any measure of conventional arms build-down - it will even be strengthened. At lower levels of conventional forces, the stabilising effects of a well-conceived residual nuclear posture would even become more apparent. The Alliance's Comprehensive Concept of Arms Control and Disarmament states this principle with unmistakeable clarity. It also stresses that our nuclear needs for the future must retain a highly stratified and diversified structure, whatever the numbers of weapons needed to retain essential deterrent options. There are now first indications that the East, beyond the facile talk of denuclearisation, may come to accept the basically stabilising effect of a cooperatively structured, nuclear element on the part of both alliances.

In London one year ago, I called on the Soviet Union to join in our concept of nuclear deterrence, at lower levels of weapons. I said, on that occasion, that it "would be very odd if the Alliance were to jeopardize its policy of deterrence just at a time when there are prospects of making the Soviet leadership understand the importance of its contribution to maintaining the sort of stability in Europe that is the necessary precondition for peaceful change".

We now hear Soviet experts speak of minimum deterrence - Gorbachev himself has used that term. This is important movement in the right direction. I, for one, find the term "minimum deterrence" misleading: what we really want is maximum deterrence with a minimum of weapons. What needs to be retained from this novel Soviet concept is that it could well provide a starting point for the establishment of stable yet relatively small deterrent structures to underpin the future East-West security equation. In this sense I find myself rather encouraged.

All of the objectives I have set out for you are only achievable if the transatlantic partnership holds good. As our Summit leaders stressed last May, none of us can do it alone. All our resources and all our imagination and moral strength are needed, on both sides of the Atlantic, to play our role of midwife of change in the East while maintaining security in difficult times of transition. Throughout its 40-year history, NATO has always had the vital role of managing the intra-Alliance relationship. We have never allowed strife and diversity of interest - so natural among 16 sovereign states - to get in the way of our common endeavour.

All Allies have equal significance, enjoy equal privileges and the common benefit of security, share the common responsibilities in ways that make each and every one indispensable. But, as a matter of sheer geography and size of the two countries, the German-American relationship has always been of pivotal importance. No Ally needs America more than the Germans; no other Allied country had a stronger and more beneficial role in the creation of the Federal Republic of Germany. Partners of uneven size and uneven power in the early decades, the two countries now grow more and more into a mature partnership based on a higher level of mutual political responsibility. I am deeply convinced that our two countries have a rewarding and an assured joint future before them and this clearly benefits the whole Alliance.

☐

The Alliance-
A Key Player
in the Future

ADDRESS GIVEN
AT THE 35TH ANNUAL ASSEMBLY
OF THE ATLANTIC TREATY
ASSOCIATION

**Brussels
26 October
1989**

Our Western values are protected by the Atlantic Alliance but they are no longer limited to the Atlantic area. This is one of the very few spiritual revolutions in history that has not required the sword or a burning dogma. Example and practice have sufficed. The world comes to us. Wherever you look, the success of our great Atlantic Alliance has transformed even the most fixed mentalities. It has created aspirations.

As a result, when it comes to the consequences: a world in immense transition, the failure of communism, the quest for new structures of peace based on the Alliance vision of freedom, human dignity and self-determination, then it is just as clear that we are not at the end, but at the beginning of a new phase of history. The Alliance will be a key player in the unfolding future. Our Summit meeting was not just or even primarily a celebration of 40 years of peace in freedom - the longest period Europe has enjoyed since Roman times. Neither was it just a Western response to the changes at work in the East. It was first and foremost an affirmation that this Alliance can shape that future according to our values - for our benefit, certainly, but for humanity's benefit as well. Our vision is threefold:

- a Europe undivided in which all peoples would exercise their inherent right of self-determination; in which all would enjoy the same freedoms and economic opportunities; and in which no nation need ever fear military intimidation or aggression from its neighbours;
- a new global order of co-operation in which East and West would work together to solve humanity's most pressing problems: drugs, terrorism, the environment, regional tensions;
- a more equal transatlantic partnership based on a strong

North America and a united and cohesive Western Europe; one which would assume its full share of the common defence and of global responsibilities.

Our ideological opponents for forty years are now caught up in a terminal crisis. Many of their leaders blame this crisis on us. If by this they mean that our societies are more dynamic, our citizens more creative, our economies more prosperous and our nations resolved to defend these benefits, then indeed I am most happy for this Alliance to take the credit. The East is not turning to the West by accident. No-one can deny that our success and resolve is a primary reason why the East does not only want to change but simply has to change. On the other hand, if these leaders mean instead that their crisis is caused not by Communism's patent failings, but by something that Mr. Shevardnadze has called Western "revanchism", then I can only echo the verdict of Dumouriez on the courtiers of Louis XVIII of France: "they have forgotten nothing, and learned nothing". But I hope that this is not their real opinion. After all, did we not hear Mr. Gorbachev acknowledge in East Berlin that "what is most important is that the citizens decide for themselves"?

Along with the momentous changes in some Communist countries, there is still sufficient uncertainty to make one wonder whether some authoritarian régimes will really listen to their peoples, and rule for them, rather than against them. We have had in recent weeks the example of others responding to the same aspirations with riot police, arrests and crackdowns. The improving human rights picture in some of these states seems regrettably to have encouraged others to move backwards. Take the example of Bulgaria forcing over 300,000 of its ethnic Turks to leave. But, despite all this, I am not pessimistic. The call for freedom cannot be suppressed forever, nor can Communist régimes survive indefinitely through repression and stagnation. People want to be responsible for their own lives, even if this means risk and uncertainty. The fact that over 50,000 East Germans were willing to abandon everything - jobs, family, friends - to flee to the West is a testament to this fundamental need of the human spirit. And those who have chosen to stay behind are not politically passive. They are organizing, speaking out, pushing for change. The writing is on the wall for repressive communist systems. The longer reform is postponed, the harder it will be - and with fewer young, energetic people to see it through.

Mr. Gorbachev is often given credit by our public opinion for unleashing these forces of change. I would see him as a determined man who is the vehicle, but not the master, of historical necessity. Mr. Gorvachev has accelerated - we must thank him for that - a transformation that was inevitable. Communism has never taken root in Eastern Europe. Stalin's famous dictum about communism in Poland, that it was "like trying to put a saddle on a cow" applies as much to his own country, the Soviet Union.

The aspirations of the peoples of Eastern Europe have been expressed beyond doubt or question : and I think the Alliance vision of Europe in the year 2000 meets them :

- self determination - the right to live as one independent nation and to enjoy one's national identity;
- the right to choose one's own government at regular intervals;
- the right to freedom of speech, travel, access to information, to organize politically;
- the right to live without fearing external military force, and to enjoy security abroad and stability at home;
- the right to equal economic and social opportunities;
- above all, a Europe undivided, of open borders, human contacts, common values and culture.

This vision is not only morally correct: it alone procures lasting stability. Not the false stability of a system of states that can be maintained only through military blocs, "satellised" Allies, ideological conformity and internal repression. In truth this is the most unstable of all systems; militarily dangerous and politically untenable. It may have kept the peace, but at a price far too heavy for us, and far too heavy for the peoples of Eastern Europe.

History does not allow stagnation. You can only have real stability through constant change and adaptation. The *status quo* is finished. This Alliance neither can, nor wants, to sustain it. It is not only our distant vision to create a new Europe. It is our immediate interest. There is more at stake than simply removing the shadow of Soviet military power and ideological hostility from our affairs. A Europe of free nations and open borders would certainly be a more stable and peaceful Europe; but it would be also one of vast new opportunities in trade, communications, education, cultural exchanges, and East-West co-operation to solve our human problems: pollution, drugs, terrorism.

So it is not a question of what we want to achieve, but how we achieve it. The break-up of the old system is inevitable; nothing we do in the West will change that. But the shape of the new system is by no means inevitable. As the midwife of change, we have a special responsibility in ensuring that it becomes both permanent and universal throughout Eastern Europe. This can be achieved only by evolution, not revolution.

The Alliance has the political initiative. Our NATO Summit Declaration is two things: a conceptual blueprint for a better Europe, and a pragmatic policy to make that a reality. Take, for instance, our offer of co-operation. We have offered these countries the largest programme of help since Stalin forced them to turn down Marshall Aid in the nineteen-forties:

- food assistance to Poland - 24 Western nations are involved; the United States has doubled its amount;
- trade facilitation, such as the recent economic agreement between the EEC and Poland, or the decision of the United States to grant Hungary most favoured nation trading status;
- private enterprise trusts to be established in Poland and Hungary; government encouragement of joint ventures;
- funds for pollution control projects;
- the twelve governments of the European Community have guaranteed a $1 billion credit to Poland and Hungary; individual governments are helping too with new credits;
- training courses and facilities for Eastern managers;
- a review of the debt burden of Poland and Hungary;
- scholarships for the study of Western institutions.

Yet, we can best help those who help themselves, and who take the necessary steps to move closer to democracy and market economies. Political and economic reform are intertwined. We must use our aid to stimulate political reform and the respect of human rights, as well as economic progress. Only in this way can we produce long-term results. We have no desire to have one year's feast, followed by ten years' famine.

The requirements for economic and political change are simultaneous. First the economic:
- reforms must not be designed merely to relieve immediate economic pressures, but to permanently introduce market mechanisms;
- measures must be taken to reduce inflation, liberalise trade, allow for individual business enterprise, and to restore values to dead currencies;
- the management of the economy must be decentralised; for instance, the rôle of the nomenklatura in economic decision-making must be reduced
- in its place must come a more impartial civil service; local managers must have more autonomy;
and then the political:
- first and foremost, the Warsaw Pact must scale back its forces in Eastern Europe to a level where an attack is impossible. Our proposals to eliminate conventional disparities and provide for stringent stabilization and verification measures show the way;
- democratic institutions must be allowed to take root;
- human rights and the undertakings of the Helsinki Final Act must be respected in full; only in this way will the Eastern governments persuade their populations to accept the sacrifices of reform, and to work to rebuild their nations;
- the Soviet Union and its allies must co-operate with us on global concerns: environmental pollution, terrorism, the proliferation of dangerous weapons, regional tensions.

Poland and Hungary will be the two test cases for our strategy. They are rapidly approaching the Rubicon of irreversible change. We must help them to cross it. This is our challenge: to give reform a scope and a pace that avoids a relapse into stagnation, or an uncontrolled slide into disarray. Of course, instability is often a by-product of necessary change. We must accept this and not be afraid of it. We must mitigate its negative effects, but, above all, turn the movement that it brings to our advantage.

We are up to it. The future rôle of NATO is determined by the context we face: first to provide a framework of stability and cohesion in a time of great change: but also, and just as importantly, to be an instrument of that change - to encourage it and to give it something solid to anchor itself on. We are not just aiming to help Eastern Europe over its immediate hurdle, thereafter to abandon it to its fate. The Alliance strives to reshape East-West relations by allowing Communism to phase itself out, building in its place new democratic and economic structures. And this Alliance is unique in being the one Western institution that can manage the integrated Western strategy that is required. Political, economic, military and human rights policies cannot be handled in isolation.

The Europe of the year 2000 will not be a more prosperous Europe if it is not a safer Europe. So our policy of promoting change has to be backed up by a policy for security. The momentous changes we are witnessing in the East are taking place within a context of East-West military confrontation that remains for now essentially unchanged, despite the promise for the future. Vast Soviet forces remain in Eastern Europe. They continue to maintain the unnatural division of our continent, to oppress Eastern Europe and to intimidate the NATO Allies. Modernized Soviet nuclear missiles continue to threaten our cities. While we welcome Mr. Gorbachev's unilateral reductions, they do not modify this fundamental geo-political reality. There is, moreover, mounting evidence that Soviet defence spending remains high - 13-17% of GNP; real growth since 1985 is estimated - still - at 3% a year on average; and new weapons systems continue to roll off the production line.

The currently envisaged Soviet unilateral reductions will still leave an intimidating military machine facing us in the East. In addition to keeping our own defences modern and effective, we have responded with a dynamic arms control policy. It is a main plank of this Alliance's political agenda, seeking cuts in military forces across the board. If, for example, our conventional forces proposal is realised, we will have succeeded in cutting the number of Soviet tanks, artillery and armoured personnel carriers in Europe by 60%.

It is the West that leads when it comes to bold, imaginative proposals. Not just ones that appeal to the public gallery; but ones that are directly negotiable in Vienna or Geneva. We are pushing for an initial agreement on conventional reductions in one year - ambitious, I grant you, but the speed with which 16 democratic and sovereign nations are merging their interests into common positions proves that, on our side at least, it is wholly feasible.

The speed with which change is happening, and our unprecedented prospects for further arms control success, have, not unexpectedly, generated new problems for us. Public expectations have been raised, and they often base themselves on two misguided propositions:

- that with a reduced threat to Western security, there is no longer justification for strong Western defences;
- that arms control alone will solve our security concerns and bring about a more stable and peaceful Europe.

On the first point, I would warn against over-hasty conclusions. One third of the globe, an entire ideological system is now in a deep and terminal crisis. No-one can predict what will happen. I wish Gorbachev success, but it would be foolhardy to place all our eggs in the basket of his political survival, or his success. Reform in the East has been born of failure. There is a race going on between political change and systemic collapse; noone can tell which will win, or when. Explosive forces are building up throughout Eastern Europe - all the more potent for having been repressed for so long. This Alliance will do all it can to help. But we would be taking enormous risks if we threw ourselves into this enterprise without a secure defence. This alone can protect us against setbacks and reversals, and against any temptation of the Soviet Union to resort to military threat or intimidation. The same people who call on this Alliance to be bold and imaginative in our political strategy - in short to take risks - cannot at the same time deny us the requisite insurance cover.

On the second point, I warn against the easy assumption that less weapons automatically imply more security. Our arms control initiatives will only bear their full fruit in the context of an overall Western strategy for promoting political change in the East. Arms control can facilitate solutions; but weapons are not the fundamental cause of tension. They are the product of unsound political relations. The function of arms control is to make the East-West security system safer; it is not to do away with that system altogether. If it is true that there can be no stability without change, there can also be no change without stability. Even in a Europe of vastly improved political relations, military forces, albeit at reduced levels, will always be the lynchpin of our security. Certainly the bright prospects for the future allow us to conceive of a security that will be more co-operative, transparent and reassuring. What I like to think of as maximum deterrence with minimum forces. But until that time, this Alliance will not take away the scaffolding from around the building before the cement has set.

When I first became Secretary General, I was asked by many people "What is NATO doing about the Gorbachev challenge?" Well, all of you who follow Alliance affairs closely now have the answer: we have taken the initiative in moving political change and arms control forward. The Alliance has demonstrated that it is a political Alliance paving the way for a new order of peace and freedom. None of you who are actively engaged in the battle for the hearts and minds of our public opinion can say that you lack a positive message to put across. Never has this Alliance had such a forward-looking and ambitious strategy. Never have we had such a great opportunity to put that strategy into effect. There are truly historic opportunities before us. We created them and we will seize them. I am looking to you to help. You have a vital rôle to play in ensuring that we will continue to have public support. And this Alliance has opened up such prospects for future achievement that today as never before, you can go about your task with optimism and confidence.

□

Atlantic Alliance and German Unity

SPEECH
AT THE ÜBERSEECLUB

Hamburg
8 February
1990

The question of European security is one that must now be looked at afresh. The rigid military confrontation of past decades is increasingly giving way to a concern for enhanced security and to the active pursuit of peace using a combination of military and political elements.

Two tasks have to be faced in the coming years:

- the development of a new security structure, and
- the creation of a new political order in Europe.

Both tasks are equally indispensable for the preservation and strengthening of peace in the long run.

The Alliance therefore faces a dual challenge. It must be a driving and guiding force in the dynamic process of change from the *status quo*, helping to establish a new continental order of peace and freedom. In the second place, it must be a source of stability, guaranteeing security in Europe, especially in the face of erratic developments in the Soviet Union and a difficult transitional period in Central and Eastern Europe.

The task of working out a new European security equation for the 21st century offers a historic opportunity. Under pressure for comprehensive change in its system the Soviet Union favours a new security order. The basic premises of Western security and stability - the presence of US troops on the European continent, the continuation of the Atlantic Alliance and an ultimate nuclear deterrent to uphold peace - are today increasingly acknowledged by the Soviet Union as being prerequisites for stability and fundamentals of a future security structure.

143

I believe the following points to be important:

- Only the transatlantic link, the continued integration of America in our security structures, can guarantee stability in the long term. The US commitment to European security is the cornerstone of the Western system that was created after the Second World War, and which has given us peace. Without the active participation of North America it will not be possible to balance the Germans' interest in unity, their neighbours' concerns and the Soviet Union's legitimate security interests, and to reach a common position.
- The Alliance, which is the concrete expression of this transatlantic link, remains indispensable for a future security scheme. At the same time, the Alliance will still have the function of guiding the ongoing arms control process.
- The starting point for the future European security structure is provided by the Vienna negotiations. Initial results must lead to yet further reductions in force levels and new defensive structures. The latest US proposal to reduce American and Soviet troops in Central Europe to less than 200,000 shows the way. Future conventional disarmament in Europe must not remain a matter of mere bean-counting, however. It must not merely cover force levels, but also build-up capability, logistics, infrastructure, modes of deployment, force structures and exercise patterns, under conditions of increased transparency.
- A new European security equation must also comprise a residual nuclear deterrent as an ultimate guarantee of peace, with agreement on a minimum level of nuclear armament. On this point, the most recent pronouncements of Soviet spokesmen, including even Gorbachev, are encouraging.
- It is necessary to develop co-operative mechanisms to promote understanding with the East - for instance more exchanges between military academies, reciprocal troop visits, seminars to enhance shared learning.
- Comparison of NATO with the Warsaw Pact is only conceivable or useful if the latter changes fundamentally to become a voluntary alliance of free and equal partners. Until this happens the two cannot properly be equated, although they often are, through thoughtlessness or for transparent reasons. Even to refer to both these alliances as military blocs is grossly misleading. The Warsaw Pact itself is no longer a bloc, let alone NATO. The Atlantic Alliance is a free association of democratic, self-determining nations of the free world, and is purely defensive in nature. Up till now the Warsaw Pact has been a military alliance lacking the legitimation of a free expression of will by the peoples involved. We hope for a change, which would decisively improve the prospects for fruitful co-operation.
- Nevertheless we cannot and will not become guarantors of the Warsaw Pact. We are arguing neither for its dissolution nor for its continuation.

Its fate will be determined by its members alone exercising free choice. This must also be allowed for in the arms control process.

- Even if the Warsaw Pact does dissolve itself that is no reason for disbanding NATO. On the contrary there is every reason to argue that our role as an agent of stability would then become even more important.

- To equate the stationing of Soviet troops in Central and Eastern Europe with the presence of American troops in Western Europe is neither acceptable nor helpful. The American and Canadian troops are here with the agreement of free parliaments and governments. The same is not true of the Soviet forces in Central and Eastern Europe - on the contrary, the free governments of Czechoslovakia and Hungary have demanded their withdrawal. Once again, the removal of Soviet troops can and indeed will lead to the reduction of American force levels, but not to a complete US withdrawal. There are also geostrategic reasons for that. The current arms control negotiations should not be used to legitimise the presence of Soviet troops in Central and Eastern Europe against the will of the stationing countries, nor to make their withdrawal conditional on that of the North American forces.

A future European political order must build on the right of free self-determination of peoples. From the debate in the West the outlines of a European architecture for peace are already visible. It is based on existing institutions which represent the outstanding accomplishment of the post-war period:

(1) The process of European integration with its goal of political union;
(2) The Atlantic Alliance;
(3) The CSCE process.

In this context the CSCE framework for a pan-European peace system assumes special significance. The CSCE system must be extended and deepened. Such an overarching structure, however, cannot replace but only complement the Atlantic Alliance. How should a body of 35 states, which still can exercise veto rights, really guarantee security. Only the Atlantic Alliance is able to supply the structural base for the growing European architecture, to overcome crises and conflicts which can never be excluded, even with the current changes in the European landscape. The Alliance is the umbrella under which European integration is able to grow dynamically and continually. EC and CSCE would be overburdened if they had to carry out the task of guaranteeing peace in the forseeable time. They do not dispose of the necessary structure nor the corresponding instruments in their present and foreseeable state of evolution.

Whether we are concerned with security arrangements or a peaceful political order in Europe, we inevitably find the German question to be central.

German unity will come. We, who have striven for the triumph of democracy and for an end to the division of Europe and of Germany, must accept the crucial role of the peoples who are shaping the new order in the revolution in the East. The timetable for the achievement of German unity will not so much be determined by planners and governments as by the course of events in the GDR, as part of the tremendous restructuring of Europe, and by the free choice of the people there and in the Federal Republic. What politicians and diplomats can do is to recognise these facts and develop a framework so that the process is smooth and harmonious and avoids crises or erratic developments with the attendant risks for all of Europe.

The Alliance has been pledged to German unity since the entry of the Federal Republic in 1954/55. This is true of the three Western powers as well as of all the other Allies. The Alliance is not an obstacle to German unity, any more than it is to European integration. It helped to bring more democracy and freedom. It seeks to overcome the division of Germany and Europe. It is promoting reform in the East.

The continued existence of NATO and progress towards German unity are perfectly compatible. Indeed I would say they were mutually dependent. Now I hear sometimes that it is not realistic to assume that a reunified Germany could exist in the Atlantic Alliance. I would confront these voices with the insight drawn from our historic experience : To make the dissolution of the Alliance a *sine qua non* of German unity would deprive both Germany and Europe of a basic force for stability. Only firm anchoring in the West can provide the fundamental stability for the difficult process in which we are engaged.

A drifting, neutral Germany cannot be a solution, given the country's geostrategic position and its political, economic and military potential, and this is the view of all the Allies. It would not even be in the enlightened self-interest of the Soviets. The history of the last two centuries demonstrates this.

Thus there is no acceptable alternative to Germany remaining anchored in the Atlantic Alliance - and belonging to the European Community. Please understand that it would be a mistake to consider the German question in terms of a dynamically unfolding future while, at the same time, viewing the role and function of the Atlantic Alliance as merely static. The latter is another part of the same series of rapid, interdependent developments.

The Soviet Union is adapting to this movement towards German unity. Foreign Minister Shevardnadze's speech in Brussels and General Secretary Gorbachev's latest pronouncements show this. Soviet security interests and their definition have changed dramatically in the past four years. The Soviets' forward deployment in Europe since 1945 sprang partly from an expansionist drive for world power, but also from deep-seated need for security. That need has lost its justification with the now unequivocal recognition that there is no threat from the West.

As a result, the Soviet perception of their security has changed. They no longer need a Western glacis. The Soviet Union will have to accept - and is probably already on the way to doing so - that its security will be enhanced rather the impaired by the loss of its Central and East European buffer zone. New, stable structures and increased prosperity as well as new and closer forms of international co-operation in Central and Western Europe will above all benefit Soviet reform process.

The Soviet Union's security interests - in stability, freedom from threat and co-operation along the borders of the Soviet state - will be better served in the long term by the intensification of the disarmament process and the further reduction of military forces, by taking advantage of the Alliance as a co-operative partner in the management of peace, and by the extension of the CSCE system and the resulting reduction of confrontation.

In addition, special arrangements could be devised to take account of Soviet security interests with a united Germany as a member of the Atlantic Alliance.

A component of such an arrangement could be a special military status for the territory of the GDR, or perhaps an agreement not to extend military integration to that territory. These are just two possibilities out of many which could be conceived. German unity and membership of the Atlantic Alliance are perfectly compatible within a security architecture which would preserve European stability in the interest of the Soviet Union as well as of other states.

The members of the Alliance must as a matter of urgency incorporate such considerations into a common concept for progress towards German unity.

The important sign is that the European Community, the Atlantic Alliance and the CSCE should be developed as a framework for German and European unity. Omission of any of these structural elements would disrupt the balance which is so vital for the future of Germany and Europe. The Soviet Union can be sure that we take their ideas seriously, and more : we will respect their legitimate security interests.

□

Nato and a new European Order

ADDRESS GIVEN
TO THE ITALIAN SENATE

Rome
19 April
1990

Rome is, of course, the "Eternal City". This wholly appropriate appelation comes not only from its contribution to Western civilization, its vibrant culture or the magnificence of its architecture, but because it is the city that one wants to return to most often.

So I am extremely grateful to my old and dear friend, Senator Giovanni Spadolini, who like me has a new incarnation since the days when we worked closely together, in trying times, as defence ministers, for his invitation to come back to Rome today. Having re-invigorated my senses in both aspects of your city - the grandeur of its ancient world, the hustle and bustle of its modern counterpart - I wish to thank you for honouring me with the opportunity to address such a distinguished gathering.

I am particularly pleased to be speaking before this audience on the importance of the Alliance for a new European order. We need at this juncture of history a combination of continuity and vision, of constancy and innovation, of devotion to the Atlantic partnership and to the unity of Europe. These have been the hallmarks of Italian policy for the past 40 years, and are precisely the qualities demanded now. Italy has always been in the forefront of the search for a future Europe, deriving strength and stability from our Alliance, in which we can achieve the true stability and peace which have eluded Europeans throughout history. My message to you is that we now have a chance, a real chance, to succeed. To do so will require the wisdom and vision to build on that which we have achieved.

Since NATO's 40th anniversary twelve months ago, we have witnessed a revolution not only on the streets of Central and

Eastern Europe but also in the assumptions that for forty years have under-pinned East-West relations. The prospect of war in Europe is at its lowest ebb in nearly half a century.

Risks to our security remain, and instability has proved explosive in the past. But the situation in Europe has nonetheless evolved to the point where the Alliance's concept of political rather than exclusively military security is coming into its own. We have an opportunity, not yet realized, to develop a new European architecture of peaceful cooperation that deals as well with potential conflicts or reversals.

With the conventional threat now diminishing, has NATO developed into something beyond the classic Alliance of nations to meet an external threat? What remains uniquely important about the Alliance in the context of a new European order ?

First and foremost, the Alliance has oriented the United States away from isolationism and towards a lasting commitment to uphold peace and stability in Europe. The US is prepared to maintain this commitment for as long as the Allies wish. Traditionally, Europe has not enjoyed stability. And the search for a new Europe is complicated by Russia's predominant military might and geography. It is the link to the United States - and Canada - which for the last forty years has given Europe security and stability. The Atlantic Alliance has not only cemented the union of destiny between Europe and North America; it has also shown that democracies are most secure and strong when they bind together.

NATO has in fact become a unique model of the collective management of broadly defined security among free nations. It has established a political as well as a military partnership. This is a major factor in the deterrence of war, and in the vitality of the values on which this partnership is based. Within the Alliance former enemies have been reconciled; all enjoy equal security; the Alliance's stabilizing framework has extended outwards to protect the neutral states of Europe, and the newly democratizing states of Central and Eastern Europe recognize that without NATO they would not have recovered their independence and liberty.

Without this stabilizing Alliance framework, Europe would become once more vulnerable to the shifting alliances and power politics of the past. Security would be "renationalized". The lessons of European history are clear on the subject of nation states searching alone to find an elusive security.

Only the Atlantic collective security system can balance and hedge the preponderance of Soviet power in Europe, and ensure that the relatively weaker feel confident *vis-à-vis* the relatively stronger.

One of the historic achievements of the Alliance has been to convert nuclear weapons into the ultimate instrument of peace keeping. The Alliance has secured nuclear deterrence; it has also facilitated its members' participation in collective nuclear planning. Given that arms control can reduce but never disinvent the nuclear weapon, Europeans would be well advised to retain the controlling structure that the Alliance represents.

NATO is not, of course, alone in striving to put in place the architecture of a future European order. But talking about one or the other institution as the basis for the future misses the essential point: it is on all our existing bodies and successes that we must build.

The European Community, for instance, is playing an important political rôle, not least in the economic reconstruction of Central and Eastern Europe. It has an ultimate goal of political union and to this end has achieved already an impressive degree of interaction among its 12 members. It is obviously the most attractive and dynamic European political organisation. Yet despite its emerging political identity, it has no security dimension, nor will it acquire one for the foreseeable future.

NATO and the EC have provided the cohesion and stability at the centre of Western success. Building on that, the Conference on Security and Cooperation in Europe (CSCE) also has a promising future as the framework for the new European architecture. Yet it lacks the legal solidity of binding obligations, a permanent institutional status, or a conflict-resolution machinery backed up by effective powers of enforcement and sanction. Given the differing values, interests and views of its 35 members, each with a right of veto, it cannot guarantee security. Essential as its work is in promoting democratic values, human rights and breaking down barriers, the CSCE cannot replace the Atlantic Alliance, which remains an essential pillar of every future European security structure.

Our challenge is how to extend security without diminishing it. Neither the European Community nor the CSCE, either alone or jointly, can substitute for the transatlantic Alliance in carrying the burdens of stability and democracy across the whole of Europe. Only the Alliance can keep the United States and Canada tied to Europe; ensure that change can unfold without fear of setbacks and reversals; co-ordinate overall Western strategy for the reconstruction of Central and Eastern Europe; and firmly anchor a united Germany in the West in conditions of maximum security for both itself and its neighbours.

In that light, the Alliance will face three tasks in the 1990s:

First is that of building a new European order, not only more just but also more durable than that of the Cold War. Europe will continue to change for many years yet. The demise of the Warsaw Pact, the end of the military confrontation of the Cold War, the imminent prospect of German unity have all fundamentally changed the terrain before the Alliance. We are already adjusting in military and political terms to the new environment, and there are two immediate and essential contributions that we will make to a future European architecture.

In supporting Gorbachev both politically and materially as long as he moves towards democracy and reform, the Allies are proving to the Soviet Union that they do not intend to take advantage of Soviet weakness, but to assist it in its difficult transformation. In particular, the Allies will respect the legitimate security interests of the Soviet Union in Europe so that it can embrace reform in full confidence. There is no doubt: we want successful reform in the Soviet Union, and for it to take place in security, safely. The second contribution is in offering the new Germany a membership in the Alliance that ensures its continued anchorage in the West. This makes the inherent right of self-determination of the Germans compatible with stability in Europe. It is in the Soviet interest as much as that of Germany's neighbours and partners.

At the same time, the Alliance will contribute to the CSCE process, speed up the establishment of solid democratic institutions, promote the respect of human and minority rights and the rule of law in all the nations of Europe. It will also use the CSCE process to break down barriers to human, cultural and economic exchanges across Europe's vanishing line of division, and to promote economic progress in the East.

Indeed our Alliance understands that peace is more than military security. It also depends on tackling the pressing problems of mankind. For this reason we have a NATO Third Dimension, our programmes dealing with science and the environment. More and more the Alliance is helping to build up scientific expertise in fields ranging from global climatic change to condensed matter physics. Italy has been a great contributor to these programmes and a guiding influence over their development. In June we are meeting in Erice to celebrate the 20th anniversary of the Committee on the Challenges of Modern Society. I want to emphasize how grateful we in NATO are for the continuing support of the Italian authorities, and particularly Prime Minister Andreotti.

The Alliance is also stimulating arms control negotiations to make the ebbing of the East-West confrontation an irreversible process. If the Alliance can bring the states of Europe to cooperate over their vital security interests, they will find it much easier to cooperate over everything else. An agreement on conventional forces, which we hope to secure this year, is thus the indispensable foundation of a new European architecture. Wherever you look - strategic nuclear arms, a chemical weapons ban, confidence building measures - we are pushing ahead.

But conflict cannot be prevented by arms control or diplomacy alone. We have not yet secured the future. Developments in the Soviet Union, for instance, are unpredictable. The prospect of a conventional disarmament treaty must not obscure the fact that the Soviet Union will remain a superpower. It is modernizing its nuclear arsenal both inside and outside its national territory. Although the Soviets are following through their promised unilateral reductions, they have restructured their remaining forces. The power of the Soviet armed forces to intimidate will remain, even with all Soviet forces back within their national borders. We must also remember that the collapse of the Soviet imperium has stirred both regional tensions and nationalism throughout much of the Soviet Union and Central and Eastern Europe.

The second task must therefore be to maintain a secure peace. Our defence structure will continue to be the main guarantee of peace as well as the necessary element for crisis management. War at the close of the twentieth century is so potentially catastrophic that we cannot take its prevention less seriously just because it is now less probable.

But within the overall premise that we maintain a credible defence capability, results in conventional arms control and the changes taking place in the East offer us more flexibility than in the past in planning our force structure. Clearly the forces NATO needs to deal with the risks in Europe today and in the future do not have to have the same level of readiness and availability as at present. These adjustments will not be limited to our obligations under a forthcoming CFE treaty; the Alliance is looking ahead to a new European security system going beyond confrontation, based on cooperation, transparency and minimal force levels commensurate with deterrence.

Third, and finally, NATO must ensure the partnership between North America and an increasingly self-aware and politically unified Europe, while managing all the complexities of their relationship. This is a fundamental political choice for partnership, and preserving what we have worked for. Erosion of the transatlantic linkage will leave all of us worse off, including our partners to the East.

The future of NATO is not tied to that of the Warsaw Pact. There is no equivalence between the two alliances. NATO is the expression of the solidarity and will of 16 democratic nations; the Warsaw Pact on the other hand has served as the instrument of Soviet domination of Central and Eastern Europe. Its future can be determined only by the free decision of the Pact's own members.

Equally, US troops in Europe cannot be compared to Soviet troops. They are here expressly at the invitation of Allied governments and parliaments. The Soviet Union now recognizes their wholly defensive intention and their reassuring influence. Moscow has even accepted President Bush's proposal for a higher ceiling of US forces in Europe than Soviet forces stationed outside Soviet territory.

To answer the question I posed at the outset, this is an Alliance **for** a vision of peace, security and prosperity. Our values are inclusive, not exclusive. NATO is not simply an Alliance against threat or intimidation, but a model of partnership, success, and a vision of a future Europe of peace in freedom. The historical developments of our day allow us finally the prospect of realizing this vision, and to go beyond confrontation to cooperation, as the Alliance has for decades hoped to do.

The Atlantic Alliance and European Security in the 1990s

ADDRESS
TO THE BREMER TABAKS
COLLEGIUM

Brussels
17 May
1990

History does not always flow evenly like a stream. There are phases in which it moves more slowly, and phases in which it moves more rapidly; phases when the momentum of events quickens; indeed when those events even outpace one another. Today we are experiencing this acceleration of history. The shape of our European political landscape is being transformed decisively. Europe is in search of a new form for itself. We still cannot tell what this will ultimately be, but certain contours are nonetheless already visible.

As is always the case in such phases of historical transition, new and bold perspectives and possibilities are being created; yet in our path we also find new risks and dangers.

The Opportunity

The opportunity: it is to finally realize our vision of a free and united Europe based on a secure and lasting order of peace. In this respect it is not of cardinal importance what we call it : whether European Peace Order, or Common European Home or European Confederation. What is important is the substantive content of such an order : human rights and free choice for all its citizens, equality before the law, openness of borders, self-determination, democracy and the protection of minority rights. This is what we have to insist on. The current debate on a future security structure for Europe is focussed far too much on procedural and structural matters. It would be better if instead we emphasized the substance of such an order. It is already contained in the three baskets of the CSCE process which we need to reinforce and to translate into a set of legally binding undertakings.

155

First and foremost are the universal values on which our Atlantic Community has been based since its very inception. These values are now in the ascendant throughout the world, and hopefully this time for good. The aspiration for freedom, democracy and a market-oriented economic system rooted in freedom is the driving force of history these days. The historical mission that falls to our generation is to assist this dynamic process, to steer it towards our vision and to undergird it with the necessary degree of stability. It thus also defines the basic task of our Atlantic Alliance which is the foremost community of destiny and of joint consultation and endeavour that we have in the free world today.

The Risks

Yet the risks bound up with the transition of our European states system are unmistakable. There is the risk of instability in internal as well as external developments, with even the danger of collapse. There are enormous problems associated with the building of democracy and with economic restructuring in Central and Eastern Europe. There are old national and ethnic rivalries that we thought had been overcome; border and minority questions are again rearing their heads. Nobody knows what is going to happen tomorrow in the Soviet Union, against the background of a Soviet military might that remains formidable. And to these risks we must add also those coming from the Third World: the proliferation of ballistic missile technology, and of chemical and nuclear weapons. Eternal peace is still nothing more than a sweet dream. Old-fashioned power politics is still the order of the day. Thus the other part of our current mission is to master these dangers and to contain or even eliminate the risks.

If we are to fulfil both parts of our historical mission, then we absolutely must have a strong, constructive partnership between the two major Western organisations : the Atlantic Alliance and the European Community. In this phase of our history, we need more urgently than ever a sense of common purpose, stability and cooperation with the United States. Without the Atlantic Alliance there can be no cohesion and unity throughout the Free World, no transatlantic partnership, no security and stability. Without the European Community there can be no closer union of the European nations, no economic prosperity, and no creative dynamism.

NATO and the EC

The Atlantic Alliance and the European Community are not rivals. They are complementary. They work in unison. Where their areas of competence overlap, we need practical understandings but not new institutions. We can come to such practical understandings because our two organisations have many common members; we can also use unbureaucratic contacts between the European Commission and the NATO International Staff. The Atlantic Alliance has an interest in a stronger and more united Europe - going all the way to political union, including a European defence identity within the broader Atlantic framework. In fact today we need this more than ever as we face enormous tasks that make it imperative to combine, not fragment all the forces of the free West, including those of North America.

The Tasks

The most important tasks are:
1. to support the countries of Central and Eastern Europe in their efforts to build democracy and successful economies. Without our help, they stand no chance;
2. to assist Gorbachev and those forces working for reform as long as their reforms seek to promote democracy, freedom, pluralism and the market economy;
3. to build a new security system for the whole of Europe;
4. to firmly anchor a united Germany in this security system as well as in the structures of the West - the European Community and NATO;
5. to extend the process of disarmament and to ensure its speedy progress;
6. as in the past, to prevent war and to make the threat of military aggression pointless.

How could we possibly complete these tasks if we abandon the Atlantic Alliance or tolerate its dissolution? That would be a serious historical mistake.

The Atlantic Alliance:
- has led the United States away from isolationism and towards a lasting commitment to uphold peace and stability in Europe; it will continue to do this in the future;
- keeps the military might of the Soviet superpower in Europe in check;
- has transformed nuclear weapons into a peace-keeping instrument. As arms control can reduce but never disinvent the nuclear weapon, Europeans would be well-advised to retain the controlling structure that the Alliance represents.

Model of Security Management - from Peace-keeping to Peace-building

The Atlantic Alliance has become a unique model of the collective management of security among free countries. It has created a political as well as a military partnership among sovereign states. This is an essential reason for its success in fostering peace. Now we must progress from peace-keeping to peace-building.

This stabilizing framework of the Alliance has also contributed to protecting the neutral states of Europe, and the newly-democratizing nations of

Central and Eastern Europe recognize that without NATO they would not have regained their independence and freedom - and indeed could not retain them.

Without the stabilizing framework of our Alliance, Europe could once again become vulnerable to the shifting alliances and power politics of the past. Security would be "renationalized". The lessons of European history are clear on the subject of states seeking alone for their security.

Our challenge is to extend security without diminishing it. Neither the European Community nor the CSCE process, either individually or jointly, can substitute for the Atlantic Alliance in preserving security and freedom for the whole of Europe. Only the Atlantic Alliance can bind the United States and Canada to Europe; only it can guarantee that change can unfold without fear of setbacks and reversals. Only it can coordinate the West's grand strategy for peace and the securing of democratic values in the new Europe and anchor a united Germany in the West under conditions of maximum security for both itself and its neighbours.

A European Security Structure

The primary task of the next decade will be to build a new European security structure, to include the Soviet Union and the Warsaw Pact nations. The Soviet Union will have an important role to play in the construction of such a system. If you consider the current predicament of the Soviet Union, which has practically no allies left, then you can understand its justified wish not to be forced out of Europe.

Such a European security structure will have the job of organizing a security partnership of the European states to overcome the rigid hostility of the Cold War years, and to progress from confrontation to cooperation. Two alternatives are currently being discussed : a structure of collective security in which the two alliances would be dissolved in favour of a cooperative security organization; or one that is built around existing structures - the Atlantic Alliance and the European Community - and which works like an overarching framework, binding them together and extending them.

Only this second alternative is a serious option for us, because, if history is anything to go by, a collective security system would only work if all the participating states had perfectly concordant interests. When one state has to guarantee the security of all the other states, it really is in no position to give any concrete guarantee to anyone in the event of a conflict. A collective security system depends on permanent goodwill on all sides. In essence it only operates until it is put to its first serious test - and then it breaks up into mutually antagonistic alliances and power blocs. The pre-war League of Nations is our best example of this. Thus we have to build the future European security architecture on existing structures and to further develop those forms of cooperation that are already available to us.

We have the following elements of such an architecture:

1. **The CSCE process**

   This already offers us the embryon of a future security architecture. Under its aegis, the 35 participating nations can shape their relationship in a spirit of togetherness and concrete cooperation. We therefore have to develop the CSCE, bringing in new elements, such as the right to free elections - and also to institutionalize it. Then we can make good use of it as a forum for regular consultations over security, confidence-building, crisis prevention and the peaceful resolution of conflicts.

   We have to extend the process of arms control and take it further to the point when no European nation or collection of nations can any longer threaten another with military force, or hope to launch a successful military aggression.

2. **The European Community**

   This is the most promising and attractive model of political integration with its goal of a political union and the prospect of associating other European nations. It even offers the prospect of a future European confederation.

3. **The Atlantic Alliance**

   This gives us history's most successful model of an Alliance of sixteen free and sovereign states for the collective preservation of their security. This Alliance is united and determined; and it is capable of fulfilling its future tasks.

   The CSCE cannot fulfil these tasks, not now or in the future. It lacks the power to decide and implement sanctions. All of its 35 member states have the right of veto. The interests, social structures and value systems that make up the CSCE are still far too diverse for them to be able in the event of conflict to formulate or to impose a common security policy. This will be all the more difficult if one or more of them are engaged in the conflict in question. This does not in any way restrict the usefulness of CSCE as a medium for confidence building. But it cannot replace the Atlantic Alliance which will remain an essential pillar of the future European security architecture.

German Membership

The other primary task is to anchor a united Germany firmly into the institutional structures of the West, the EC and NATO.

Three basic considerations determine our Alliance policy:

1. Neutrality or non-alignment of the united Germany are not acceptable

for us. They would destabilize Europe and take us back to the days of balance of power diplomacy, of alliances and counter-alliances.

2. The united Germany must not be subjected to any discriminatory special régimes. They would only produce resentment sooner or later. On this point too, history teaches us a sobering lesson.

3. We have to find solutions that respect the legitimate security interests of all the participants - including the Soviet Union. I emphasize: **all** participants; in other words not only the Soviet Union. That nation has a right to expect that German unification and Germany's membership of the Atlantic Alliance will not prejudice its security. But it is also clear that it cannot expect us to put NATO's existence on the line and thus give it something that it never succeeded in obtaining in the past, even at the height of its power. The West cannot respond to the erosion of the Warsaw Pact with the weakening or even dissolution of the Atlantic Alliance; the only response is to establish a security framework that embraces both alliances : in other words one that draws the Soviet Union into a cooperative Europe.

We are already in the process of examining our strategy and our Alliance tasks, and of adapting them to changed circumstances. Yet nobody can expect us to deprive NATO of its core security function and its ability to prevent war. Our strategy and our Alliance are exclusively defensive. They threaten no-one, neither today nor tomorrow. We will never be the first to use our weapons. We are prepared for radical disarmament, right down to the minimum level that we must retain to guarantee our security.

This will also be true of a united Germany in NATO. The very fact that we are ready not to deploy NATO troops beyond the territory of the Federal Republic gives the Soviet Union firm security guarantees. Moreover we could conceive of a transitional period during which a reduced number of Soviet forces could remain stationed in the present-day GDR. This will meet Soviet concerns about not changing the overall East-West strategic balance. Soviet politicians are wrong to claim that German membership of NATO will lead to instability. The opposite is true. Europe including the Soviet Union would gain stability. It would also gain a genuine partner in the West ready to cooperate.

We have left behind us the old friend/foe mind-set and the confrontational outlook. We do not need enemies nor threat perceptions. We do not look upon the Soviet Union as the enemy. We want that nation to become our partner in ensuring security. On the other hand, we expect the Soviet Union not to see us as a military pact directed against it or even threatening it. Instead we wish the Soviet Union to see our Alliance as an open and cooperative instrument of stability in an over-arching European security system. We are not proposing something to the Soviet Union which is against its interests. What we have to offer can only be to its advantage. I am confident that this insight will gradually gain ground in Moscow, especially as the other Warsaw Pact countries see things the same way as we do.

The Political Role

From what I have said, I think it is clear how crucial NATO's political role will be in the future. We do not have to invent such a political role for ourselves. From its very inception, the Atlantic Alliance was more than just a military pact, even if during the Cold War years the military aspects perforce overshadowed the political ones. It has always been a community of values and a community of destiny among free nations, and today more so than ever on both counts. Thus in today's changed circumstances the Alliance's new political tasks are a logical extension of this fundamental *raison d'être*.

1. As **a community of destiny** the Alliance has the task of coordinating the policies of its members:
   - to shape East-West relations;
   - to help construct a new democratic and peaceful European states system;
   - to guide and verify arms control.
2. As **a community of values:**
   - to shape West-West relations; in other words, to maintain a vibrant transatlantic partnership;
   - to bring the various interests of its members into harmony and to identify the common denominator;
   - to tackle new security problems and to develop collective solutions;
   - in short: to shape the future course of peace.

Yet no matter how crucial the political character of the Atlantic Alliance now is, and no matter how important its political tasks, we must never forget one thing : its primary function is to maintain peace; only on that basis can we successfully deploy our efforts to build a more peaceful order.

Defence

Neither policies to promote détente, nor arms control nor diplomacy by themselves can prevent war. We cannot dispense with military efforts in the context of a coherent and credible defence posture. For this reason NATO will also remain a defensive Alliance. Even if there is now no danger of a direct attack by the Soviet Union, there are still considerable risks to our security. The situation in the Soviet Union itself is extremely unstable and we cannot base our security solely on the good intentions of a Soviet leader. People and intentions can change.

The Soviet Union still has enormous military capabilities; under any scenario it will still be the dominant European power on the Eurasian continent.

If we allow our defence to fall away and our Alliance to fall apart, the Soviet Union could be tempted in a crisis to use force against us, or at least to threaten us with force. Who would then respond?

Our defence efforts are thus indispensable for the foreseeable future to guarantee peace and to provide us with the necessary element for crisis management. War at the close of the twentieth century is so potentially catastrophic that we cannot take its prevention less seriously merely because it is now less likely.

Nevertheless the changed threat perception and the progress of arms control now enable us to adjust our defence efforts, our defence planning and strategy to today's different circumstances. We have already begun this work. A series of NATO ministerial meetings this spring and summer - culminating in a Summit early in July - will point the way ahead.

We will review our strategy and adjust it to the changed circumstances. We will significantly reduce types and numbers of our nuclear weapons, and we will gain the initiative also in the field of nuclear disarmament. In the future we will meet our task of war prevention and defence with fewer soldiers and weapons, with a lower level of readiness, less stationed troops and a higher dependence on force mobilization. We are going to modify the operational implementation of our strategic principle of forward defence. Electronic intelligence and command and communications systems will become more important. So will multinational units. In the next set of arms control negotiations, we will try to engage the Soviet Union in the quest for a common definition of minimal deterrence. A minimum of nuclear weapons will, however, also be needed in the future to prevent war. A denuclearization of Germany or of Europe as a whole would only leave us vulnerable to nuclear blackmail and would make conventional war once again feasible. The complete elimination of nuclear weapons would not bring more, but less security.

One thing is of particular importance : that we maintain a coherent, integrated defence and defence planning structure, including German forces. It would not be a good thing if each Ally were to reduce according to its fancy, without prior consultation within the Alliance and with the other Allies.

From all I have said, it is clear that NATO is by no means obsolete. Quite the reverse. For each of its three roles, it is indispensable.

1. In its role as a political alliance and community of values for the free world:
    as an instrument of change and peace-building.
2. In its role as the transatlantic alliance:

as the link and foundation that binds North America and Europe together in a community of destiny.

3. In its role as a security alliance:
   as an instrument to preserve peace and as a framework of stability that is the precondition of positive change.

A Changing Alliance

At the same time, our Alliance is changing with the new times and through time. Already during the last two years it has begun to adjust to changed circumstances in the definition of its tasks, substance and policies. This adjustment will continue for some time yet. The centre of gravity of our Alliance is shifting

- from confrontation to cooperation,
- from a military to a political Alliance,
- from deterrence to protection against risks and the guarantee of stability,
- from peace-keeping to peace-building,
- from a US-led Alliance to a genuine partnership with the Europeans now playing an equal leadership role.

The forthcoming NATO Summit will consecrate this new sharing of leadership roles within the Alliance, and it will produce a broad-ranging strategy for the changing Europe of the nineties.

Europe's Alternatives

Europe has a basic choice : either it lapses back into the old power politics and balance of power diplomacy of past centuries or it moves ahead along the road leading to a new order of peace and freedom, whether this be based on multinational or supranational cooperation. Our choice is clear : we are going forward. Our Alliance together with the European Community is the most successful model of such multinational cooperation. It is and will remain our best guarantee for a future of security and freedom.

□

L'Alliance Atlantique et la Sécurité Européenne dans les années 1990

DISCOURS
PRONONCE DEVANT
LE BREMER TABAKS
COLLEGIUM

Bruxelles
17 mai
1990

L'Histoire n'est pas un long fleuve tranquille. Elle passe par des phases de ralentissement et d'accélération, des phases au cours desquelles les événements se pressent et vont même, parfois, jusqu'à s'emballer. Nous vivons actuellement l'une de ces phases où l'Histoire se fait plus dense. Le visage de l'Europe se transforme radicalement. L'Europe est à la recherche d'une forme nouvelle. Nous n'en connaissons encore aucun élément définitif, mais ses premiers contours se dessinent pourtant déjà.

Comme toujours dans de telles périodes de transition, on voit s'ouvrir des chances et des perspectives nouvelles et audacieuses, mais des risques et des dangers nouveaux nous guettent au bord de la route.

Les chances

Concrétiser notre vision d'une Europe libre et unie, dotée d'une plus grande sécurité et durablement plus pacifique. En fait, il importe peu de trouver une appellation : ordre de paix européen, maison commune européenne, confédération européenne. Ce qui importe c'est le contenu proprement dit, à savoir : droits de l'homme et droit à des élections libres pour tous les citoyens, égalité devant la loi, ouverture des frontières, autodétermination, démocratie et protection des minorités. C'est sur ces points que nous devons insister. Les discussions actuelles sur un nouvel ordre de sécurité se polarisent trop sur des questions de procédure et de structure. En réalité, il serait plus important de mettre l'accent sur le fond même d'un tel ordre. Sa substance est déjà présente dans les trois Corbeilles de la CSCE qu'il faut encore enrichir et rendre juridiquement contraignantes.

165

Il s'agit des valeurs universelles sur lesquelles s'est construite notre communauté de valeurs atlantique dès son origine. Ces valeurs viennent d'entamer - et vont, espérons le, poursuivre longtemps - leur marche triomphale à travers le monde. L'élan vers la liberté, la démocratie et un ordre économique libéral et ouvert aux forces du marché est le moteur du processus historique que nous traversons. La mission historique qui incombe à notre génération est d'encourager cette dynamique, d'adapter le cours de l'Histoire à notre vision et de lui donner la stabilité nécessaire. Elle définit le rôle fondamental de notre Alliance atlantique, communauté de destin et d'action devenue une référence dans le monde libre.

Les risques

Mais les risques de bouleversement des Etats en Europe sont incalculables. L'instabilité de l'évolution tant intérieure qu'extérieure peut aller jusqu'au danger d'effondrement. L'instauration de la démocratie et l'introduction des réformes économiques en Europe du Centre et de l'Est posent d'énormes problèmes. D'anciennes rivalités nationales et ethniques que l'on croyait dépassées depuis longtemps se réveillent, et des problèmes de frontières et de minorités éclatent à nouveau. Nul ne sait ce qui se passera demain en Union soviétique, avec en toile de fond un potentiel militaire toujours impressionnant. A cela s'ajoutent, dans le tiers monde, les dangers résultant de la diffusion de la technologie des missiles, des armes chimiques et nucléaires. Un monde éternellement en paix reste une illusion séduisante. Pourtant, la politique de puissance continue à déterminer le cours des choses. L'autre partie de notre mission actuelle est d'agir sur ces dangers et d'atténuer les risques, voire de les supprimer.

Les deux grandes organisations de concertation mises en place dans le monde occidental - l'Alliance atlantique et la Communauté européenne - sont absolument indispensables à l'accomplissement des deux parties de notre mission historique. Dans cette phase de notre histoire, nous avons besoin plus que jamais d'union, de stabilité et de coopération avec les Etats-Unis. Sans l'Alliance atlantique, il n'y a ni cohésion ni unité du monde libre, il n'y a pas non plus d'association transatlantique, ni de sécurité et de stabilité. Sans la Communauté européenne, il n'y a pas de croissance harmonieuse de l'Europe, pas de prospérité économique, pas de dynamique.

L'OTAN et la Communauté européenne

Il n'y a aucune rivalité entre l'Alliance atlantique et la Communauté européenne. Elles se complètent l'une l'autre et agissent ensemble. Les points sur lesquels leurs domaines de compétences se recoupent appellent une coordination, mais pas d'institutions nouvelles. Cette coordination se fait par les Etats membres des deux Organisations et par des contacts informels entre la Commission de la Communauté et le Secrétariat international de l'OTAN.

L'Alliance atlantique a intérêt à voir une Europe plus forte et plus unie - allant jusqu'à l'union politique et englobant même la sécurité - se développer dans un cadre de sécurité atlantique. Et cela d'autant plus que nous devons faire face à d'énormes tâches qui exigent le regroupement et non l'éparpillement des forces du monde libre occidental comprenant l'Amérique du Nord.

Les tâches à accomplir

Les tâches les plus importante sont les suivantes :
1. Apporter notre concours aux pays d'Europe du Centre et de l'Est pour la mise en place de la démocratie et de l'économie. Sans nous, ils n'y parviendront pas.
2. Aider Gorbatchev et les forces réformistes à poursuivre les réformes dans la voie de la démocratie, la liberté, le pluralisme et l'économie de marché.
3. Construire un ordre de sécurité paneuropéen.
4. Ancrer solidement une Allemagne unie dans cet ordre de sécurité, ainsi que dans les structures de l'Ouest - Communauté européenne et OTAN.
5. Elargir le processus du désarmement et l'accélérer.
6. Continuer d'exclure l'éventualité de la guerre et rendre inutile toute menace de recours à la force.

Comment pourrions-nous faire face à ces tâches, si nous abandonnons l'Alliance atlantique et si nous la laissons se dissoudre ? Ce serait une erreur historique fatale.

En effet, l'Alliance atlantique :
- a sorti les Etats-Unis de l'isolationnisme pour les amener à prendre un engagement durable envers la paix et la stabilité en Europe, conduite qu'elle maintiendra à l'avenir;
- a réussi à tenir en échec la supériorité militaire de l'Union soviétique en Europe;
- a transformé les armes nucléaires en instruments de dissuasion. On peut certes réduire les armes nucléaires par le désarmement, mais il est impossible de nier leur existence; c'est pourquoi les Européens seraient bien avisés de conserver la structure de contrôle que représente l'Alliance.

Modèle de gestion de la sécurité :
du maintien de la paix à l'organisation de la paix

L'Alliance atlantique est devenue un modèle exceptionnel de gestion collective de la sécurité réalisé entre pays libres. Elle a établi une association à la fois politique et militaire entre des Etats souverains. C'est là une des raisons essentielles de son succès dans l'instauration de la paix. Il s'agit maintenant de passer du maintien de la paix à l'organisation de la paix.

Le cadre stabilisateur de l'Alliance a également joué un rôle à l'extérieur en protégeant les Etats européens neutres; les nouveaux Etats démocratiques d'Europe du Centre et de l'Est reconnaissent d'ailleurs que, sans l'OTAN, ils n'auraient pu regagner leur indépendance et leur liberté et qu'ils ne pourraient pas non plus les conserver.

Sans la stabilité qu'offre notre Alliance, l'Europe pourrait à nouveau se montrer sensible aux renversements des alliances et à la politique de puissance du passé. La sécurité se trouverait "renationalisée". Mais les enseignements de l'histoire européenne sont sans équivoque, s'agissant de la recherche d'une sécurité isolée par des Etats individuels.

Le défi que nous avons à relever est d'élargir le champ de la sécurité sans la diminuer. Ni la Communauté européenne ni la CSCE ne peuvent, isolément ou ensemble, se substituer à l'Alliance atlantique pour garantir la stabilité et la liberté de l'Europe tout entière. Seule l'Alliance atlantique peut lier les Etats-Unis et le Canada à l'Europe, elle seule peut assurer que le changement s'instaurera sans crainte de revers ou de volte-face. Elle seule peut coordonner la stratégie globale de l'Occident pour la paix et la garantie des valeurs démocratiques dans une Europe nouvelle. Elle seule peut ancrer à l'Ouest une Allemagne unie dans des conditions de sécurité maximales pour ce pays et pour ses voisins.

Ordre de sécurité européen

La tâche primordiale de la prochaine décennie est la mise en place d'un ordre de sécurité européen qui englobe l'Union soviétique et les Etats du pacte de Varsovie. L'Union soviétique aura un rôle important à jouer dans la construction de cet ordre de sécurité. Si l'on considère la situation de l'Union soviétique, qui se retrouve pratiquement sans alliés véritables, il est compréhensible et justifié qu'elle ne souhaite pas être écartée de l'Europe.

Dans ce cadre européen, l'une des tâches à accomplir est d'organiser une association de sécurité des Etats européens qui aille au-delà de l'affrontement de la guerre froide pour passer de la confrontation à la coopération. Deux solutions sont en présence : une structure de sécurité collective qui absorbera les alliances existantes, et une organisation de sécurité en coopération qui se fondera sur les structures existantes - l'Alliance atlantique et la Communauté européenne pour se surimposer à elles, les relier et les compléter.

Pour nous, cette dernière solution est la seule valable, l'Histoire nous ayant enseigné qu'un système de sécurité collective ne fonctionne que lorsqu'il y a concordance d'intérêts entre les Etats en présence. Si chacun est le garant de la sécurité de tous, en cas de conflit il n'y a plus de garantie pour personne. Un système de sécurité collective repose sur l'hypothèse d'une bonne volonté durable de toutes les parties. Il ne fonctionne, en fait, que jusqu'au moment où il est véritablement mis à l'épreuve, et il s'effondre alors dans l'affrontement des alliances et des pactes. La Société des nations nous en a fourni un excellent exemple. Il s'agit donc de construire le futur ordre de sécurité européen sur les structures existantes et de perfectionner les formes de coopération dont nous disposons.

Divers éléments permettront la mise en place d'un tel ordre :

1. **La CSCE**

   La CSCE nous offre les grandes lignes d'une future architecture de sécurité. Sous son égide, les 35 Etats participants peuvent façonner leurs relations dans un esprit de communauté et de collaboration concrète. Il faut donc l'étoffer, l'enrichir de nouveaux éléments - tels ceux du droit à des élections libres - et institutionnaliser le processus. La CSCE pourrait alors servir de cadre à des consultations régulières sur la politique de sécurité, les mesures de confiance, la prévention des crises et le règlement pacifique des conflits.

   Aussi faut-il élargir le processus de désarmement et le poursuivre de telle sorte qu'aucun Etat ou groupe d'Etats en Europe ne se trouvent plus jamais en mesure d'exercer une menace militaire, ou n'aient même de chances de lancer une attaque avec succès.

2. **La Communauté européenne**

   C'est le modèle le plus porteur d'avenir et le plus prestigieux d'une intégration d'Etats ayant pour objectif l'union politique et pour perspective l'association d'autres Etats européens, voire la réalisation d'une confédération européenne.

3. **L'Alliance atlantique**

   Nous avons là le modèle exemplaire d'une alliance de seize Etats libres et souverains, engagés dans la défense collective de leur sécurité. Cette alliance, solidaire et unie, pourra, même dans l'avenir, accomplir sa mission. Ce n'est pas le cas de la CSCE, qui n'a pas les moyens de décréter et de faire exécuter des sanctions. Chacun des 35 Etats dispose d'un droit de veto. L'éventail des intérêts, la structure des sociétés et les systèmes de valeur de ces pays sont trop différents pour qu'ils puissent, en cas de crise, garantir conjointement la sécurité et l'imposer, surtout si un ou plusieurs d'entre eux sont parties à ce conflit. L'importance de la CSCE, comme cadre propre à créer la confiance n'en est en rien diminuée. Mais la CSCE ne peut se substituer à l'Alliance atlantique, qui restera un pilier essentiel de la future structure européenne de sécurité.

Appartenance de l'Allemagne

L'autre tâche primordiale consiste à ancrer solidement une Allemagne unie dans les structures d'alliance de l'Occident, c'est-à-dire la Communauté européenne et l'OTAN.

169

La politique de notre Alliance repose sur trois principes :
1. Nous n'accepterons pas qu'une Allemagne unie soit neutre ou indépendante des blocs. Cette formule entraînerait la déstabilisation de l'Europe, qu'elle rejetterait à l'ère de la politique des équilibres entre les Etats-nations et du système d'alliances et de contre-alliances.
2. L'Allemagne unie ne devra pas faire l'objet de discriminations qui pourraient ultérieurement conduire au désastre. Là aussi, le spectre de l'histoire se profile.
3. Il s'agit de trouver des solutions qui respectent les intérêts de sécurité légitimes de tous les participants, y compris des Soviétiques. J'insiste : **tous** les participants - c'est-à-dire pas seulement l'URSS. L'Union soviétique est en mesure et en droit d'attendre que le processus d'unification et l'appartenance de toute l'Allemagne à l'Alliance atlantique ne portent pas atteinte à sa sécurité. Mais il est tout aussi vrai qu'elle ne peut pas attendre que nous mettions l'OTAN en sommeil, lui accordant ainsi ce qu'elle n'a jamais pu obtenir, même à l'apogée de sa puissance. L'Occident ne peut pas, pour compenser l'érosion du Pacte de Varsovie, amputer l'Alliance atlantique ou la dissoudre, mais seulement adopter des mesures de sécurité qui dépassent l'Alliance, c'est-à-dire intégrer l'Union soviétique dans une Europe de la coopération.

Nous procédons actuellement à un examen de notre stratégie, de notre potentiel nucléaire et conventionnel et des missions de l'Alliance, en vue de les adapter aux nouvelles circonstances. Nul ne peut cependant escompter que nous dépouillerons l'OTAN de la pièce maîtresse de sa sécurité et de sa capacité de prévenir la guerre. Notre stratégie, comme notre alliance, sont exclusivement défensives. Elles ne menacent ni ne menaceront personne. Nous n'utiliserons jamais nos armes en premier. Nous sommes favorables à un désarmement d'envergure, allant jusqu'au minimum inaliénable pour notre propre sécurité. Cela vaut aussi pour une Allemagne unie, membre de l'OTAN. Cette affirmation et l'assurance que les troupes de l'OTAN ne dépasseront pas le territoire de la République fédérale d'Allemagne, offrent à l'Union soviétique de solides garanties de sécurité. On peut en outre imaginer que, pendant une période de transition, des troupes soviétiques, en nombre réduit, resteront stationnées sur le territoire de l'actuelle RDA. Cette formule répondra au souhait de l'Union soviétique de ne pas voir modifié le rapport des forces. Il est faux de prétendre, comme le font les hommes politiques soviétiques, que l'appartenance de l'Allemagne à l'OTAN serait facteur d'instabilité. C'est l'inverse qui est vrai. L'Europe - et donc aussi l'Union soviétique - y gagne en stabilité. Qui plus est, cette dernière trouve également à l'Ouest de véritables partenaires prêts à coopérer. Nous ne pensons plus en termes d'ami-ennemi et de confrontation. Nous n'avons pas besoin d'ennemi, nous n'avons pas besoin de cette image. Nous ne voyons pas dans l'Union soviétique l'ennemi - nous souhaitons qu'elle devienne pour nous un partenaire dans les questions de sécurité. A l'inverse, nous attendons qu'elle ne considère pas notre Alliance comme un bloc militaire dirigé contre elle ou même menaçant sa sécurité mais comme un instrument de stabilité sans exclusive et ouvert à la coopération, dans un futur ordre de sécurité supérieur. Nous n'exigeons rien de l'Union soviétique qui puisse lui causer un préjudice. Ce que nous lui proposons est dans son intérêt. Je suis certain que cette conception fera son chemin à Moscou, d'autant que les autres pays du pacte de Varsovie partagent notre vision de la situation.

Rôle politique

Tout ceci montre bien l'importance du rôle politique de l'OTAN dans l'avenir. Ce rôle ne doit pas être inventé de toutes pièces. Depuis sa création, l'Alliance atlantique est plus qu'une simple alliance militaire, même si le militaire a pris le pas sur le politique au temps de la guerre froide. Elle était déjà une communauté de valeurs et une communauté de destin d'Etats libres. Elle l'est aujourd'hui plus que jamais. De ce fait, de nouvelles tâches politiques surgissent, face aux bouleversements actuels.

1. Communauté de destin, l'Alliance doit coordonner la politique des Etats membres :
   - Façonner les relations Est-Ouest.
   - Contribuer à l'instauration d'une nouvelle Europe, démocratique et consacrant l'état de droit.
   - Orienter la maîtrise des armements et en vérifier l'application.
2. Communauté de valeurs, elle doit :
   - Faconner les relations entre les pays occidentaux, c'est-à-dire préserver le lien transatlantique.
   - Harmoniser les divers intérêts des Etats membres et leur trouver un dénominateur commun.
   - Aborder les nouveaux problèmes qui se posent dans le domaine de la sécurité et mettre au point des solutions communes.
   - En bref : organiser la paix.

Si important que soit l'élément politique dans le caractère et les tâches de l'Alliance atlantique, on ne peut et on ne doit pas se cacher que le maintien de la paix reste la pierre angulaire des efforts à déployer pour organiser la paix.

Défense

Ni la politique de détente, ni la maîtrise des armements, ni la diplomatie ne peuvent à elles seules prévenir la guerre. L'effort militaire, que traduit une défense cohérente et crédible, est indispensable. C'est pourquoi l'Alliance atlantique demeure aussi une alliance défensive. Même si la menace d'une attaque directe de l'Union soviétique ne se profile pas actuellement, il subsiste des risques non négligeables, dont nous devons nous protéger. La situation en Union soviétique est extrêmement instable. Nous ne pouvons pas fonder notre sécurité uniquement sur les bonnes intentions d'un dirigeant soviétique. Les personnes et les intentions peuvent changer. L'Union soviétique conserve un potentiel militaire énorme, et quoi qu'il puisse arriver, elle restera la puissance militaire dominante du continent eurasiatique. Si nous baissions notre garde ou si nous laissions notre Alliance se dissoudre, la tentation serait forte, en cas de crise, d'employer la force contre nous ou du moins de nous en menacer. Qui prendrait une telle responsabilité ?

Parce qu'il est le garant de la paix et un élément nécessaire de la gestion de crise, notre dispositif de défense reste inaliénable. La guerre, à la fin du 20ème siècle, serait un tel cataclysme que nous ne pouvons pas nous employer moins sérieusement à la prévenir sous prétexte qu'elle est moins vraisemblable. D'ailleurs, la modification de la menace et le désarmement nous permettent d'adapter aux nouvelles circonstances notre dispositif, nos plans et notre stratégie de défense. Nous avons déjà commencé. Nos réunions ministérielles - qui culmineront, cet été, avec l'organisation d'un Sommet au début du mois de juillet - montreront la voie à suivre.

Nous allons réexaminer notre stratégie et l'adapter à l'évolution des circonstances. Nous allons réduire sensiblement le type et le nombre de nos armes nucléaires et nous allons prendre l'initiative également dans le domaine du désarmement nucléaire. Nous pourrons désormais prévenir la guerre et assurer notre défense en réduisant le nombre des soldats et les armes, le niveau de préparation, notre présence mais en faisant une plus large part à la mobilisation. Nous modifierons les modalités de mise en oeuvre de notre principe stratégique de défense en avant. Les moyens électroniques de reconnaissance et de commandement seront plus déterminants. Les groupements multinationaux prendront plus d'importance. Nous nous efforcerons, dans la poursuite des négociations sur le désarmement avec les Soviétiques, de parvenir à un accord sur un concept de dissuasion minimale. Cependant, un minimum d'armes nucléaires sera toujours indispensable à l'avenir pour prévenir la guerre. La dénucléarisation de l'Allemagne ou même de toute l'Europe nous exposerait au chantage nucléaire et rendrait une guerre conventionnelle de nouveau possible. L'élimination totale des armes nucléaires ne reviendrait pas à accroître la sécurité, mais à la diminuer.

Il est en effet particulièrement important que nous maintenions - et ce, avec l'Allemagne - une défense et une planification de la défense cohérentes et intégrées. Il ne serait pas bon que chacun réduise à sa guise, sans concertation avec l'Alliance et les Alliés.

En conclusion, l'OTAN n'est nullement dépassée. Elle est, au contraire, irremplaçable dans son triple rôle :
1. Dans son rôle d'alliance politique et de communauté de valeurs du monde libre,

comme instrument du changement et de l'organisation de la paix

2. Dans son rôle d'alliance transatlantique,
   comme lien et fondement de la communauté de destin des pays
   d'Amérique du Nord et d'Europe

3. Dans son rôle d'alliance sécuritaire,
   comme instrument du maintien de la paix et comme cadre de stabilité
   pour le changement.

Transformation de l'Alliance

Il est vrai que notre Alliance est en mutation. Elle évolue dans le temps et avec le temps. Depuis deux ans déjà, elle s'adapte à la nouvelle donne de la définition des tâches, des questions de fond et de la politique. Ce processus se poursuit. Le centre de gravité de notre Alliance se déplace, passant :

- de la confrontation à la coopération,
- du militaire au politique,
- de la dissuasion à la protection contre le risque et à la garantie de la stabilité,
- du maintien de la paix à l'organisation de la paix,
- du leadership des Etats-Unis à un authentique partenariat, dans lequel les Européens assument des responsabilités égales.

Le prochain sommet de l'OTAN entérinera notre nouvelle conception des rôles et lancera une stratégie élargie pour l'Europe nouvelle des années 90.

Quelle alternative pour l'Europe ?

L'Europe se trouve devant une alternative fondamentale : ou elle retombe dans l'ancien système politique de puissance et d'équilibre des siècles passés, ou elle avance sur la voie d'un nouvel ordre de paix et de liberté résultant d'une coopération internationale ou supranationale. Notre choix est clair : nous allons de l'avant. Notre Alliance est, avec la Communauté européenne, le modèle le plus accompli de ce partenariat entre Etats. Elle est et demeure notre meilleure garante d'un avenir sûr et libre.

Opening remarks at the Ministerial Meeting of the North Atlantic Council

Turnberry
7-8 June
1990

On behalf of the North Atlantic Council I would like to express our deep appreciation to the United Kingdom Authorities for the warm welcome they have extended to us here in Turnberry.

This is the time to create a new European order, an order for a Europe which is undivided, free and at peace. As members of the Atlantic Alliance, we are taking the decisions and devising the policies necessary to that task. Our Alliance has to play a major rôle in this endeavour. We have consistently promoted and contributed to change, and will continue to do so: that is the central message of our meetings this Spring. If we want to be able to meet the challenge of change, we have to change ourselves. We are equipping the Alliance for its rôle as a partner in stability and progress.

The two fundamental elements of the policy of this Alliance, defence and dialogue, have borne fruit. In pursuing the path we decided upon decades ago, we have helped to create a new world which is now unfolding and which we must continue to nourish.

The Harmel Report of 1967 made a fundamental observation about overcoming the post-war division of Europe. Harmel warned that "No final and stable settlement in Europe is possible without a solution of the German question which lies at the heart of present tensions in Europe. Any such settlement must end the unnatural barriers between Eastern and Western Europe, which are most clearly and cruelly manifested in the division of Germany." Now that this is happening, we can and will add a new third dimension to our policy: cooperation. We intend to move beyond confrontation to cooperation with all the states who have an interest in Europe.

This Alliance will continue to guarantee the safety and stability of Europe. We have entered a period with prospects for cooperation and the peaceful management of change, and for changing the ways we think about security. The greatly reduced risk of military conflict in Europe and the conclusion of an agreement on conventional arms control will provide the foundation.

The results of our recent Ministerials are already giving concrete shape to our vision, and we trust that the Soviet Union will finally and fully appreciate this new dimension. We seek a framework of cooperation which adds to the security of all and diminishes the security of no one. We want to build a cooperative framework. A CFE agreement is the essential first step. We support an enhanced and strengthened CSCE. Such an invigorated CSCE will be an important complement to the Alliance, while not substituting for it.

The Atlantic Alliance will remain an essential pillar of any future European security structure. A unified Germany, firmly anchored in the structures of the West and fully participating in the strengthened CSCE, will make a critical contribution. Europe, including the Soviet Union, will gain the stability which must, after so many centuries of conflict, be the underpinning of a truly cooperative Europe. In such circumstances, the Soviet Union has everything to gain: peace, security, stability and genuine partnership.

The Alliance does not have to invent its political rôle: history has given it to us. Our agenda is ambitious, but not unrealistic. I look forward very much to our meeting here in Turnberry and our forthcoming Alliance Summit in London. Both will make important contributions to this effort and further chart the course ahead.

Allocution d'ouverture à la Réunion Ministérielle du Conseil de l'Atlantique Nord

Turnberry
7 et 8 juin
1990

Au nom du Conseil de l'Atlantique Nord, je voudrais exprimer aux autorités du Royaume-Uni notre profonde reconnaissance pour le si chaleureux accueil qu'elles nous ont réservé à Turnberry.

Le moment est venu de créer un nouvel ordre européen, un ordre pour une Europe qui soit sans division, libre et en paix. En tant que membres de l'Alliance atlantique, nous prenons les décisions et nous concevons les politiques nécessaires à cette fin. Notre Alliance doit jouer un rôle majeur dans cette entreprise. Nous avons toujours apporté nos encouragements et notre contribution au changement, et nous continuerons de le faire : tel est le message central de nos réunions de ce printemps. Si nous voulons être à même de relever le défi du changement, nous devons changer nous-mêmes. Nous donnons à l'Alliance les moyens de jouer son rôle comme partenaire dans la stabilité et le progrès.

Les deux éléments fondamentaux de la politique de l'Alliance - la défense et le dialogue - ont porté leurs fruits. En suivant la voie que nous nous sommes tracée, il y a plusieurs décennies, nous avons contribué à créer un monde nouveau que nous voyons se développer aujourd'hui et que nous devons continuer de bâtir.

Le rapport Harmel, publié en 1967, contenait une observation fondamentale sur le dépassement de la division de l'Europe de l'après-guerre. Il y était souligné que "aucun règlement définitif et stable en Europe n'est possible sans une solution de la question allemande, qui est au coeur des tensions actuelles en Europe. Tout règlement de ce genre devra faire disparaître les barrières artificielles entre l'Europe de l'Est et l'Europe de l'Ouest, barrières dont la division de l'Allemagne constitue la manifestation la plus évidente et la plus cruelle".

A présent que ce stade a été atteint, nous pouvons, et nous allons, ajouter une nouvelle troisième dimension à notre politique : la coopération. Nous comptons dépasser la confrontation pour coopérer avec tous les Etats qui ont un intérêt en Europe.

Notre Alliance continuera de garantir la sécurité et la stabilité en Europe. Nous sommes entrés dans une période qui offre des perspectives de coopération et de gestion pacifique du changement, et d'ajustement de notre manière de penser à propos de la sécurité. La forte réduction du risque de conflit militaire en Europe et la conclusion d'un traité sur la maîtrise des armements conventionnels en seront les fondements.

Les résultats de nos récentes réunions ministérielles donnent déjà forme concrète à notre vision, et nous ne doutons pas que l'Union soviétique finisse par reconnaître pleinement cette nouvelle dimension. Nous recherchons l'instauration d'un cadre de coopération qui ajoute à la sécurité de tous et ne réduise la sécurité d'aucun. Nous voulons construire un cadre de coopération. La conclusion d'un traité sur les FCE en est la première étape essentielle. Nous sommes partisans d'une CSCE améliorée et renforcée. Une CSCE ainsi revigorée sera un important complément de l'Alliance, que, cependant, elle ne saurait remplacer.

L'Alliance atlantique restera un pilier essentiel de toute structure de sécurité européenne future. Une Allemagne unifiée fermement ancrée dans les structures de l'Ouest et participant pleinement à la CSCE revigorée apportera une contribution vitale. L'Europe, y compris l'Union soviétique, acquerra la stabilité qui doit, après tant de siècles de conflit, former la base d'une véritable Europe de la coopération. Dans de telles circonstances, l'Union soviétique a tout à gagner : la paix, la sécurité, la stabilité et un partenariat authentique.

L'Alliance n'a pas à s'inventer un rôle politique : l'histoire le lui a donné. Notre programme d'action est ambitieux, mais pas irréaliste. J'attends beaucoup de la réunion que nous allons tenir ici, à Turnberry, et du Sommet de l'Alliance à Londres. Tous deux apporteront une importante contribution à cette action et préciseront nos orientations futures.

La Sécurité Européenne et l'Avenir de l'Alliance

DISCOURS PRONONCE
A L'INSTITUT FRANCAIS
DES RELATIONS
INTERNATIONALES

Paris
21 juin
1990

C'est un grand plaisir pour moi que de m'adresser aujourd'hui à un auditoire sélectionné par l'Institut Français des Relations Internationales. J'ai conscience de parler à beaucoup des meilleurs spécialistes français des questions internationales. Depuis sa fondation en 1978, l'IFRI a hautement contribué, sous la direction de Thierry de Montbrial, à promouvoir les études et les recherches internationales en France, et a encouragé les spécialistes français à se produire dans des rencontres internationales et à entreprendre avec des collègues étrangers des travaux en commun. Au premier rang de ces entreprises internationales ont figuré les travaux menés avec des instituts correspondants dans des pays de l'Alliance atlantique.

Je n'ai pas besoin de vous dire, Mesdames et Messieurs, à quel point nous sommes aujourd'hui dans un monde en mouvement, dans une Europe dont la configuration d'aujourd'hui aurait été impensable il y a un an, et dans une société internationale dans laquelle les notions traditionnelles ont donc besoin d'être réajustées par rapport à ces changements. Il serait impensable, dans cette conjoncture, que l'Alliance atlantique, qui a si fortement contribué au maintien de la paix en Europe durant plus de 40 ans, se contente de célébrer cette réussite et qu'elle ne cherche pas à évoluer elle aussi. L'Alliance doit bâtir sur ses succès pour participer aussi pleinement au nouvel ordre européen qu'elle a participé à l'ancien.

Or, non seulement l'Alliance le doit-elle, mais elle le fait. Lors de nos fréquentes réunions récentes, nous avons jeté les bases d'une remise à jour de notre Alliance, tout en conservant ce qui fait l'essentiel de son apport à la sécurité européenne : un ferme point d'ancrage, permettant le maintien de la paix sur

179

notre continent. La tâche est en effet complexe qui consiste à créer une **nouvelle communauté des Etats en Europe,** ce qui devrait être la conclusion logique de l'évolution qui se produit sous nos yeux depuis huit mois, si celle-ci se poursuit. Cette nouvelle communauté, que l'on peut qualifier, comme le Président Mitterrand, de "confédération", ou comme les Allemands, d'"ordre de paix européen", ou, comme les Américains, de "nouvelle architecture", devra reposer sur des principes clairement établis : la liberté, l'Etat de droit, la démocratie, appuyés sur l'égalité devant la loi, l'ouverture des frontières, l'auto-détermination et la protection des minorités. Ce sont ces principes qui comptent plus que les structures institutionnelles, car ce sont eux qui devront former la substance du nouvel ordre.

Il convient en effet de comprendre que le concept même de sécurité, à une époque comme la nôtre, ne peut être conçu que de manière plus globale, plus large, qu'à une période où existait une menace massive et clairement identifiable. Aujourd'hui, la menace s'exprime davantage en termes de risques multiples, multiformes, et plus difficiles à identifier, du fait du caractère imprévisible des développements en URSS. Qui peut aujourd'hui prédire comment l'Union soviétique se comportera, face aux défis formidables que représentent pour elle l'unité de son empire et l'affaiblissement de sa position internationale? L'instabilité et l'incertitude forment la toile de fond des développements à venir. Autant de risques potentiels contre lesquels il convient de nous garder. C'est là notre tâche. L'Alliance atlantique demeure donc, mais dans un sens plus large qu'auparavant, une Alliance pour la sécurité.

La sécurité des Etats membres de notre Alliance est donc moins que jamais une notion purement militaire, parce que les défis auxquels nous avons à faire face appellent des solutions qui dépassent très largement le cadre militaire. La sécurité implique aujourd'hui la stabilité, qui a évidemment des dimensions économiques et sociales, voire culturelles, aussi bien que des aspects militaires, **la synthèse de ces aspects multiformes de notre sécurité ne pouvant, quant à elle, n'être que politique.** Notre concept de sécurité en conformité avec l'appel universel du Traité de Washington ne peut pas ignorer et les nouveaux risques militaires et les défis posés par les évolutions dans le Tiers Monde; ceux-ci se caractérisent par les différences croissantes de richesse, une démographie explosive, la prolifération balistique, nucléaire et chimique. Je fais, en particulier, référence au Proche-Orient et au pourtour de la Méditerranée, dont l'évolution affecte directement la sécurité européenne. Joints aux conflits de l'avenir sur le partage des ressources mondiales, ces risques doivent donc figurer plus pleinement dans nos délibérations et dans nos consultations dans la mesure où ils affectent notre sécurité. Evidemment, il n'est pas question que l'OTAN se transforme en gendarme du monde, ni d'agir en tant qu'Alliance en dehors de notre zone géographique. Mais **la sécurité est indivisible.** Déjà, ce même Traité de Washington définissait aussi les tâches de notre Alliance, d'une manière générale, en faisant référence - je cite - aux "libres institutions" qu'il convenait de renforcer, et aux "principes sur lesquels ces institutions sont fondées" avant que d'en venir aux articles concernant l'attitude à prendre en cas d'attaque contre l'un des signataires. Notre Alliance n'est en effet nullement "un personnage à la recherche d'un rôle" : ses tâches sont bien fixées : **elle doit maintenir la sécurité de ses membres.** Elle doit cependant le faire dans des circonstances nouvelles, qui impliquent une adaptation.

Le Rapport Harmel contenait une observation fondamentale sur le dépassement de la division de l'Europe de l'après-guerre. Il y était souligné qu'"aucun règlement définitif et stable en Europe n'est possible sans une solution de la question allemande, qui est au coeur des tensions actuelles en Europe. Tout règlement de ce genre devra faire disparaître les barrières artificielles entre l'Europe de l'Est et l'Europe de l'Ouest, barrières dont la division de l'Allemagne constitue la manifestation la plus évidente et la plus cruelle".

C'est pourquoi - ce stade aujourd'hui atteint - il est nécessaire de donner à la **défense** et au **dialogue** qui ont été définis par le Rapport Harmel comme les deux axes de la politique de l'Alliance atlantique une nouvelle dimension comprenant les deux volets traditionnels : la dimension de la **coopération**.

La défense demeure nécessaire, y compris dans sa composante dissuasive, ce n'est pas à un auditoire français que je l'apprendrai. Dans un monde de plus en plus instable, dans une Europe où le poids politico-militaire de l'Union soviétique demeurera considérable, il convient de s'assurer contre les dangers possibles. Quant au dialogue, il est depuis longtemps une règle d'or de nos diplomaties.

Nous sommes en route, si le cap est tenu, vers une Europe libre et entière, dont l'Alliance constituera un élément essentiel. Ce nouvel ordre demande en effet à être organisé de manière stable. A cette stabilité, notre Alliance peut apporter une **contribution militaire.** Ce sera l'objet de la première partie de mon exposé.

Et une **contribution politique.** Ce sera l'objet de ma seconde partie.

C'est seulement ainsi que ce **nouvel ordre de sécurité européen** prendra son sens. Ce sera l'objet de la troisième partie de mon exposé.

I. MAINTENIR LA CONTRIBUTION MILITAIRE DE L'ALLIANCE A LA STABILITE EUROPEENNE

Face aux risques que j'ai évoqués plus haut, notre Alliance doit évidemment ajuster sa stratégie, son rôle militaire, au changement des circonstances, tout en ne perdant pas de vue ses principes de base, qui demeurent valables : nous continuerons à avoir besoin d'un mélange adéquat de forces nucléaires et conventionnelles. L'arme nucléaire continuera de réduire le danger de conflagration militaire parce qu'elle fait courir à l'agresseur potentiel des risques crédibles, inacceptables et incalculables. Elle rend donc l'agression absurde. La dissuasion constitue donc toujours le dernier rempart de la sécurité, et cela même dans une situation où le niveau des forces conventionnelles en Europe serait plus proche de la parité. Par conséquent, un minimum d'armes nucléaires sera indispensable à l'avenir pour prévenir la guerre. La dénucléarisation de l'Allemagne ou même de toute l'Europe nous exposerait au chantage nucléaire et rendrait une guerre conventionnelle de nouveau possible. L'élimination totale des armes nucléaires ne reviendrait pas à accroître la sécurité, mais à la diminuer. Toutefois nous allons réduire de manière sensible et les catégories et le nombre d'armes nucléaires. Le Président Bush a à cet égard émis un signal positif en décidant de renoncer à la modernisation des armes nucléaires à courte portée en Europe. Les négociations imminentes sur les forces nucléaires à courte portée doivent nous permettre de nous entendre avec les Soviétiques sur un concept commun de dissuasion minimale.

Les quinze Etats participant à notre système commun de planification de la défense ont décidé lors de la dernière réunion du Comité des Plans de Défense de réévaluer notre stratégie militaire afin de l'adapter aux circonstances nouvelles.

Cela sera facilité par le rééquilibrage et la réduction des forces conventionnelles en Europe, qui devraient constituer le résultat principal du traité FCE dont nous espérons la conclusion cette année. Dans ce contexte, il faudra changer l'application de la doctrine de la défense de l'avant pour tenir compte des réalités nouvelles. Ce sera l'une des tâches du réexamen que je viens de mentionner que d'examiner les modalités de ce changement. A l'avenir nous devrons maintenir notre mission de prévention de la guerre et de défense avec moins d'hommes et moins d'armes, et moins de préparation et de manoeuvres, tout en dépendant davantage que par le passé de notre capacité de mobilisation.

Une organisation militaire fondée sur de plus petits nombres a en effet particulièrement besoin de concentration et de capacité d'action rapide. Nous aurons donc de plus en plus besoin d'unités mobiles, flexibles, à déploiement rapide. Dans ce contexte, et vu la réduction du nombre des troupes, il conviendra de créer des unités multinationales intégrées au niveau du corps et de la division. De même faudra-t-il augmenter nos capacités d'interopérabilité et évidemment notre coopération en matière d'armements. C'est la réponse aux bouleversements actuels.

Cependant, c'est au rôle politique de notre Alliance qu'il faut maintenant attacher la plus grande importance.

II. UNE CONTRIBUTION POLITIQUE DE PLUS EN PLUS IMPORTANTE A LA STABILITE

Je l'ai dit en commençant cet exposé, la dimension politique de la sécurité l'emporte aujourd'hui sur les autres. Le facteur militaire de la puissance internationale décroît aujourd'hui relativement aux autres déterminants de la puissance, et ce sont les crises et les tensions politiques, l'injustice, la répression, la dictature, la détermination d'employer la force et la volonté de domination politique qui constituent le véritable danger pour la paix. Nous sommes fermement convaincus que la paix n'a pas de meilleure garantie que des sociétés ouvertes et démocratiques, dont le développement économique est assuré. Il est donc essentiel, dans le cadre d'une politique de sécurité, d'aider les mouvements réformateurs en Europe centrale et orientale, ainsi qu'en URSS, et de contribuer ainsi à la démocratisation, à la prospérité et à la coopération dans cette zone. Le soutien à la réforme constitue donc un volet essentiel de cette dimension politique de la sécurité dont je pense qu'elle devient centrale, et qui garantit à mes yeux le meilleur type de sécurité. Dans cette optique, l'unification de l'Allemagne peut apporter une contribution essentielle, car elle représente le symbole de la réforme et du dépassement de la division de l'Europe en deux, division dont celle de l'Allemagne constituait le centre.

Notre Alliance, quant à elle, est la seule institution qui puisse envisager les questions politiques et de sécurité dans une dimension transatlantique. Elle constitue le garant de la présence américaine en Europe, dont nous savons qu'elle demeure indispensable à la stabilité de notre Continent. Il convient que les Etats-Unis participent pleinement à l'élaboration et à la mise en oeuvre du nouvel ordre européen.

L'Alliance atlantique a par conséquent un rôle éminent à jouer pour coordonner la politique de ses pays membres dans le domaine des rapports Est-Ouest comme dans le domaine des relations transatlantiques. Elle apporte une contribution essentielle à l'articulation d'une coopération avec les pays de l'Est, pour parvenir à un ordre de paix paneuropéen, et pour poursuivre et vérifier le processus de maîtrise des armements; et, "last but not least" à l'ancrage d'une Allemagne unie dans les structures de sécurité de l'Occident. Sa tâche essentielle consiste aujourd'hui à construire la paix autant qu'à la préserver. Elle est devenue un modèle unique et exemplaire de gestion collective de la sécurité entre des pays libres. Elle a créé un partenariat politique aussi bien que militaire entre des Etats souverains qui à l'avenir tirera sa validité de la recherche en commun de solutions collectives aux problèmes de demain.

L'unité de l'Allemagne a toujours constitué l'un des objectifs essentiels de notre Alliance, et nous nous félicitons évidemment des progrès effectués dans cette direction. Nous souhaitons que les pourparlers "2 + 4" parviennent à un règlement définitif qui n'impose plus aucune limitation à la souveraineté allemande. C'est pourquoi notre Alliance affirme le droit de l'Allemagne, que lui reconnaît l'Acte Final d'Helsinki, de participer à l'Alliance qu'elle choisira. L'Alliance soutient entièrement les points sur l'unité allemande que le Président Bush a définis sur la base de consultations approfondies avec les Alliés. L'Allemagne unie doit être membre de l'OTAN, mais nous tenons compte des intérêts légitimes de l'URSS en lui donnant des garanties de sécurité valables.

L'Europe - et donc aussi l'Union soviétique - gagnera en stabilité du fait de cette solution. Nous n'exigeons rien de l'Union soviétique qui soit susceptible de lui nuire. Ce que nous lui proposons est dans son intérêt. Pourquoi ? Parce que cette solution ne menace pas l'Union soviétique mais, au contraire, lui donnera à la longue des partenaires voire des amis dont elle a un besoin pressant pour sortir de son isolement. Je suis certain que cette conception fera son chemin à Moscou, d'autant que plusieurs membres du Pacte de Varsovie partagent nos vues sur ce point.

III. UN NOUVEL ORDRE EUROPEEN DE COOPERATION

Pour réussir, ce nouvel ordre doit se fonder sur des institutions déjà existantes. Je pense en particulier à **trois institutions**: la Communauté européenne, l'Alliance atlantique et la CSCE.

La Communauté européenne

C'est le modèle le plus porteur d'avenir et le plus prestigieux d'une intégration d'Etats ayant pour objectif l'union politique et pour perspective l'association d'autres Etats européens, voire la réalisation d'une confédération européenne. La Communauté européenne a un rôle essentiel à jouer comme facteur de réussite économique et moteur d'une unité économique et politique européenne à venir. Son dynamisme créateur, qui est extraordinaire, en fait une structure de soutien essentielle pour l'Europe de demain, qui s'étendra au-delà de ses propres frontières à l'Europe centrale et orientale. La CEE a eu le rôle unique de diriger les énergies nationales des grands pays industriels de l'Europe vers des directions nouvelles, et d'amarrer l'Allemagne à un cadre politique et économique qui peut maintenant inclure le territoire de la RDA. Tout ordre européen implique donc la réalisation du Grand Marché Intérieur, et également des compétences accrues de la CEE dans le domaine de la politique étrangère et de la sécurité. C'est seulement ainsi que toute l'Europe pourra bénéficier du considérable dynamisme de la Communauté. Il n'y a aucune rivalité entre l'Alliance atlantique et la Communauté européenne. Elles se complètent l'une l'autre. L'Alliance atlantique a intérêt à voir émerger une Europe forte et unie. Plus les membres européens de notre Alliance s'uniront, plus ils contribueront de manière concrète à notre Alliance, et plus réels seront leur influence et leur rôle au sein de l'OTAN. Les points sur lesquels les domaines de compétence de la CFE et de l'Alliance se recoupent peuvent appeler une coordination, mais ne nécessitent pas d'institutions nouvelles.

L'Alliance atlantique

Deuxième institution, l'Alliance est indispensable à tout nouvel ordre de sécurité européen. Ni la CEE, ni la CSCE, ne peuvent remplir les tâches politiques et militaires de notre Alliance. Il est incontestable que notre Alliance est en mutation. Elle évolue dans le temps et avec le temps. Depuis deux ans déjà, elle s'adapte à la nouvelle donne de la définition des tâches, de l'ordre du jour et de la politique. Ce processus se poursuit. Le centre de gravité de notre Alliance se déplace, passant :
- de la confrontation à la coopération,
- du militaire au politique,
- de la dissuasion à la protection contre le risque et à la garantie de la stabilité,
- du maintien de la paix à la construction de la paix,
- d'une situation où les Etats-Unis assumaient la plus large part des responsabilités à un authentique partenariat, au sein duquel les Européens jouent un rôle d'une égale importance.

La CSCE

Troisième institution, la CSCE nous offre les grandes lignes d'une future architecture de coopération européenne. Elle est en effet la seule à rassembler 35 Etats et à leur permettre de façonner concrètement leurs relations. Aujourd'hui, elle lie les Européens, les Nord-Américains, et les Soviétiques, dans un code de comportement commun. Mais elle peut devenir davantage. C'est ce que recouvre l'expression "d'institutionnalisation", qui a connu une grande fortune récemment.

L'institutionnalisation revient à donner un cadre à des consultations régulières sur la politique de sécurité, les mesures de confiance, la prévention des crises, et le règlement pacifique des conflits, en particulier dans les zones où l'affaissement du Pacte de Varsovie a laissé un vide. Il faut en effet éviter l'isolement d'un certain nombre de pays d'Europe centrale et orientale, qui souhaitent participer légitimement à la construction de l'Europe de demain. Ces Etats ont besoin d'une institution dans laquelle leur voix soit entendue et qui contribue à leur sécurité. La CSCE doit donc devenir un organisme réellement consultatif. Il faut donc renforcer les procédures de consultation permanente entre les 35 Etats, pour que la CSCE puisse aborder tous les problèmes qui affectent ses Etats membres. Un secrétariat international léger pourrait contribuer à la permanence de la CSCE, en organisant et en préparant ces consultations.

Même à l'avenir, la CSCE ne pourra pas se substituer à l'Alliance atlantique. Elle n'a pas les moyens de prendre et de faire exécuter des sanctions; car chacun des 35 Etats y dispose d'un droit de veto. Les intérêts de chacun de ses membres, leurs structures sociales, et leurs systèmes de valeurs sont trop différents les uns des autres pour leur permettre en cas de crise de garantir conjointement la sécurité et d'imposer des solutions, surtout si l'un ou plusieurs d'entre eux sont impliqués dans cette crise. Cela ne diminue en rien l'importance de la CSCE en tant que cadre propre à créer la confiance et à promouvoir la coopération. Elle peut contribuer par exemple à résoudre pacifiquement les crises entre Etats nées de problèmes nationaux, dont on voit bien qu'elles constituent une cause d'instabilité en Europe centrale et orientale. A cet égard, rendre obligatoires certaines dispositions de la Troisième Corbeille pourrait être utile. La mise en forme juridique des engagements humanitaires pris par les 35 constituerait un facteur de réduction des tensions. De même, sont utiles et doivent être développés les mesures de confiance et les échanges d'information, qui créent des habitudes de vivre ensemble. Mais la CSCE, comme je l'ai dit, ne peut se développer que si elle s'appuie sur l'existence de notre Alliance. C'est là sa force. C'est là aussi sa limite.

* * *

Il convient, pour assurer à l'Europe une sécurité véritable, stable et durable, de faire en sorte que les intérêts légitimes de tous les Etats européens - y compris l'URSS - soient intrinsèquement reconnus dans toute réorganisation de l'Europe. Les pays de l'Alliance se sont déclarés "prêts à contribuer activement à l'édification et au resserrement des relations de confiance entre tous les pays européens, y compris entre les membres des deux Alliances".

L'Alliance atlantique tend la main à ses partenaires de toute l'Europe pour créer un système européen qui satisfasse les exigences de sécurité de chacun, sans souci de triomphalisme. Elle est prête, sérieusement et pratiquement, à coopérer dans ce but. L'Europe se trouve devant une alternative fondamentale : ou elle retombe dans l'ancien système politique de puissance et d'équilibre de la puissance des siècles passés, ou elle avance sur la voie d'un nouvel ordre de paix et de liberté résultant d'une coopération internationale ou supranationale. Notre choix est clair : nous allons de l'avant. Notre Alliance est, avec la Communauté européenne, le modèle le plus accompli de ce partenariat entre Etats. Elle est et demeure notre meilleure garantie d'un avenir sûr et libre.

*O*pening Statement to the NATO Summit Meeting

London
5 July
1990

The Cold War belongs to history. Our Alliance is moving from confrontation to cooperation. We are building a new Europe, a Europe drawn together by the unfettered aspiration for freedom, democracy and prosperity. Never before has Europe had such a tangible opportunity to overcome the cycle of war and peace that has so bedevilled its past.

We have a clear vision of Europe's future. We set it out in our 40th Anniversary Summit Declaration just one year ago. Now at our meeting today we must chart the further course towards the realization of that vision of a Europe whole and free. Our objective is not only the preservation of peace but the building of peace.

In the past few weeks a series of ministerial meetings have drawn up the basis for this Alliance's contribution to the new Europe. Already we are responding to change with change and with initiative. We are adapting our Alliance, reaching out to all who wish to build the same Europe as we do. Today we will renew our offer of cooperation and give it concrete form. We look at the Soviet Union and the countries of Central and Eastern Europe as potential partners and friends. A policy of cooperation is the logical extension of our Harmel Doctrine. The Alliance is now realizing its full potential as a framework of stability and an instigator of peaceful change.

Europe is not yet immune from future risk or danger. This Alliance, which has contributed so much to overcoming Europe's painful division, must play its full part alongside other Western institutions in extending the stability and security we enjoy to all European nations. NATO's impact will be critical in four areas :

First in clearing away the legacy of the Cold War years by concluding a CFE agreement and continuing the process of arms control. We must bring the military situation rapidly into line with the new political realities of Europe.

Second in helping to erect a new European architecture that binds all our nations together. The Alliance will play a central role, as this meeting shows. We will set out our concrete proposals for giving the CSCE a more prominent role as the genesis of this new order.

Third in continuing to press for a settlement of the external aspects of German unity satisfactory to all the parties concerned. Full German membership of our Alliance - and it alone - offers stability to a Europe in transition.

Fourth, and finally, our Alliance will continue to prevent war, a task that is no less relevant simply because the most direct threat to peace on our continent has now receded. There are many potential instabilities, both within and without Europe, that we must plan for prudently today if we are not to be their victim tomorrow.

Our Alliance cannot be successful in its new tasks if it fails to fulfil the oldest and most fundamental one: the preservation of peace. We must retain a secure defence. It is not an obstacle to change but the very precondition for change, and our weapons never were, and never will be, a threat to anyone.

Neither North America nor Europe can be secure and successful unless they stay together. Now that Europe is stronger and more integrated it can provide for an even closer and more successful transatlantic partnership by assuming its share of global responsibilities. United there is no challenge this Alliance cannot meet.

Finally, allow me on behalf of all Allies to express our appreciation for the hospitality and warm welcome that Her Majesty's Government, under Prime Minister Margaret Thatcher, has extended to us here in London.

Déclaration d'ouverture au Sommet de l'OTAN

Londres
5 juillet
1990

La guerre froide appartient désormais au passé. Laissant derrière elle une période d'affrontement, notre Alliance s'engage sur la voie de la coopération. Nous construisons une Europe nouvelle, une Europe cimentée par l'aspiration, libre de toutes entraves, à la liberté, à la démocratie et à la prospérité. Jamais le continent n'a eu une occasion aussi réelle de dépasser le cycle de la guerre et de la paix qui a empoisonné son histoire.

Nous avons pour l'Europe un projet précis, que nous avons d'ailleurs exposé dans la déclaration faite au sommet du Quarantième anniversaire, il y a tout juste un an. A notre réunion d'aujourd'hui, il nous appartiendra de tracer la suite de l'itinéraire qui mène à l'aboutissement de ce projet, à savoir l'avènement d'une Europe entière et libre. Notre objectif n'est pas seulement de préserver la paix, mais de la consolider.

Ces dernières semaines, une série de réunions ministérielles a permis de définir les éléments de base à partir desquels l'Alliance pourra apporter sa contribution à une Europe nouvelle. Déjà, nous répondons au changement par le changement, en faisant preuve d'esprit d'initiative. Nous adaptons l'Alliance, tendant la main à tous ceux qui souhaiteraient bâtir l'Europe chère à notre coeur. Nous désirons maintenant renouveler cette offre de coopération et lui donner une forme concrète. Nous voulons voir dans l'Union soviétique et dans les pays d'Europe centrale et orientale des partenaires et des amis en puissance. Le choix d'une politique de coopération n'est que le prolongement logique de la doctrine Harmel. A présent, l'Alliance exploite pleinement ses atouts, confirmant ainsi le rôle prééminent qu'elle est appelée à jouer dans l'instauration de la stabilité et du changement pacifique.

189

Mais l'Europe n'est pas encore à l'abri de tout danger. L'Alliance, qui a tant contribué à l'effacement de la douloureuse division de l'Europe, doit assumer toutes ses responsabilités, aux côtés d'autres institutions occidentales, pour faire profiter chaque nation européenne de la stabilité et de la sécurité dont bénéficient ses propres membres. L'OTAN exercera une influence déterminante dans quatre domaines; il s'agira :

Premièrement, de liquider l'héritage de la guerre froide, par la conclusion d'un accord sur les forces conventionnelles en Europe, et de poursuivre le processus de maîtrise des armements. Il nous incombe en effet d'adapter sans tarder la situation militaire aux nouvelles réalités politiques européennes.

Deuxièmement, d'aider à la mise en place d'une nouvelle architecture européenne qui unisse toutes les nations. A cet égard, l'Alliance jouera un rôle central, comme en témoigne le présent sommet. Nous présenterons des propositions concrètes en vue de conférer à la CSCE un rôle plus important dans l'édification de cet ordre nouveau.

Troisièmement, de maintenir sa pression en faveur d'un règlement des aspects extérieurs de l'unité allemande qui soit satisfaisant pour toutes les parties intéressées. L'appartenance pleine et entière de l'Allemagne à notre Alliance - et à elle seule - est un gage de stabilité pour une Europe en transition.

Enfin, notre Alliance continuera à prévenir la guerre, tâche qui n'est pas devenue moins importante du seul fait que la menace la plus directe qui pesait sur la paix en Europe se soit maintenant estompée. Il subsiste de nombreux risques d'instabilité, tant à l'intérieur qu'à l'extérieur du continent, et il nous faut aujourd'hui nous prémunir contre ces dangers si nous ne voulons pas en être demain les victimes.

L'Alliance ne parviendra pas à mener à bien ses tâches nouvelles si elle échoue dans sa mission la plus ancienne et la plus fondamentale : la sauvegarde de la paix. Nous devons conserver une défense solide qui, loin de constituer une entrave au changement, en est le préalable indispensable. Jamais nos armes n'ont été une menace pour quiconque, jamais elles ne le seront.

L'Amérique du Nord comme l'Europe ne pourront profiter de la sécurité et de la prospérité que si elles demeurent solidaires. L'Europe d'aujourd'hui - plus forte et mieux intégrée - peut apporter sa contribution au resserrement de liens transatlantiques toujours plus fructueux, en exerçant les responsabilités qui lui reviennent sur l'échiquier mondial. Il n'existe aucun défi qu'une Alliance unie ne puisse relever.

Permettez-moi enfin d'exprimer, au nom de tous les Alliés, notre profonde gratitude au Gouvernement de Sa Majesté et à son Premier ministre, Madame Margaret Thatcher, pour leur hospitalité et leur chaleureux accueil.

A common Europe- Partners in Stability

SPEECH TO MEMBERS
OF THE SUPREME SOVIET
OF THE USSR

Moscow
16 July
1990

It is not only a great honour for me to be here in Moscow but also a rare pleasure - one indeed that I hope will not be rare at all in the future. It is my second visit to your great country, to this land that has done so much to shape our European, and also universal culture. One thinks, on the literary side, of Pushkin, Tolstoy and my favourite author Dostoevsky; on the musical side of Tchaikovsky, Prokofiev and Shostakovich; and on the scientific side of Lomonosov and Sakharov; to name those that, for me, are the most obvious.

Your country endured immense suffering in the Second World War, a sacrifice which has earned the Soviet people our respect and sympathy.

When I first visited your country in 1960, I was 25 years old, a student. It was still the time of the Cold War. Europe was divided. NATO and the Warsaw Pact confronted each other. Far too many of our resources went into armaments, and to what purpose? Where did it lead us except into even more sterile confrontation? It was to nobody's benefit. In short, a waste of energy, imagination and sacrifice; money that could have been better spent building those democratic, industrially advanced and prosperous societies that we know are inherently peaceful, and thus our best guarantee of lasting stability and security.

Now 30 years later I come again. This time as Secretary General of the North Atlantic Treaty Organization. This visit in itself symbolizes the dramatic changes of the past year. The Cold War now belongs to the past. A new Europe is emerging, a Europe drawn together by the unfettered aspiration for freedom, democracy and prosperity. Certainly age-old fears and suspicions cannot be banished overnight; but they can be overcome. Never before has Europe had such a tangible opportunity to overcome the cycle of war and peace that has so bedevilled its history.

We in the Alliance intend to seize this opportunity. We wanted and welcome this. And our Alliance has done its share in helping to bring it about. Yet the Soviet leadership also deserves much of the credit for the promising new era that opens before us. President Mikhail Gorbachev initiated the new thinking in your country. It was he who realized the imperative need not only to change fundamentally the structures of your society, but also the entire pattern of East-West relations.

I have come to Moscow today with a very simple message: we extend our hand of friendship to you. And I have come with a very direct offer: to cooperate with you. The time of confrontation is over. The hostility and mistrust of the past must be buried. We see your country, and all the other countries of the Warsaw Treaty Organization, no longer as adversaries but as partners in a common endeavour to build what you call a Common European Home, erected on the values of democracy, human freedoms, and partnership.

There is a way that leads us beyond confrontation and towards a Europe whole and free :
- through the building of new structures, a new architecture that includes all of us;
- through arms control negotiations to reduce weapons to the minimum, and to increase stability and reassurance;
- through cooperation between us in all fields, political, economic, scientific, cultural.

We have to draw the consequences from the changes we see. Our Alliance has done so and will continue to do so. At the London Summit 10 days ago, we decided to change our Alliance in the most far-reaching way since its inception forty one years ago. We have no interest in a confrontational system. NATO's future is as a supporting pillar of a new and peaceful order of cooperation in Europe in which military power plays a lesser role in international relations; less dominant, threatening noone and dedicated to the role of reassurance against risks and the prevention of war.

How has NATO changed, you may well ask. Which concrete steps have we taken?
- We are reducing our defence budgets and scaling back our forces;
- We are reviewing our force structures, and changing our military strategy;
- we are reducing the readiness of our active units, reducing training requirements and the number of exercises;

- we are relying less on nuclear forces in Europe; we have proposed to the Soviet Union the elimination from Europe of all nuclear artillery warheads;
- we have offered to negotiate on short range nuclear forces in Europe once a CFE treaty is signed;
- and also, following agreement on CFE, we have offered immediately to proceed to follow-on negotiations to build on that agreement, including measures to limit manpower in Europe.

These changes will be carried out as Soviet Forces return home and the conventional arms control agreement is implemented. Moreover this Alliance wishes not only to eliminate tension by reducing weapons, but also by increasing confidence and transparency. So we are pushing hard for an Open Skies agreement; we are proposing discussions on military strategy and doctrine. Above all we want to consult and to discuss our security with you.

Our security must increasingly become cooperative in an age when no nation can provide for its security alone or in isolation from its neighbours. NATO will maintain a secure defence, as will the Soviet Union. We live in an uncertain world with many risks and instabilities, and will continue to do so. And that security will require us to maintain a mix of nuclear and conventional forces in Europe, as the Soviet Union will also do. Yet our goal is clear : to reduce military forces in Europe to a minimum. We wish to explore with you a common concept of war prevention at minimum levels. Our aim is a military posture that gives maximum reassurance. Our own history in the Alliance shows that this is possible.

Our aim is a Europe in which military aggression or threat becomes materially impossible and politically meaningless. At our NATO Summit we moved boldly ahead to put the structures of such a secure Europe in place.

Firstly in enhancing our dialogue with you and the other members of the Warsaw Treaty Organization. We have invited President Gorbachev to come to Brussels to address the North Atlantic Council. We have proposed the establishment of diplomatic contacts with NATO. We have proposed a joint declaration on non-aggression, to be concluded between the member states of NATO and the Warsaw Treaty Organization.

Secondly in pursuing the arms control process with vigour and determination. A conventional arms control agreement is the key that will unlock the syndrome of confrontation between us. It is the indispensable first step in building a Europe whole and free; so I call on the Soviet Union to help us conclude this treaty now. This agreement will lay the basis of cooperation and mutual reassurance that will enable us to create an enduring peace in Europe. It makes possible all that we foresee can be accomplished in this decade.

The conventional arms control process, coupled with talks on short range nuclear forces and an agreement on additional Confidence Building Measures, will give all of us in Europe, including the Soviet Union, guarantees that change in Europe will not be prejudicial to legitimate security interests. Soviet security will be enhanced as much as Allied security.

Thirdly, the NATO Summit in London set forth our ideas for building on the CSCE to bring all of Europe closer together in new or expanded structures of cooperation. To be effective, CSCE must serve first and foremost to protect democracy and freedom throughout Europe, and tackle the problems involved in the transition to efficient market economies. Thus NATO has proposed a range of initiatives to strengthen the existing Helsinki principles and establish new forms of cooperation : initiatives such as the right to free and fair elections, commitments to uphold the rule of law, guidelines for economic and environmental cooperation.

To enable the CSCE to perform these tasks, and to amplify and give more structure to wider political dialogue, NATO has proposed new institutional forms for the CSCE, most notably a programme for regular high-level consultations among member governments; CSCE review conferences once every two years; a small CSCE secretariat; a CSCE centre for the Prevention of Conflict; and a Parliamentary Assembly of Europe. Our aim is to have a CSCE that allows all the nations of Central and Eastern Europe to play a full role in building with us the future European order.

One thing is clear: we intend to steer change in Europe so that there are no losers, only winners. This applies also to the case of German unity. Germany's membership in the Alliance will increase stability for all. It is as much in the interests of the Germans as their neighbours in East and West, including the Soviet Union. Many in your country ask if NATO is not gaining a unilateral advantage from this outcome. We take such questions seriously. That is why we are not only striving to understand your security interests, but also to respect them and to offer you tangible guarantees that German unification will not shift the balance of power in Europe. Rather, it is really the gateway to overcoming division, and to partnership.

In short, NATO sees its future role as putting in place new structures of cooperation across Europe that will make it impossible for a situation like the Cold War ever to return. We want to work together with you in helping to manage the two crucial tasks in Europe today :

- to promote constructive change;
- to provide stability so that change can take place in optimal conditions, with diminished risk of setbacks and reversals.

Nevertheless, some in your country may still ask us : what have we to gain from this historical upheaval that is reshaping the world? The answer is the Soviet Union gains partners that will help in its great domestic task of reform and renewal. Partners who will cooperate to ensure that the Soviet Union is an active and constructive part of the dynamic Europe of advanced industrial economies and technological inter-dependence of the 21st century. True security, like prosperity, comes from the stability, prosperity and growth that only freedom, inter-dependence and partnership can bring. Beyond confrontation, we can address the immense global challenges of today and tomorrow : environmental degradation, drugs, terrorism, hunger, population, the proliferation of immensely destructive military technologies in the Third World. Together we can achieve a great deal.

Our generation is lucky. We have a historically unique opportunity which may not repeat itself. An opportunity to create a new world, a world of co-operation, where none of us feel threatened. We cannot afford to miss the chance. The Alliance I have the honour to represent wants partners in the building of a new Europe and a more just and equal world order. Your country has much to offer. Indeed it is vital to this whole process of historical change. Let us look to a common future, and work for it with trust and imagination. And let our children be even luckier than we are.

□

*U*ne Europe commune- Partenaires dans la stabilité

DISCOURS PRONONCE
DEVANT DES MEMBRES
DU SOVIET SUPREME
DE L'URSS

Moscou
16 juillet
1990

Pour moi, être accueilli à Moscou est non seulement un grand honneur, mais un plaisir rare, dont j'espère d'ailleurs qu'il se fera beaucoup moins rare dorénavant. C'est donc mon deuxième séjour dans votre grand pays, qui a tant contribué à façonner la culture européenne, et, de fait, la culture universelle. Je pense aux écrivains Pouchkine, Tolstoï. et aussi Dostoïevski, mon auteur préféré; je pense aux compositeurs Tchaïkovski, Prokofiev et Chostakovitch; je pense, enfin, aux savants Lomonossov et Sakharov. Et je ne cite là que ceux dont les noms me viennent immédiatement à l'esprit.

Pendant la seconde guerre mondiale, le peuple soviétique a enduré d'immenses souffrances, et son sacrifice lui a valu notre respect et notre compassion.

La première fois que je suis venu dans votre pays, en 1960, j'avais vingt-cinq ans et j'étais étudiant. La guerre froide sévissait toujours. L'Europe était divisée. Entre l'OTAN et le Pacte de Varsovie, c'était la confrontation. Une part bien trop grande de nos ressources était engloutie par les budgets militaires. Dans quel but ? Où cela nous a-t-il conduits, si ce n'est à une confrontation plus stérile encore, qui ne profitait à personne ? Bref, nous assistions au gaspillage de l'énergie, de l'imagination, des efforts, de l'argent qu'il aurait été préférable de consacrer à l'édification de ces sociétés démocratiques, industrialisées et prospères dont nous savons qu'elles sont intrinsèquement pacifiques, et qu'elles constituent ainsi notre meilleure garantie d'une stabilité et d'une sécurité durables.

Et me voici de retour, trente ans plus tard, cette fois en qualité de Secrétaire général de l'Organisation du Traité de

197

l'Atlantique Nord. C'est une visite qui, par elle-même, reflète les changements spectaculaires survenus au cours des douze mois écoulés. La guerre froide appartient désormais au passé. Une Europe nouvelle prend forme, une Europe cimentée par l'aspiration, débarrassée de toutes entraves, à la liberté, à la démocratie et à la prospérité. Bien évidemment, on ne peut dissiper du jour au lendemain des craintes et des soupçons dont l'origine remonte aussi loin dans le temps, mais il est possible de les surmonter. Jamais l'Europe n'a eu une occasion aussi réelle de dépasser le cycle de la guerre et de la paix qui a tant empoisonné son histoire.

L'Alliance atlantique compte saisir cette occasion qu'elle a appelée de ses voeux, et dont elle se félicite. Et, il faut le reconnaître, elle a joué un grand rôle dans l'apparition de la situation actuelle. Il n'empêche que nous sommes grandement redevables à la direction soviétique de l'avènement de l'ère prometteuse qui s'ouvre maintenant. Le président Mikhaïl Gorbatchev est le chantre de la "nouvelle pensée" qui a pris son envol dans votre pays. Il a compris qu'il était impératif de changer non seulement les fondements de votre société, mais aussi la structure générale des relations entre l'Est et l'Ouest.

Je suis venu à Moscou avec un message très simple : nous vous offrons notre amitié. J'ai aussi une proposition très directe à vous faire : coopérer. L'époque de la confrontation est révolue. Oublions l'hostilité et la méfiance du passé. Nous voyons dans votre pays, et dans tous les autres Etats membres de l'Organisation du Traité de Varsovie, non plus des adversaires, mais bien des partenaires, engagés avec nous dans une entreprise commune : la construction de ce que vous appelez la maison commune européenne, bâtie sur les principes de la démocratie, des libertés fondamentales et de la coopération.

Nous pouvons laisser derrière nous la confrontation et avancer sur la voie d'une Europe entière et libre; il s'agit pour cela :

- de construire de nouvelles structures, une nouvelle architecture qui englobe chacun d'entre nous;
- de négocier sur la maîtrise des armements, pour réduire au maximum nos arsenaux et pour renforcer la stabilité et la confiance mutuelle;
- de coopérer dans tous les domaines : politique, économie, sciences, culture.

Nous devons tirer les conséquences des mutations que nous observons. Comme par le passé, notre Alliance continuera à le faire. Au Sommet de Londres, dix jours plus tôt, nous avons décidé de faire subir à celle-ci le remaniement le plus radical qu'elle ait connu depuis sa naissance, il y a quarante et un ans de cela. Nous ne voyons aucun intérêt dans un système nourri par la confrontation. L'OTAN sera désormais le pilier d'un ordre de coopération européen nouveau et pacifique, à l'intérieur duquel la puissance militaire occupera une place moins importante dans les relations internationales : elle perdra sa prééminence, ne menacera personne et assumera une fonction de protection et de prévention des conflits.

Mais, nous demanderez-vous, en quoi l'OTAN a-t-elle changé ? Quelles mesures concrètes avons-nous prises ?

- nous réduisons nos budgets de la défense, ainsi que nos forces elles-mêmes;
- nous réexaminons nos structures de forces et modifions notre stratégie militaire;
- nous abaissons le niveau de préparation de nos unités d'active en réduisant les normes d'entraînement et le nombre des exercices;
- nous restreignons le rôle attribué aux forces nucléaires en Europe; nous avons proposé à l'Union soviétique l'élimination de toutes les ogives d'artillerie nucléaire présentes sur ce continent;
- nous avons proposé d'engager des négociations sur les forces nucléaires à courte portée en Europe une fois signé un traité sur les FCE;
- et, également après la conclusion d'un accord sur les FCE, nous avons proposé d'entamer immédiatement des négociations qui, mettant à profit cet accord, devraient déboucher notamment sur des mesures de limitation des effectifs en Europe.

Ces changements seront introduits tandis que les forces soviétiques seront rapatriées et que l'accord sur la maîtrise des armements conventionnels sera mis en oeuvre. En outre, l'Alliance souhaite éliminer la tension non seulement par la réduction des armements, mais aussi par l'accroissement de la confiance et de la transparence. C'est pourquoi nous nous employons à obtenir la conclusion d'un accord sur le "Ciel ouvert"; nous proposons l'ouverture de pourparlers sur la stratégie et la doctrine militaires. Par-dessus tout, nous recherchons la consultation et le dialogue avec vous sur notre sécurité.

Notre sécurité doit, de plus en plus, être placée sous le signe de la coopération, dès lors qu'aucun pays ne peut assurer sa sécurité à lui seul ou en s'isolant de ses voisins. L'OTAN maintiendra une défense sûre, tout comme l'Union soviétique. Nous vivons, et continuerons de vivre, dans un monde incertain, marqué par tant de risques et tant d'instabilités. Et cette sécurité exigera que nous conservions une combinaison de forces nucléaires et de forces conventionnelles en Europe, comme le fera également l'Union soviétique. Cependant, notre objectif est clair : nous voulons réduire le niveau des forces militaires en Europe à un minimum. Nous voulons rechercher avec vous un concept commun de prévention de la guerre à des niveaux de forces minimums. Notre but est de parvenir à des dispositifs militaires qui apportent un maximum d'assurances. L'histoire des membres de l'Alliance eux-mêmes montre que c'est possible.

Notre but est une Europe dans laquelle l'agression militaire ou la menace d'agression militaire deviennent matériellement impossibles et politiquement dénuées de sens. Au Sommet de l'OTAN, nous avons pris des initiatives audacieuses en vue de mettre en place les structures d'une Europe connaissant une telle sécurité.

Premièrement, nous entendons développer le dialogue avec vous et avec les autres membres de l'Organisation du Traité de Varsovie. Nous avons invité le Président Gorbatchev à venir à Bruxelles prendre la parole devant le Conseil de l'Atlantique Nord. Nous avons proposé l'établissement de contacts diplomatiques avec l'OTAN. Nous avons proposé que les Etats membres de l'OTAN et de l'Organisation du Traité de Varsovie adoptent une déclaration commune sur la non-agression.

Deuxièmement, nous poursuivons le processus de maîtrise des armements avec vigueur et détermination. Un accord de maîtrise des armements conventionnels est la condition essentielle de la disparition du syndrome de confrontation entre nous. Il est indispensable comme première étape de la construction d'une Europe entière et libre; aussi, j'appelle l'Union soviétique à nous aider à conclure maintenant ce traité. Il jettera les bases de la coopération et de la confiance mutuelle qui nous permettront de créer en Europe un état de paix durable. Il rendra possible tout ce que nous prévoyons comme pouvant être accompli au cours de cette décennie.

Le processus de maîtrise des armements conventionnels, s'ajoutant à des conversations sur les forces nucléaires à courte portée et à un accord sur des mesures de confiance supplémentaires, donnera à tous les Européens, y compris à l'Union soviétique, la garantie que le changement en Europe ne portera pas atteinte à leurs intérêts légitimes en matière de sécurité. La sécurité de l'Union soviétique sera renforcée tout autant que la sécurité des Alliés.

Troisièmement, le Sommet de Londres a indiqué comment on pourrait, selon nous, exploiter le processus de la CSCE pour parvenir à un resserrement des liens à l'échelle de l'Europe entière dans le cadre de structures de coopération nouvelles ou élargies. Pour porter ses fruits, la CSCE doit permettre par-dessus tout de protéger la démocratie et la liberté dans l'ensemble de l'Europe, et s'attaquer aux problèmes que pose le passage à des économies de marché efficaces. Ainsi, l'OTAN a proposé une série d'initiatives de nature à renforcer les actuels principes d'Helsinki et à établir de nouvelles formes de coopération; ces initiatives concernent notamment le droit à des élections libres et loyales, l'engagement de maintenir la primauté du droit, et les directives relatives à la coopération dans les domaines de l'économie et de l'environnement.

Afin de permettre à la CSCE d'accomplir ces tâches, et aussi de développer et de structurer davantage un dialogue politique plus large, l'OTAN a proposé de nouvelles formes institutionnelles pour la CSCE, et tout particulièrement un programme de consultations régulières de haut niveau entre les Etats membres, des conférences-bilans de la CSCE tous les deux ans, un secrétariat léger pour la CSCE, un centre CSCE pour la prévention des conflits, et une assemblée parlementaire de l'Europe. Notre objectif est d'arriver à une CSCE qui permette à tous les pays d'Europe centrale et orientale de jouer un rôle plein et entier en édifiant avec nous l'ordre européen de demain.

Une chose est claire : nous entendons conduire le changement en Europe de façon qu'il n'y ait pas de perdants, et que tous gagnent. Cela vaut aussi pour l'unité allemande. L'appartenance de l'Allemagne à l'Alliance accroîtra la stabilité pour tous. Elle est autant de l'intérêt des Allemands que de celui de leurs voisins de l'Est et de l'Ouest, y compris l'Union soviétique. Dans votre pays, nombreux sont ceux qui demandent si l'OTAN ne retire pas de cette évolution un avantage unilatéral. Nous prenons de telles questions très au sérieux. C'est pourquoi nous nous efforçons, non seulement de comprendre vos intérêts en matière de sécurité, mais aussi de les respecter, et de vous garantir de façon tangible que l'unification de l'Allemagne ne va pas modifier l'équilibre des forces en Europe. En fait, cette unification va réellement permettre de surmonter la division de l'Europe, et ouvrir la voie au partenariat.

En bref, l'OTAN voit son rôle futur comme consistant à mettre en place, dans toute l'Europe, de nouvelles structures de coopération qui rendront impossible à tout jamais le retour à une situation telle que la Guerre froide. Nous voulons travailler avec vous à la gestion des deux tâches cruciales qui s'imposent à l'Europe d'aujourd'hui :
- promouvoir un changement constructif;
- assurer la stabilité pour que ce changement puisse avoir lieu dans des conditions optimales avec un moindre risque de retours en arrière et de revirements.

Néanmoins, certains, dans votre pays, pourraient encore nous demander: "qu'avons-nous à gagner à ce bouleversement historique qui est en train de changer la face du monde ?" La réponse est que l'Union soviétique y gagne des partenaires qui l'aideront dans sa grande oeuvre nationale de réforme et de renouveau. Des partenaires qui coopéreront pour faire en sorte que l'Union soviétique soit un élément actif et constructif de l'Europe dynamique des économies industrielles avancées et de l'interdépendance technologique du 21ème siècle. La vraie sécurité, comme la prospérité, passe par la stabilité, la prospérité et la croissance que seuls la liberté, l'interdépendance et le partenariat peuvent apporter. Au-delà de la confrontation, nous pouvons nous attaquer aux immenses défis du monde d'aujourd'hui et de demain : la dégradation de l'environnement, la drogue, le terrorisme, la faim, les problèmes démographiques, la prolifération de technologies militaires à énorme pouvoir de destruction dans le Tiers monde. Ensemble, nous pouvons faire beaucoup.

Notre génération a de la chance. L'Histoire nous offre une occasion unique, qui pourrait ne pas se représenter. Une occasion de créer un monde nouveau, un monde de coopération, où aucun de nous ne se sente menacé. Nous ne pouvons pas nous permettre de la laisser passer. L'Alliance que j'ai l'honneur de représenter cherche des partenaires dans l'édification d'une Europe nouvelle et d'un ordre mondial fait de plus de justice et d'égalité. Votre pays a beaucoup à offrir. Son importance est même vitale pour tout ce processus de changement historique. Regardons vers un avenir commun, et employons-nous à le bâtir, avec confiance et imagination. Et veillons à ce que nos enfants aient encore plus de chance que nous.

Building a new Europe

Prague
6 September
1990

A year ago it would have seemed unimaginable that a Secretary General of NATO visit Czechoslovakia as the official guest of your government. Yet today a new Europe has emerged which makes the once impossible now seem wholly natural; a Europe drawn together by the unfettered aspiration for freedom, democracy and economic prosperity.

Your proud nation, always loyal to the traditions of Thomas Masaryk and Eduard Benes, has played its part in bringing about this historic change. In 1968 the Prague Spring proved that the love of your countrymen for freedom could not be extinguished, despite the dark years that followed. Charter 77 and other courageous groups stuck doggedly to the principles of the CSCE Final Act and its humanitarian provisions, thus creating, even at the worst periods of repression by the state, an area of freedom about them.

Today Czechoslovakia is engaged in a bold process of democratic and economic renewal. This will not be easy, as we all know, but your country has a long democratic heritage and a tradition of industrial enterprise which bodes well for your ultimate success. For your nation in its history and culture is quintessentially a Western one. With energy and vision, your new leaders are proving that Czechoslovakia intends also to play a key role in building the new European order. Their proposals for a new European security architecture and their staunch defence of human rights and freedoms are an inspiration to us all.

It is, of course, not only in the relations between government and people that the Cold War is over. Also in the relations between nations we see a new spirit of cooperation - a common

203

desire not to be held back by the fears and suspicions that have bedevilled all previous attempts to create a European family of nations. Indeed I would say that never has Europe had such a palpable opportunity to break out of the infernal cycle of peace and war and create a durable order of peace and prosperity. It is the privilege of our generation to have this historically unique opportunity to make a fresh start.

We in the Alliance are determined to seize this opportunity. Certainly, and even with all the changes we see, age-old fears and suspicions, stereotyped images and popular misconceptions, will not be banished overnight. But they can be overcome, as President Havel has so eloquently stated. The active participation of Czechoslovakia in the Pentagonal Initiative, and its role in bringing the newly born democracies of Central Europe together, show also how quickly bridges can be built over old divisions. We now have a chance to spend our energy, imagination and money on building those democratic, free-market societies that we know are inherently peaceful, and thus our best guarantee of lasting stability, security and prosperity.

I have come to Prague today with the same, very simple message that I took to Moscow in July and which I will take to Warsaw next week; for it is a message that is addressed with equal conviction to all our former adversaries who are now our friends and partners. We extend the hand of friendship to you. We wish to cooperate with you. The time of confrontation is over. The hostility and mistrust of the past must be buried. We need to work together. Only in this way can we build the Common European Home or the European Confederation or the new European Order, call it what you will. We all know what we mean : a Europe of democracy, human rights and partnership in which the whole sustains the parts and the parts sustain the whole. We must go forward together; or we will be condemned to go backwards separately.

There is a way that leads us beyond confrontation and towards a Europe whole and free :

- through the building of new structures of cooperation, a new European architecture that includes all of us;
- through arms control negotiations to reduce weapons to the minimum, and to increase stability and reassurance;
- through cooperation between us in all fields, political, economic, scientific, cultural.

We need to look afresh at our objectives and tasks. This our Atlantic Alliance has done, and will continue to do. At the London Summit in early July we decided to change our Alliance in the most far-reaching way since its inception forty one years ago. We have no interest in a confrontational system. For NATO has a new, even more valuable role to play as a supporting pillar of a new and peaceful order of cooperation in Europe. In such an order military power will play a lesser role; less dominant, threatening no-one and dedicated to the role of reassurance against risks and the prevention of war.

How has NATO changed, you may well ask. Which concrete steps have we taken?
- We are reducing our defence budgets and scaling back our forces;
- we are reviewing our force structures, and changing our military strategy;
- we are reducing the readiness of our active units, reducing training requirements and the number of exercises;
- we are relying less on nuclear forces in Europe; we have proposed to the Soviet Union the elimination from Europe of all nuclear artillery warheads;
- we have offered to negotiate on short-range nuclear forces in Europe once a CFE treaty is signed. We have already convened a meeting of our Alliance's Special Consultative Group to draw up a mandate for these talks;
- and also, following agreement on CFE, we have offered immediately to proceed to follow-on negotiations to build on that agreement, including measures to limit manpower in Europe.

These changes will be carried out as Soviet forces leave the territories of Czechoslovakia and Hungary, as they have already agreed to do so, and also the territory of the present - day GDR in the transition period following German unification. They will also be conditional on the implementation of a CFE treaty which will give all participating states firm guarantees against military aggression or intimidation. Moreover the Atlantic Alliance wishes not only to eliminate tension by reducing weapons, but also by increasing confidence and transparency. Thus we are pushing hard for an Open Skies agreement; we are proposing discussions on military strategy and doctrine. Above all we want security to be something that we discuss and decide upon together.

No nation these days can provide for its security alone or in isolation from its neighbours. Nations seeking total security by their own efforts only create insecurity around them. So we must never re-nationalize European security. On the contrary real security can be achieved only through cooperation and sharing.

This does not, of course, mean that NATO or any European nation has to be defenceless. We live in an uncertain world with many risks and instabilities. Indeed the present Gulf crisis has brought this home to us with a vengeance. This crisis is not like previous regional disputes in which the interests of only a few nations were directly at stake; nor is it only, or even primarily, about oil. If our principal common objective - which must be the complete Iraqi withdrawal from Kuwait and the release of all hostages - is not fulfilled, the entire international community will be exposed to grave danger. Danger from the precedent of a large, powerful country cynically taking over a smaller neighbour; danger even more ominously from the ambitions that successful aggression will undoubtedly engender in dictatorships that increasingly have access to technologies of mass destruction.

Thus it is of crucial importance not only for Kuwait, and peace in the Middle East, but for our common effort to create a more durable and just international order after the Cold War that the United Nations sanctions against Iraq should work. We in the Alliance are determined to maintain our solidarity, and we will do our utmost to build further on the new-found effectiveness of the United Nations as the guarantor of international law and stability. I salute the robust stance that Czechoslovakia has taken on this issue and trust that we can continue to work together until we can prove to Iraq - and all potential belligerents - that naked aggression cannot succeed.

Our Alliance must maintain a secure defence and we expect no less of other nations. NATO will maintain a mix of conventional and nuclear forces in Europe as the ultimate guarantee of peace. Yet our goal is clear : to reduce military forces in Europe to a minimum so that no nation needs to threaten others to feel secure itself. A military posture that gives maximum reassurance is possible. Our Alliance's experience with its integrated defence structure proves this; for could any of you seriously imagine 16 sovereign and democratic states deciding to launch or support an attack?

Our aim is a Europe in which military aggression or threat becomes materially impossible and politically meaningless. At our NATO Summit we moved resolutely ahead to put the structures of such a secure Europe in place.

Firstly in creating a new dialogue with your country and all the other members of the Warsaw Treaty Organisation. We have invited President Gorbachev to come to Brussels to address the North Atlantic Council - an invitation that I was able to deliver in person in Moscow last July and which he readily accepted. After the recent visit of Minister Dienstbier, we also look forward to a visit by President Havel.

We have proposed the establishment of diplomatic contacts with NATO, to which Czechoslovakia has favourably responded. We look also to a multiplication of military as well as diplomatic contacts and exchanges. We have proposed to negotiate a joint declaration on non-aggression between the member states of NATO and of the Warsaw Treaty Organisation.

Secondly in pursuing the arms control process with vigour and determination. A conventional arms control agreement is the key that will unlock the syndrome of confrontation among the old adversaries of the two alliances. Thus it is the indispensable first step in building a Europe whole and free; which is why I am counting on the Czechoslovak government to do all it can to help us conclude this treaty now. This agreement will lay the basis of cooperation and mutual reassurance that will enable us to create an enduring peace in Europe. It is the secure foundation on which the new European order must be built if it is to last.

The conventional arms control process, coupled with talks on short range nuclear forces and an agreement on additional Confidence Building Measures, will give all of us in Europe guarantees that change and renewal will not be prejudicial to anyone's legitimate security interests. This is particularly important in the case of your neighbour, the Soviet Union. Understandably that country fears exclusion from the new Europe and is experiencing the impact of change most acutely. So it is essential that we use the arms control process to convince the Soviet Union that it has nothing to fear, but indeed everything to gain from helping a process of change - that it has done so much to initiate - to continue to its natural destination - a Europe whole and free.

Thirdly the NATO Summit in London set forth our ideas for building on the CSCE to bring all of Europe closer together in new or expanded structures of cooperation. Czechoslovakia, of course, also attaches key importance to an enhanced role for the CSCE as the genesis of a future European order. Your government in this respect has made a number of important and interesting proposals. In the weeks leading up to the CSCE Summit, we will strive to bring these ideas together into a coherent concept.

To be effective, however, CSCE must serve first and foremost to protect democracy and freedom throughout Europe, and tackle the problems involved in the transition to efficient market economies. Thus NATO has proposed a range of initiatives to strengthen the existing Helsinki principles and establish new forms of cooperation : initiatives such as the right to free and fair elections, commitments to uphold the rule of law, guidelines for economic and environmental cooperation. In applying to become a member of the Council of Europe, Czechoslovakia has demonstrated that it attaches the same importance to these values as we do in our Alliance.

To enable the CSCE to perform these tasks, and to amplify and give more structure to wider political dialogue, NATO has proposed new institutional forms for the CSCE, most notably a programme for regular high-level consultations among member governments; CSCE review conferences once every two years; a small CSCE secretariat; a CSCE centre for the Prevention of Conflict; and a parliamentary Assembly of Europe. Our aim is to have a CSCE that allows all the nations of Central and Eastern Europe to play a full role in building with us the future European order.

Will you, however, permit me to sound on the subject of CSCE just one note of caution? I know that there are many in the nations of Central and Eastern Europe, as in our Alliance nations, who see CSCE as a replacement for the existing security organisations. I will not comment on the Warsaw Treaty Organisation for its continuation is clearly dependent on the free choice of its members. Yet NATO will remain an essential supporting pillar of a successful CSCE.

The CSCE can certainly enhance security. But it cannot substitute for the Atlantic Alliance. It does not have the means to take sanctions or ensure their implementation. The interests of each of its members, their social structures and value systems, at least for the foreseeable future, are too diverse to enable them to act collectively to preserve security in the event of crisis. This does not in any way diminish the importance of CSCE as a framework for creating confidence and promoting cooperation. It can, for instance, contribute to the peaceful resolution of disputes between states arising from problems with national minorities. We indeed see already how much instability they can cause in Central and Eastern Europe. In this respect the introduction into law of those commitments on human rights contained in the Helsinki Final Act can be a useful step forward. At the same time, we can and will develop confidence building measures and information exchanges that will enable us to live more harmoniously together. Yet, in the final analysis, CSCE will live up to its promise only if it is complementary to a strong Atlantic Alliance on which it can rely. Consequently, it will be all the more successful to the extent that we do not burden it with unrealistic expectations from the outset.

The existence of a strong and coherent new Atlantic Alliance is in the interest of Czechoslovakia as much as of any other European nation. It provides stablility for change and maintains the transatlantic link with the United States of America and Canada. This is indispensable for peace, and the freedom and security of the whole of Europe.

Yet even such a well-established and resilient institution as NATO cannot shoulder alone the burden of ensuring cooperation, prosperity and peaceful progress across Europe. Fortunately for this purpose we also have the European Community. It is the other essential component in our Western institutional framework and it too is undergoing a process of change and renewal in its striving to achieve an ever closer union of its members. While NATO provides the stability and the transatlantic link, the European Community provides dynamism, creativity and the basis of an ever more fruitful economic inter-dependence. Together with an expanded role for the CSCE, both a strong NATO and a strong European Community are the prerequisites for a Europe of progress and prosperity. None can succeed without the others.

At a time when the entire international system is being transformed, no government or alliance can fully control the powerful forces that make change inevitable. But by working together we can steer that change and produce an outcome in which there are no losers, only winners. I am vastly more hopeful in this respect now that agreement has been reached on membership of a united Germany in our Alliance. This will increase stability for all. It is the gateway to overcoming division, and to establishing a partnership between Western Europe and the newly democratising nations which will be a key factor in their economic and social modernization.

In short, NATO sees its future role as putting in place new structures of cooperation across Europe that will make it impossible for a situation like the Cold War ever to return. We want to work together with you in helping to manage the two crucial tasks in Europe today :
- to promote constructive change;
- to provide stability so that change can take place in optimal conditions, with diminished risk of setbacks and reversals.

Here in Prague I hardly need to emphasize the benefits that cooperation between us will bring. The 21st century will bring new challenges, some of which could threaten our survival even more than nearly half a century of Cold War. Environmental degradation is one which your government is particularly concerned about; terrorism another which has been the subject of some fruitful discussions between Czechoslovakia and Alliance member nations in recent weeks. You too are aware as we are of the destabilizing potential of such things as drugs, hunger, population growth and the proliferation of immensely destructive military technologies in the Third World. Thus a dynamic Europe of advanced industrial economies and technological inter-dependence is not only essential for our material prosperity, but also for our security and stability at home and abroad. Without such cohesion Europe could well be the victim of these global challenges; together we can help to solve them.

My visit to this great European city of Prague today symbolizes a new era; but it is also a concrete invitation : to work together using our combined resources and ingenuity to create a new world, a world of cooperation where none of us feel threatened. We cannot escape the responsibility that this unique opportunity brings. Czechoslovakia which has contributed so much to our European political and intellectual culture, is a key partner in the building of a new Europe and a more just and equal world order. Let us therefore make today the start of that new relationship and work for that brighter future with trust and imagination.

□

Construire une Europe nouvelle

DISCOURS AU MINISTERE DES AFFAIRES ETRANGERES DE LA REPUBLIQUE TCHEQUE ET SLOVAQUE

Prague
6 septembre
1990

Il y a un an, il eût semblé inimaginable qu'un Secrétaire général de l'OTAN se rende en Tchécoslovaquie en qualité d'invité officiel de votre gouvernement. Pourtant, aujourd'hui, la naissance d'une Europe nouvelle fait que ce qui était naguère impossible paraît maintenant tout à fait naturel; cette Europe est réunie par une aspiration, sans entraves, à la liberté, à la démocratie et à la prospérité économique.

Votre fière nation, toujours fidèle aux traditions de Thomas Masaryk et Edouard Benès, a joué son rôle dans la réalisation de ce changement historique. En 1968, le Printemps de Prague a prouvé que l'amour de vos compatriotes pour la liberté ne pouvait être étouffé, malgré les années sombres qui l'ont suivi. Charte 77 et d'autres groupes courageux ont soutenu avec ténacité les principes de l'Acte Final de la CSCE et ses dispositions humanitaires, créant ainsi autour d'eux, même aux pires moments de la répression exercée par l'Etat, une zone de liberté.

Aujourd'hui, la Tchécoslovaquie s'est engagée dans un audacieux processus de renouveau démocratique et économique. Nous savons tous que la tâche ne sera pas facile, mais votre pays a un long héritage démocratique et une tradition d'entreprise industrielle qui est de bon augure pour votre succès final. Car votre nation, par son histoire et sa culture, appartient, dans sa quintessence, au monde occidental. Avec dynamisme et prévoyance, vos nouveaux dirigeants apportent la preuve que la Tchécoslovaquie entend également jouer un rôle clé dans l'édification du nouvel ordre européen. Leurs propositions visant une nouvelle structure de sécurité en Europe et leur défense résolue des droits de l'homme et des libertés sont une source d'inspiration pour nous tous.

Ce n'est pas, bien entendu, seulement dans les relations entre le gouvernement et le peuple que la Guerre froide est terminée. Nous voyons aussi dans les rapports entre nations un nouvel esprit de coopération, un désir commun de ne pas être prisonnier des craintes et des suspicions auxquelles se sont heurtées toutes les précédentes tentatives de création d'une famille de nations européenne. Je dirais même que l'Europe n'a jamais eu une occasion aussi tangible de sortir du cycle infernal de la paix et de la guerre et de créer un ordre durable de paix et de prospérité. Notre génération a le privilège de voir s'offrir à elle cette occasion, unique dans l'histoire, de prendre un nouveau départ.

Nous, les membres de l'Alliance, sommes résolus à saisir cette occasion. Certes, et même avec tous les changements auxquels nous assistons, les craintes et les suspicions du fond des âges, les images stéréotypées et les idées fausses ancrées dans la mémoire populaire ne vont pas disparaître du jour au lendemain. Il est cependant possible d'en triompher, comme l'a dit avec tant d'éloquence le président Havel. La participation active de la Tchécoslovaquie à l'Initiative pentagonale et le rôle qu'elle joue dans la réunion des nouvelles démocraties de l'Europe centrale montrent également avec quelle rapidité on peut jeter des ponts surmontant les vieilles divisions. Nous avons à présent une chance de consacrer notre énergie, notre imagination et nos ressources financières à l'édification de ces sociétés démocratiques à économie de marché qui, nous le savons, sont pacifiques par nature, et nous offrent ainsi la meilleure garantie d'une stabilité, d'une sécurité et d'une prospérité durables.

Je suis venu à Prague aujourd'hui porteur d'un message très simple, celui-la même que j'ai porté à Moscou au mois de juillet et que je porterai à Varsovie la semaine prochaine; car il s'agit d'un message que nous adressons avec une égale conviction à tous nos anciens adversaires, qui sont désormais nos amis et nos partenaires. Nous vous offrons notre amitié. Nous souhaitons coopérer avec vous. Le temps de la confrontation est révolu. Il faut enterrer l'hostilité et la méfiance du passé. Nous devons travailler ensemble. C'est de cette façon seulement que nous pourrons édifier la maison commune européenne, ou la confédération européenne, ou le nouvel ordre européen - peu importe le nom qu'on lui donne. Nous savons tous ce que nous entendons par là : une Europe de la démocratie, des droits de l'homme et du partenariat, dans laquelle le tout renforce les parties et les parties renforcent le tout. Nous devons avancer ensemble; sinon, nous serons condamnés à reculer séparément.

Il existe une voie qui nous conduit, au-delà de la confrontation, vers une Europe entière et libre:
-par l'édification de nouvelles structures de coopération, d'une nouvelle architecture européenne qui englobe chacun de nous;
-par des négociations sur la maîtrise des armements en vue de réduire au maximum nos arsenaux et d'accroître la stabilité et la confiance mutuelle;

-par une coopération entre nous dans tous les domaines - politique, économique, scientifique, culturel.

Nous devons considérer d'un oeil nouveau nos objectifs et nos tâches. C'est ce que notre Alliance atlantique a fait, et continuera de faire. Lors du Sommet que nous avons tenu à Londres au début du mois de juillet, nous avons décidé de modifier notre Alliance de la façon la plus profonde depuis sa création, il y a quarante et un ans. Un système de confrontation n'offre pour nous aucun intérêt. Car l'OTAN a un rôle nouveau, encore plus important, à jouer : celui de pilier d'un ordre de coopération européen nouveau et pacifique. Dans le cadre d'un tel ordre, la puissance militaire jouera un rôle moindre; elle sera moins prépondérante, ne menacera personne et aura pour vocation de fournir des assurances contre les risques et de prévenir la guerre.

Comment l'0TAN a-t-elle changé, me demanderez-vous? Quelles mesures concrètes avons-nous prises?

- Nous réduisons nos budgets de la défense et le niveau de nos forces;
- nous réexaminons nos structures de forces et modifions notre stratégie militaire;
- nous abaissons le niveau de préparation de nos unités d'active, en réduisant les normes d'entraînement et le nombre des exercices;
- nous tablons moins sur les forces nucléaires en Europe; nous avons proposé à l'Union soviétique l'élimination de toutes les ogives d'artillerie nucléaire présentes sur ce continent;
- nous avons offert de négocier sur les forces nucléaires à courte portée en Europe lorsqu'un traité sur les FCE aura été signé; nous avons déjà prévu une réunion du Groupe consultatif spécial de notre Alliance pour élaborer un mandat en vue de ces pourparlers;
- nous avons également offert de passer, dès la conclusion d'un accord sur les FCE, à de nouvelles négociations dans le prolongement de cet accord, notamment sur des mesures de limitation des effectifs en Europe.

Ces changements interviendront à mesure que les forces soviétiques quitteront le territoire de la Tchécoslovaquie et de la Hongrie, comme l'URSS l'a déjà accepté, ainsi que le territoire de l'actuelle RDA au cours de la période de transition qui suivra la réunification de l'Allemagne. Ces changements dépendront également de la mise en oeuvre d'un traité sur les FCE qui offrira à tous les Etats participants de solides garanties contre l'agression et l'intimidation militaires. L'Alliance atlantique n'entend pas seulement éliminer les tensions par la réduction des armements : elle veut aussi accroître la confiance et la transparence. C'est pourquoi nous mettons tout en oeuvre pour obtenir la conclusion d'un accord sur le régime du "Ciel ouvert"; nous proposons l'ouverture de discussions sur la stratégie et la doctrine militaires. Nous souhaitons avant toute chose que la sécurité soit débattue et définie en commun.

Aucun pays ne peut aujourd'hui assurer sa sécurité à lui seul ou en s'isolant de ses voisins. Les pays qui recherchent une sécurité absolue par des efforts individuels ne font que créer l'insécurité autour d'eux. Nous ne devons donc plus jamais ramener la sécurité européenne au niveau purement national. La véritable sécurité ne peut d'ailleurs s'obtenir que par la coopération et le partage.

Il ne faut pas en déduire, évidemment, que les pays de l'OTAN ou tout autre pays européen doivent rester sans défense. Nous vivons, en effet, dans un monde fait d'incertitudes, qui comporte de nombreux risques et facteurs d'instabilité. La crise actuelle dans le Golfe persique nous le rappelle pour de bon. Elle ne s'apparente pas aux précédents conflits régionaux où seuls les intérêts de quelques pays étaient directement en cause; il ne s'agit pas davantage d'une crise dont le pétrole est l'enjeu exclusif ni même essentiel. Si notre objectif commun - à savoir la restauration du gouvernement légitime du Koweït et la libération de tous les otages - n'est pas atteint, c'est l'ensemble de la communauté internationale qui se trouvera exposée à un grave danger, celui du précédent créé par un pays, grand et puissant, qui annexe avec cynisme un pays voisin plus petit, et aussi - ce qui est plus inquiétant encore - d'une agression victorieuse qui ne manquera pas de nourrir les ambitions de dictatures qui ont de plus en plus accès aux technologies de destruction massive.

Il est donc crucial, non seulement pour le Koweït et la paix au Proche-Orient, mais aussi pour notre action commune qui vise à instaurer un ordre international plus durable et plus juste au lendemain de la Guerre froide, que les sanctions imposées par les Nations Unies à l'encontre de l'Irak soient suivies d'effets. Tous les pays de l'Alliance sont déterminés à préserver leur solidarité, et nous mettrons tout en oeuvre pour unir toujours plus nos efforts à ceux de l'Organisation des Nations Unies, qui a retrouvé son efficacité comme garant du droit international et de la stabilité à l'échelle mondiale. Je salue la ferme attitude que la Tchécoslovaquie a adoptée face à la crise, et je ne doute pas que nous pourrons continuer d'oeuvrer ensemble pour prouver à l'Irak - et à tous les autres belligérants potentiels - que l'agression brutale est vouée à l'échec.

Notre Alliance doit maintenir une défense solide, et nous n'en attendons pas moins des autres pays. L'OTAN conservera en Europe une combinaison de forces conventionnelles et nucléaires qui sera l'ultime garant de la paix. Notre objectif est cependant clair : nous voulons réduire les forces armées en Europe à un niveau minimum, de telle sorte qu'aucun pays ne doive plus en menacer d'autres pour se sentir en sécurité. Il est possible de concevoir un dispositif militaire qui offre les meilleures assurances de sécurité mutuelle. Notre Alliance en a d'ailleurs fait l'expérience positive avec sa structure de défense intégrée; qui parmi vous pourrait sérieusement imaginer que seize Etats souverains et démocratiques puissent un jour décider de lancer une attaque ou de la soutenir?

Notre objectif est une Europe dans laquelle l'agression ou la menace militaires deviendront matériellement impossibles et politiquement dénuées de sens. A la réunion au sommet de l'OTAN, nous sommes allés résolument de l'avant pour mettre en place les structures propres à garantir cette sécurité de l'Europe.

Tout d'abord, nous voulons instaurer un nouveau dialogue avec votre pays et avec tous les autres membres de l'Organisation du Traité de Varsovie. Nous avons invité le président Gorbatchev à prendre la parole devant le Conseil de l'Atlantique Nord à Bruxelles; j'ai eu le plaisir de lui transmettre personnellement cette invitation à Moscou au mois de juillet, et il l'a volontiers acceptée. A la suite de la récente visite de votre ministre des Affaires étrangères, M. Dientsbier, au siège de l'OTAN, nous espérons vivement pouvoir y accueillir le président Havel.

Nous avons proposé l'établissement de liaisons diplomatiques avec l'OTAN, et la Tchécoslovaquie a répondu favorablement à cette proposition. Nous comptons également multiplier les contacts et les échanges militaires aussi bien que diplomatiques. Nous avons proposé la signature d'une déclaration commune de non-agression entre les pays membres de l'OTAN et ceux de l'Organisation du Traité de Varsovie.

Ensuite, nous poursuivons le processus de maîtrise des armements avec vigueur et détermination. La conclusion d'un accord sur la maîtrise des armements conventionnels permettra aux anciens adversaires des deux alliances de se débarrasser du syndrome de la confrontation. Il constituera donc la première étape indispensable vers l'édification d'une Europe entière et libre; aussi, je compte sur le gouvernement tchécoslovaque pour qu'il nous apporte toute son aide afin que nous puissions maintenant conclure ce Traité. Cet accord jettera les bases de la coopération et de la confiance mutuelle grâce auxquelles nous pourrons construire une paix durable en Europe. Il sera le fondement solide sur lequel devra nécessairement reposer le nouvel ordre européen si l'on veut en assurer la pérennité.

Le processus de maîtrise des armements conventionnels, combiné avec des pourparlers sur les forces nucléaires à courte portée et avec un accord sur des mesures de confiance supplémentaires, donnera à tous les pays européens la garantie que le changement et le renouveau ne porteront atteinte aux intérêts légitimes de personne en matière de sécurité. Ceci est particulièrement important pour l'Union soviétique, qui est votre voisin. On peut comprendre que ce pays craigne de se voir exclu de l'Europe nouvelle, et il subit d'une manière particulièrement aiguë les effets du changement. Il est donc essentiel que nous nous servions du processus de maîtrise des armements pour convaincre l'Union soviétique qu'elle n'a rien à craindre, mais au contraire tout à gagner d'un processus de changement dont elle est d'ailleurs l'un des principaux initiateurs et qu'elle peut aider à conduire vers sa destination naturelle : une Europe entière et libre.

Enfin, la réunion au sommet de l'OTAN à Londres nous a permis d'exposer nos idées concernant un resserrement des liens entre tous les pays d'Europe par la mise en place de structures de coopération nouvelles ou élargies dans le cadre de la CSCE. La Tchécoslovaquie, elle aussi, accorde bien évidemment une importance cruciale à l'accroissement du rôle de la CSCE dans l'avènement d'un nouvel ordre européen. A cet égard, votre gouvernement a fait un certain nombre de propositions importantes et intéressantes. Au cours des semaines qui nous séparent du Sommet de la CSCE, nous nous efforcerons de faire la synthèse de ces idées dans un concept cohérent.

Pour être efficace, la CSCE doit permettre avant tout de protéger la démocratie et la liberté dans l'Europe tout entière, et s'attaquer aux problèmes liés au passage à des économies de marché performantes. Aussi l'OTAN a-t-elle proposé une série d'initiatives pour renforcer les principes contenus dans l'Acte final d'Helsinki et pour établir de nouvelles formes de coopération. Ces initiatives concernent notamment le droit à des élections libres et loyales, l'engagement de maintenir la primauté du droit, et des directives pour la coopération dans les domaines de l'économie et de l'environnement. En présentant sa demande d'adhésion au Conseil de l'Europe, la Tchécoslovaquie a montré qu'elle attache à ces valeurs la même importance que notre Alliance.

Pour permettre à la CSCE d'accomplir ces tâches, et pour élargir et structurer davantage le dialogue politique, l'OTAN a proposé de nouvelles formes institutionnelles pour la CSCE, et tout particulièrement un programme de consultations régulières de haut niveau entre les gouvernements des Etats membres, des conférences-bilans de la CSCE tous les deux ans, un secrétariat léger pour la CSCE, un centre CSCE pour la prévention des conflits et une assemblée parlementaire de l'Europe. Nous souhaitons que la CSCE soit le lieu où tous les pays d'Europe centrale et orientale puissent participer pleinement avec nous à l'édification du nouvel ordre européen.

Je voudrais cependant, si vous me le permettez, faire une mise en garde s'agissant de la CSCE. Nombreux sont ceux, parmi les pays d'Europe centrale et orientale engagés sur la voie de la démocratie, et aussi parmi les pays membres de l'Alliance, qui considèrent que la CSCE est appelée à se substituer aux organisations de sécurité existantes. Je m'abstiendrai de parler de l'Organisation du Traité de Varsovie, dont le maintien dépend naturellement du libre choix de ses membres. Mais je tiens à souligner que l'OTAN, pour ce qui la concerne, demeurera un pilier essentiel sur lequel la CSCE devra fonder sa réussite.

La CSCE peut certainement accroître la sécurité. Mais elle ne saurait remplacer l'Alliance atlantique. Elle n'a pas les moyens de prendre des sanctions, ni d'en assurer l'application. Les intérêts de chacun de ses membres, leurs structures sociales et leurs systèmes de valeurs resteront trop divers, au moins dans l'avenir prévisible, pour qu'ils puissent agir collectivement afin de préserver la sécurité en cas de crise. Cela ne diminue en rien l'importance de la CSCE comme cadre de l'instauration de la confiance et de la promotion de la coopération. Elle peut, par exemple, contribuer au règlement pacifique des différends qui peuvent surgir entre Etats à la suite de problèmes concernant des minorités nationales. Et, de fait, nous voyons déjà à quel point de tels différends peuvent engendrer l'instabilité en Europe centrale et orientale. A cet égard, l'introduction dans les textes de loi des engagements sur les droits de l'homme contenus dans l'Acte final d'Helsinki peut marquer un progrès. Dans le même temps, nous allons, car nous le pouvons, élaborer des mesures de confiance et développer des échanges d'informations qui nous permettront de vivre ensemble dans une plus grande harmonie. Mais, en dernière analyse, la CSCE ne tiendra ses promesses que si elle est complémentaire d'une Alliance atlantique forte, sur laquelle elle puisse se reposer. Ainsi, ses chances de succès seront d'autant plus grandes si nous n'y plaçons pas, dès le départ, des espoirs irréalistes.

L'existence d'une nouvelle Alliance atlantique forte et cohérente est de l'intérêt de la Tchécoslovaquie tout autant que de n'importe quel autre pays européen. Elle permet le changement dans la stabilité, et maintient le lien transatlantique avec les Etats-Unis d'Amérique et le Canada. C'est indispensable à la paix, et à la liberté et à la sécurité de l'ensemble de l'Europe.

Cependant, même une institution aussi solidement établie et aussi capable d'adaptation que l'OTAN ne peut supporter à elle seule la charge qu'il faut endosser pour assurer la coopération, la prospérité et le progrès pacifique à travers l'Europe. Heureusement, il y a aussi, pour cela, la Communauté européenne. C'est l'autre composante essentielle de notre cadre institutionnel occidental, et elle connaît, elle aussi, une période de changement et de renouveau dans l'action qu'elle mène pour parvenir à une union encore plus étroite entre ses membres. Si l'OTAN apporte la stabilité et le lien transatlantique, la Communauté européenne apporte le dynamisme, la créativité, et la base d'une interdépendance économique toujours plus fructueuse. De même qu'une CSCE dotée d'un rôle élargi, une Alliance atlantique forte et une Communauté européenne forte sont les conditions préalables à une Europe de progrès et de prospérité. Aucune ne peut réussir sans les autres.

A un moment où nous voyons se transformer l'ensemble du système international, aucun gouvernement, aucune alliance ne peut parfaitement maîtriser les puissantes forces qui rendent le changement inévitable. Mais, en oeuvrant ensemble, nous pouvons orienter ce changement de manière que, à son terme, il n'y ait pas de perdants, et que tous gagnent. Je suis infiniment plus optimiste à cet égard maintenant qu'il y a accord sur l'appartenance d'une

Allemagne unie à notre Alliance. Cette solution est de nature à accroître la stabilité pour tous. Elle ouvre la voie à l'élimination de la division et à l'établissement d'un partenariat entre l'Europe occidentale et les nations ayant récemment engagé un processus de démocratisation, partenariat qui sera un facteur clé dans la modernisation économique et sociale de ces pays.

En bref, l'OTAN voit son rôle futur comme consistant à mettre en place, dans toute l'Europe, de nouvelles structures de coopération qui rendront impossible le retour à une situation semblable à celle de la Guerre froide. Nous voulons travailler avec vous à la gestion des deux tâches cruciales qui s'imposent à l'Europe d'aujourd'hui :
- promouvoir un changement constructif;
- assurer la stabilité pour que ce changement puisse se dérouler dans des conditions optimales, avec un moindre risque de retours en arrière ou de revirements.

Il n'est guère besoin que je souligne ici, à Prague, les bénéfices qu'apportera la coopération entre nos pays. Le 21ème siècle nous placera devant de nouveaux défis, dont certains pourraient menacer notre survie encore plus gravement que ne l'avait fait près d'un demi-siècle de Guerre froide. La dégradation de l'environnement est l'un des périls dont votre gouvernement s'inquiète tout particulièrement; le terrorisme est un autre sujet de préoccupation, qui a donné lieu, ces dernières semaines, à des discussions fructueuses entre la Tchécoslovaquie et des pays membres de l'Alliance. Vous mesurez tout aussi bien que nous les risques de déstabilisation que comportent des fléaux tels que la drogue, la faim, la croissance démographique et la prolifération dans le Tiers monde de technologies militaires à énorme pouvoir de destruction. Ainsi, une Europe dynamique, composée de pays industriellement avancés et technologiquement interdépendants, est indispensable, non seulement à notre prospérité matérielle, mais aussi à notre sécurité et à notre stabilité à l'intérieur de nos frontières comme à l'extérieur. Sans une telle cohésion, l'Europe risque bien d'être dépassée par ces défis mondiaux; ensemble, nous pouvons contribuer à y répondre.

La visite que je fais aujourd'hui à Prague, grande cité européenne, symbolise une ère nouvelle; mais c'est aussi une invitation concrète à mettre en commun nos ressources et notre génie propre pour bâtir un monde nouveau, un monde de coopération où aucun d'entre nous ne se sentira menacé. Nous ne pouvons nous dérober à la responsabilité que cette chance exceptionnelle nous impose. La Tchécoslovaquie, qui a tant contribué à notre culture politique et intellectuelle européenne, est un partenaire clé dans l'édification d'une Europe nouvelle et d'un ordre mondial fait de plus de justice et de plus d'égalité. Faisons donc d'aujourd'hui le début de cette nouvelle relation entre nous, et employons-nous ensemble, avec confiance et imagination, à préparer cet avenir meilleur. ☐

*A*ddress given to a Conference sponsored by the United States Mission to NATO on the Future of the Atlantic Alliance

Brussels
19-21
September
1990

My subject today is the future of the Atlantic Alliance. It is not an exercise in prediction, something which is always hazardous and even more so in the fast moving, unpredictable world in which we live these days. We have just lived through two years of decisive historical change, old problems have lost much of their salience. New problems have appeared on the scene and become more acute. The security environment which gave birth to NATO and with which it has lived for forty years has suddenly gone. Of course, the Alliance has not been on the sidelines. It has shaped change and it has adapted to change. In the process it has been prepared to be imaginative and even radical as we saw last July at our London Summit. Yet the question remains, what overall concept are all of these structural transformations designed to serve? How has historic change affected our Alliance? What consequences have we drawn? And how far advanced is our task of re-conceptualising NATO's security mission in a world that, with the passing of the Cold War, has become more peaceful, yet as the Gulf crisis illustrates, remains unacceptably dangerous?

From the moment Communism began to crumble, this Alliance made a fundamental judgement: that the opportunities this gave us to shape a better, more secure and more just world far outweighed the risks that the demise of the bi-polar system would bring. For the most significant development is the peaceful revolution in the Soviet Union as well as in Central and Eastern Europe and the far reaching détente, indeed the really genuine and durable détente, between the two super powers and the two blocs, and I dare not speak about blocs any more, as blocs have disappeared. This promises to lead to a lasting reconciliation and to permit the construction of a new European peace order, based on a partnership in security in place of Cold War confrontation and this indeed, I consider, still to be the most important part of our Alliance, to build such a new and lasting peaceful order of co-operation and security in Europe.

Yet barely has this new order begun to take shape when the Gulf crisis has erupted to subject it to its first serious test. The North-South conflict which we had all tended somewhat to forget has returned suddenly to centre-stage, and against the background of global problems such as the distribution of resources, population growth and energy supplies which have been exacerbated by religious fundamentalism, proliferation of ballistic missile technology, nuclear and chemical weapons and by terrorism and drugs.

Europe too, has by no means become a haven of tranquillity. The fate of glasnost and perestroïka is still uncertain and it is an open question where the development of the Soviet Union will ultimately lead. Clearly, it is our hope, it is our strong wish and it is the intention of our co-operation with the Soviet Union to help and assist the forces of reform. We are interested, let me repeat this here once again, in the success of Gorbachev and those who together with him are trying to shape a new Soviet Union. We cannot yet tell if the courageous revolutions of the peoples of Central and Eastern Europe, driven by the quest for freedom, will actually produce successful democracies and economic reforms. In many places ethnic problems, border disputes and power struggles have raised their head. Nationalism, a force that most of us believed to be extinct or at least approaching extinction, is trumpeting its resurrection in many parts of Europe. Thus, while it would be irresponsible and inaccurate to claim that the risks associated with change threaten our Western security as much as the strategic presence of the Soviet Union in Central Europe during the Cold War years, it would be equally foolhardy for us to treat such risks as the innocuous side effects of this historical upheaval.

This Alliance can stamp its imprint on events; it has done so, it will continue to do so. Our vision of a Europe whole and free, and of a more secure and co-operative international order, is a realistic possibility. We are no dreamers, we are realistic politicians, and it indeed is possible to build this new Europe. Yet the ambivalence of an era of enormous change with its opportunities and risks means that we can have an influence only if we are united, determined, and strong enough in political and also in defence terms.

My central message is a very simple one: we will only succeed in shaping history, driving the historic process of transformation, if we maintain the cohesion of our Alliance, which is the most important instrument of historic change that exists on earth at this very moment.

As I told the Ambassadors and Permanent Representatives yesterday, I have just come back from Poland and Czechoslovakia, and I went to the Soviet Union in July. Clearly many hopes are directed towards our Alliance. We did not discuss in Poland or Czechoslovakia the question of membership, but clearly the feeling is that this Alliance is the decisive factor of stability which can to a large extent influence the future development of Europe.

Our Alliance has always been a community of destiny for nations that are drawn together by common values, convictions, and basic interests, a political Alliance thus, but equipped with military means. Today when the time of direct threat to our security has dwindled, its political role is becoming ever more significant. That political role lies in the shaping of East-West relations, in the construction of a new European security architecture, in steering the arms control process, maintaining a healthy transatlantic relationship which does not go by itself, and in meeting new challenges to our security. In all these areas the Alliance can and must strive to ensure the development, discussion and formulation of a coordinated Western approach. Where else could this task be carried out if not in this Alliance? The European Community will certainly play an increasingly important role in these areas but it cannot replace the Alliance, for only the Atlantic Alliance incorporates the United States and Canada as well as important states on the European periphery that are not members of the European Community. And it is obvious today, looking at the development of the whole of Europe, how important the flanks and not only the southern flank, but also the northern flank, have become.

Without the North American democracies, European security for the foreseeable future can neither be built nor maintained. Again, let me give you one impression from my travels through some of the Central and Eastern European countries, including the Soviet Union : there is a clear desire to see the United States and Canada remain in Europe, of course with reduced forces, but remain nonetheless. So the first reason why NATO will be indispensable in the future as at the moment or in the past is that it is the main vehicle of Western consent and Western political input.

Let me make one thing very clear from the outset, there is absolutely no question of NATO claiming responsibility for every problem on this earth, for this would clearly overburden its capacities and to nobody's benefit. Manifestly NATO is and will remain a security Alliance - an Alliance that guarantees the security of its members. Yet the notion of security has to be looked at in a much more comprehensive way. It has today become less than ever a purely military concept. In addition to its military component, there is an important political and an important economic dimension. It incorporates disarmament questions, weapons proliferation, terrorism. Also security can clearly be affected by events outside our Treaty area as demonstrated by the present Gulf crisis.

Who could deny that the maintenance of an uninterrupted supply of oil is a vital issue for the security of all the members of the Alliance? This Alliance has a long tradition in dealing with so-called 'out of area' problems, yet the Gulf crisis presents many different and new features. For it is a challenge to the West on several levels: the moral issue of seeing a small state taken over by a larger neighbour; the political issue of seeing an aspiring regional power acquire weapons of mass destruction; the economic issue of a major disruption in the supply of oil at a crucial moment in the economic reconstruction of Central and Eastern Europe and with many Third World states in a precarious situation. Again I would refer to my experiences in Poland and Czechoslovakia. If you held a discussion with their leaders, you would see how much this crisis is already affecting their policies and their attempts to reconstruct their economies. There is also the issue of long-term stability in the already explosive area that is the Middle East, and last but not least the human challenge of thousands of refugees and hostages whose lives have been put at risk. So this is clearly a political struggle that has a direct bearing on our Western security, and not only on our Western security of course, which neither we, nor the international community at large can afford to lose. For if the prize of applying the United Nations mandated sanctions and implementing the five Security Council resolutions will undoubtedly be high, we have to realise that the prize of allowing the Iraqis to escape with impunity will undoubtedly be higher still and will have to be paid sooner or later.

Notwithstanding the enormous effort being made by the United States in leading the international community against the Iraqi aggression, the first lesson of the Gulf crisis is clearly that the sanctions will work only if all the members of that community stay together and share the responsibilities and burdens in both the economic and military domains equitably. Let me gratefully recognize the constructive role played from the outset by our former adversary and now partner, the Soviet Union.

The role of NATO in the context of the Gulf crisis has been questioned and even severely criticized by some, especially in the United States. I fully understood the concerns and the emotions which lead to such a reaction, but first let me state some facts. NATO has never before in the history of regional conflict shown such a high degree of solidarity. We were the first international organization to strongly condemn the Iraqi aggression. We have consulted virtually on a daily basis on the events as they have unfolded. Two special meetings of Foreign Ministers have contributed effectively to maintaining and reinforcing our solidarity. All Allied member countries have contributed in one way or another to the implementation of the United Nations sanctions and to the support of those Allies who are directly committed to the defence of Saudi Arabia.

Two member countries, the United Kingdom and France, have meanwhile deployed, or are going to deploy ground forces, in addition to those of the United States in Saudi Arabia. The Alliance has strongly reaffirmed its commitment to the security of Turkey, giving Turkey clear backing for its active, courageous and important role in the execution of the sanctions. In short, given the constraints imposed on the Alliance, it has done as an organization what it could to be helpful in implementing the United Nations sanctions and in supporting the United States and other Allies in the deterrence of further aggression.

Let me also very clearly state my personal opinion that some Allies could and should do more. Among other steps it would be helpful if, in addition to Great Britain and France, other Allies could also send ground troops to the Gulf as suggested by the United States of America.

Looking to the future, it seems obvious that we have to draw lessons from the current crisis. The main question is, should the Alliance as such play an increased role in dealing with regional conflicts which directly affect the security of its member nations? I believe that we all have to think carefully about that. Of course, nobody thinks of NATO dealing with all regional crises and all global challenges, but being the decisive security Alliance of the Western World, can we afford to be limited to consultations in cases where the security of our member nations is at stake? This is a legitimate and an essential question and we have to deal with it. My only advice is not to burden our solidarity and cohesion, which is very firm, by such a debate at this very moment. Our primary goal now must be to maintain solidarity and to do what is necessary in practical terms to reach a successful solution to the crisis. We should discuss the consequences of this crisis on our Alliance and for our Alliance's future after the crisis is over. I myself intend then to participate actively in such a debate, because as you can imagine, I have very clear ideas and convictions about that.

A further and indeed indispensable role of the Alliance is in maintaining and reinforcing the transatlantic security community plus ensuring the continuing commitment by the United States and Canada to Europe. If NATO were to disappear tomorrow, the community of destiny that the Alliance has established between the North American and European democracies would be damaged, severely damaged. Both continents whose populations will represent less than 10% of the world total by the end of the century would be isolated and at a time when their active solidarity will be as necessary to face the challenges of tomorrow as those of yesterday. Without a close working relationship to North America, how can the European democracies balance the continuing enormous military might of the Soviet Union, even in the cooperative context towards which we are striving? How could they respond to the immense challenge of social and economic reconstruction in Central and Eastern Europe? Finally, how could they meet the challenges of the North-South agenda I referred to earlier and to which Europe, with its numerous Mediterranean neighbours and trading economies must of course be especially sensitive.

Finally, the Alliance is altogether indispensable in guaranteeing stability in Europe and even beyond. This is no less true in times of a reduced direct and immediate threat to our security. I would even say more so, for the threat posed by the massive Soviet military presence in Central Europe was in its way predictable and relatively easy to quantify. Now we see new risks to our security that are less easy to predict and to quantify, and which consequently cannot be managed in the same way that we dealt with the European balance of military power in the past. The new risks, therefore, are no longer confined to military attack on our territory but are as likely to originate from a breakdown in regional stability which could either spill over into our Alliance's own area or alternatively be exploited against our interests and solidarity. So clearly we need a continued coherent defence. This Alliance will not only be a political Alliance but also a military Alliance in the future with reduced manpower, with reduced arms and equipment in a much more stable environment, clearly able to deter anybody from envisaging the use of military means, able to prevent war in the future, and to deal with risks affecting the security of our member nations. This role of ensuring stability, which is clearly recognised as I said to you even by our neighbours in the East, is one that cannot be transferred from the Atlantic Alliance to another body. Neither the European Community nor the CSCE whether individually or together, can maintain stability across Europe.

The European Community despite its ultimate objective of political union and the dynamism of European integration, and I fully subscribe to it not only as a European but also as the Secretary General of this Alliance, does not have a close link with North America nor at present sufficient capacities in the security field. We perceive the wider responsibilities that result from its increasingly powerful economic position, yet more time will be needed for the Community to evolve and endow itself with the requisite tools. The CSCE, despite its contribution to enhancing security with the implementation of confidence building measures and through crisis management functions, does not have the integrated defence structure and as yet the common social and value systems that alone can guarantee cohesion and effectiveness to deter or defend against aggression. So clearly the Atlantic Alliance has a future role, as a bedrock of stability and as the essential supporting pillar, security pillar, of a new European order.

Let me briefly comment on the tasks ahead. The first task is to build a new Europe based on four pillars: the North Atlantic Alliance; the European Communities; the Council of Europe; and an institutionalized CSCE process embracing all the European nations, including the Soviet Union. In my talk with the Soviet leadership, I could transmit the unanimous attitude of all our member nations of our Alliance as such, that clearly we want to build this new Europe together with the Soviet Union, on a basis of equal rights and equal participation. It would be foolish, and nobody is foolish, at least inside our Alliance, to try to exclude or isolate the Soviet Union. What could that produce if not instability and additional risk? So clearly this new Europe will include the Soviet Union and I think our view is shared by many member countries of the Warsaw Treaty Organisation that the CSCE structure, as important as it is, cannot replace or substitute for NATO.

The next task ahead is to build a close relationship with the countries of Central and Eastern Europe. The third task will be to proceed with arms control in the way we described in the London Declaration. The fourth task is to fully implement the changes which the London Summit asked us to carry out, and that means especially to change our military strategy. Indeed we have begun to do so along the lines stated in the London Declaration. I have not enough time to go into details but there are a lot of my colleagues present this morning who could do it at least as well as I could.

Then of course, we have to manage the membership of a united Germany in NATO along the lines which we agreed upon with Germany and with the Soviet Union.

And last but not least, we have to meet those global challenges which clearly affect our own security. I am confident that we can meet these challenges. The Alliance is in good shape; solidarity and cohesion have made it possible for our policies to be successful and this success has certainly put the wind in our sails, and this in turn has further strengthened the unity and resolve of the Alliance. It has successfully passed the test of overcoming the obstacles to the full NATO membership of a united Germany. That too is cause for optimism.

At the same time I will not hide that I see some concerns or difficulties on our path that we have to avoid or to overcome. I am fully confident that we can do so, so I am just giving you a hint of what I see as problem areas which we have to deal with in the future.

One concerns the potential developments in Europe. I have mentioned the role of the European Community. The EC is clearly playing the key role in the process of European political and economic unity, and I do not doubt that it will also give itself an identity in the security field in the course of time. This is legitimate and it is not only legitimate; I think it is in the interest of our Alliance, as has been stated by the London Summit Declaration. So we should not see the relation between our Alliance and the European Community as one of competitors or even of rivals. But clearly since the European Community will deal more and more with political questions and with security questions and we are dealing partly with the same questions, there is an overlap. This overlap can and must be dealt with through timely coordination and information which can be done without additional mechanisms or organisational structures by our member nations, by contacts between the staff.

If I look at some proposals made last week about military instruments for the European Community, these are long-term goals, and the discussions and events of the last days have proved that they will not come into place as early as some may hope. My answer would be the same : clearly there has to be coordination from the very first moment on. Clearly this can and should take place only in the context of our Alliance as is acknowledged by all our member nations. But that does not mean that the Alliance somehow supervises. It does mean that now and for the foreseeable future the decisive instrument of Western security will remain this Alliance. Clearly, NATO can and should not be reduced to a purely military role.

I point to a second concern : a development in the United States that would point to the vanishing Soviet threat and the special burden that the United States has to bear on account of its global responsibilities as a reason for a complete or nearly a complete American withdrawal from Europe. These tendencies would be further strengthened by a European policy of going it alone, or by a perception that, in important policy areas, the United States is presented by its European Allies with *faits accomplis*. The process of reciprocal decoupling must be avoided at all costs, since there is unanimous attitude of all our member countries that for the foreseeable future, the Northern Americans have an indispensable role to play in ensuring stability. Another certain danger resides in the growing sense of popular euphoria regarding security questions which admittedly has been dampened down somewhat in the wake of the Gulf crisis. Naturally, the desire for a peace dividend is not only understandable but also justified, and naturally a phased reduction of our troop strength, equipment and defence budgets is a common objective of all Allies. We have already begun to do this. This process can be continued, yet it must be predicted very closely on the results of arms control negotiations and on Soviet reductions and must also be coordinated within the Alliance so that at the end of this process there is certainly a smaller defence but one that is still coherent and consistent with a military balance in Europe tomorrow and our residual military requirements.

Let me state once more very clearly, knowing that many journalists are here today and that this is a speech on the record, that if I point to such concerns, it is not because I consider that they already constitute dangers to our Alliance, or I because I believe that we could not overcome them. We are dealing with them, and I think we have started to deal with them very successfully. We will master them, I have no doubt about that. I only want to prevent complacency and a false sense of self-confidence or indeed a premature and inappropriate feeling of triumphalism. So in the future, as much as in the past, determination, leadership quality, courage, perseverance, cohesion, solidarity will prove essential if we are to keep our Alliance on track and we have to keep it on track simply because there is no alternative. With this Alliance, with its cohesion, with its leadership, we can build the new Europe we are striving for, together with our newly won partners in Central and Eastern Europe. So I think a whole and free Europe in a more peaceful and just world is within our reach, and we will not fail.

□

Address to the North Atlantic Council on the occasion of German Unification

Brussels
3 October
1990

Today, the 3rd of October 1990, is a decisive landmark in the history of our Alliance. This is a day of undiminished rejoicing, not only for the Germans, but for the whole of our Alliance. We have reached one of the most important and longstanding objectives of our Alliance.

The German people have exercised at long last their right of self-determination. Germany has overcome its painful, unnatural division. Thus a vital step has been taken to overcome the division of Europe. Without our Alliance this would not have been possible. Over twenty years ago our Harmel Report stated that German unity could never be for this Alliance a purely national question. No permanent peace, no new European order of freedom, democracy and prosperity could be built around a divided Germany, or in opposition to the wishes of the Germans themselves to live within a single nation. Today we put nearly half a century of confrontation and frustration behind us. Our policy of secure defence and the active pursuit of détente has proved the recipe for peaceful change. With German unity finally realised, the way is clear for this Alliance to achieve its ultimate objective : a lasting order of peace, freedom and justice in Europe.

Less than a year has passed since that night of celebration when the Berlin Wall came down. In that time we have all been witnesses of the historic process of a divided nation growing together again. This unique task of merging two incompatible political and social systems has demanded an unparalleled effort. Yet by their imagination, courage and determination, the German authorities, loyally supported by their partners in the

227

Alliance and in the European Community, have created the climate of confidence needed for success.

And there have been the external aspects of German unification. This process again was a unique task in history. It had to lay the groundwork in the centre of Europe for the new European order we are building in the CSCE process, based on the supporting pillars of the European Community and the Atlantic Alliance.

The same imagination and boldness displayed by the Federal German authorities in working out the internal modalities of German unity were displayed also by the US, UK and French Authorities in close consultation with all other Allies. And again our Alliance stood the test of solidarity and cohesion. Strong reservations and even opposition in the Soviet Union based on decades of fear and distrust had to be overcome. Our Alliance has met this challenge, standing firmly together. Our London Summit showed that the new Germany would be part of a new, transformed Alliance; an Alliance that desired cooperation not confrontation, and which extended the hand of friendship to the Soviet Union and to all the other nations of Central and Eastern Europe. Thus again our Alliance contributed decisively to the final lifting of Soviet objections to the full NATO membership of a united Germany. We gratefully acknowledge the contribution and consent of the Soviet leadership and people.

We now include the whole of Germany in our Alliance as we reassess our strategy and our force posture. I do not doubt that we will rapidly succeed in this endeavour.

The unification of Germany in conditions of peace, freedom and prosperity is a vindication of our perseverance; and also of our values which have proved infinitely more powerful than military force, ideology and repression. Those universal values are the forces that drive history and move human progress. In the decades since its foundation, our Alliance has been a decisive factor in the resurrection of a democratic Germany after the war up to the final achievement of regaining its unity. The Alliance has provided the framework of security in which the ruined, impoverished Federal Republic of the immediate post-war years could rebuild its democracy and anchor itself irrevocably in the West.

On behalf of our Atlantic Alliance, I congratulate the German nation on the achievement of its unity. I salute and welcome the united Germany as a loyal member of our Alliance and an active partner in the building of a Europe whole and free.

All our best wishes accompany you.

□

Discours au Conseil de l'Atlantique Nord à l'occasion de l'unification de l'Allemagne

Bruxelles
3 octobre
1990

Ce 3 octobre 1990 marque un point décisif dans l'histoire de l'Alliance: aujourd'hui, en effet, non seulement les Allemands, mais l'ensemble de l'Alliance, peuvent se réjouir sans arrière-pensée, car nous voici arrivés à l'un des objectifs les plus importants et les plus longtemps attendus de notre Alliance.

Le peuple allemand, enfin, a pu exercer son droit à l'autodétermination. L'Allemagne, enfin, a surmonté sa séparation douloureuse et contre nature. En même temps, une étape vitale a été franchie pour surmonter la division de l'Europe. Sans notre Alliance, cela n'aurait pu se faire. Voici plus de vingt ans que le Rapport Harmel affirmait que pour l'Alliance, l'unité de l'Allemagne ne saurait être une question purement nationale. On ne saurait construire de paix permanente, de nouvel ordre européen de liberté, de démocratie et de prospérité autour d'une Allemagne divisée, ni à l'encontre du désir des Allemands eux-mêmes de vivre dans une nation unique. Aujourd'hui, nous laissons derrière nous presque un demi siècle de confrontation et de frustration. Il s'est avéré que notre politique de défense et de sécurité et que la poursuite active de la détente étaient bien les ingrédients d'un changement pacifique. L'unité allemande étant enfin réalisée, la voie est libre qui permettra à l'Alliance d'atteindre son objectif ultime: un ordre durable de paix, de liberté et de justice en Europe.

Moins d'une année s'est écoulée depuis cette nuit de fête que fut la Chute du Mur de Berlin. Pendant tout ce temps, nous avons tous été les témoins du processus historique d'une nation divisée qui se reconstitue. Cette tâche unique de fusion de deux systèmes politiques et sociaux incompatibles a exigé un effort sans pareil. Pourtant, grâce à leur imagination, à leur courage et à leur détermination, les autorités allemandes, soutenues loyalement par leurs partenaires de l'Alliance et de la Communauté européenne, ont créé le climat de confiance qui était nécessaire au succès.

Puis il y eut les aspects externes de l'unification allemande. Ce processus fut lui aussi une tâche unique dans l'histoire. Il fallait en effet creuser au centre de l'Europe les fondations du nouvel ordre européen que nous construisons grâce aux travaux de la Conférence sur la sécurité et la coopération en Europe, en prenant appui sur ces deux piliers que sont la Communauté européenne et l'Alliance Atlantique.

Les autorités des Etats-Unis, du Royaume-Uni et de la France, en étroite consultation avec tous les autres Alliés, ont aussi fait preuve de la même imagination et de la même hardiesse que les autorités de l'Allemagne fédérale en élaborant les modalités internes de l'unité allemande. Et, une fois encore, notre Alliance a résisté à l'épreuve de la solidarité et de la cohésion. Il fallait surmonter les réserves tenaces et même hostiles qui, en Union soviétique, avaient survécu à des décennies de crainte et de méfiance. Notre Alliance a relevé le défi en restant fermement solidaire. Le Sommet de Londres a montré que la nouvelle Allemagne s'intégrerait à une Alliance neuve et transformée; une Alliance qui souhaite la coopération et non la confrontation, et qui tend une main amicale à l'Union soviétique et à toutes les autres nations de l'Europe du Centre et de l'Est. Ainsi, notre Alliance contribue encore de façon décisive à lever définitivement les objections que l'Union soviétique pouvait opposer à une pleine participation à l'OTAN d'une Allemagne unifiée. C'est avec gratitude que nous donnons acte aux dirigeants et au peuple soviétiques de leur contribution et de leur consentement.

Désormais, en réévaluant notre stratégie et le dispositif de nos forces, nous englobons toute l'Allemagne dans notre Alliance. Je ne doute pas que nous réussirons rapidement dans cette entreprise.

L'unification de l'Allemagne dans des conditions de paix, de liberté et de prospérité est une justification de notre persévérance; et aussi de nos valeurs qui se sont révélées infiniment plus puissantes que la force militaire, l'idéologie et la répression. Ces valeurs universelles sont les forces qui mènent l'histoire et qui font progresser l'humanité. Au cours des décennies qui ont suivi sa fondation, notre Alliance a été un facteur décisif de la résurrection d'une Allemagne démocratique, depuis l'après-guerre jusqu'à la réalisation finale de son retour à l'unité. L'Alliance a fourni le cadre de sécurité dans lequel la République fédérale de l'immédiat après-guerre, ruinée et appauvrie, pouvait rebâtir sa démocratie et s'ancrer irrévocablement dans l'Occident.

Au nom de notre Alliance Atlantique, je félicite la nation allemande d'avoir réalisé son unité. Je salue et accueille l'Allemagne unifiée comme membre loyal de notre Alliance et comme partenaire actif de la construction d'une Europe entière et libre.

Tous nos meilleurs voeux vous accompagnent. □

The Future of the Atlantic Alliance

SPEECH DELIVERED
TO THE NATIONAL DEFENCE
INSTITUTE

Lisbon
5 November
1990

I am making today what my French friends would call a "visite éclair" to Lisbon. Yet, even in a crowded programme of meetings with the President, Prime Minister and senior ministers, I am delighted to have this opportunity to address a wider audience publicly on the future of our Atlantic Alliance. And I wish to thank the National Defence Institute for giving me this platform and for bringing together this distinguished audience of opinion leaders, officials and military officers all bound by a common interest in security and defence questions.

Today it has become fashionable to speak of an "identity crisis" of the Alliance, because the security environment that gave birth to NATO, and with which it has lived for forty years, has suddenly gone. Some commentators argue that our Alliance has become the victim of its own success or has fulfilled a kind of long-standing dream : to create a peaceful Europe in which a politico-military Alliance like NATO would be altogether superfluous. Others do not go that far, but believe nonetheless that security is today less important or can be had more easily. Well, it is of course true that Europe and the wider world have changed - dramatically and permanently. Old problems have lost much of their saliency. New problems have appeared on the scene or become more acute. Yet, for my part, however much I welcome this change for having made our world order significantly more cooperative and potentially secure, I see nothing that convinces me that security itself is less important. Indeed in a time of rapid change, it becomes more important.

In the first place, the lesson of the past two years is that change itself can be sudden and unpredictable - which means things can change for the worse as well as for the better. The Gulf crisis illustrates this. Peace, like democracy, will always require vigilance.

Europe has not yet found its final new shape. Nor has it become a haven of tranquility. The fate of glasnost and perestroïka is still uncertain, and it is an open question where the dramatic current developments in the Soviet Union will ultimately lead. Notwithstanding all our encouragement and concrete assistance, we equally cannot yet tell if the courageous revolutions of the peoples of Central and Eastern Europe, driven by the quest for freedom, will actually produce successful democracies and economic reforms. In many places old ethnic problems, border disputes and power struggles have reared their heads. Nationalism, a force we believed was approaching extinction, is trumpeting its resurrection with fanfare in many parts of Europe.

If states give up their defences or allow collective structures of security like NATO to disintegrate, they will only create vacuums around them. These might sooner or later tempt potential aggressors or create insecurity in other states. The result would be a return to the disastrous power politics and unstable alliances of past centuries. Defence would be renationalized. Even in a time of peace we would thereby sow the seeds of future instability as nations once again compete with each other and against each other for their security.

Finally there are new challenges disturbing developments beyond Europe which we cannot disregard. The Iraqi aggression against Kuwait is the deliberate attempt to eliminate a UN member from the world map - what Sir Michael Howard has termed : "state murder".

It is also a challenge to the West on several levels : the moral issue of seeing a small state taken over by a larger neighbour; the political issue of seeing an aspiring regional power acquire weapons of mass destruction; the economic issue of a major disruption in the supply of oil at a crucial moment in the economic reconstruction of Central and Eastern Europe and with many Third World states in a precarious situation; the issue of long term stability in the already explosive area that is the Middle East and, last but not least, the human challenge of thousands of refugees and hostages whose lives have been put at risk. Thus the Gulf crisis combines an act of brutal annexation - something of which history of course gives us many sad examples - with a host of new issues which make this crisis not only a threat to our security but also to our efforts to build a new order based on restraint, cooperation and the rule of law. For both reasons it is a struggle that neither we, nor the international community at large, can afford to lose.

Thus it would be foolhardy for us to treat the residual risks, whether in Europe or the wider world, as the innocuous side-effects of historical upheaval. This Alliance can stamp its imprint on events. Our vision of a Europe whole and free, and of a more secure and cooperative international order, is a realistic possibility. Yet the ambivalence of an era of enormous change - with its opportunities and risks - means that we can have an influence only if we are united and determined; and if we maintain a secure defence.

The most important vehicle for this collective enterprise is the Atlantic Alliance. From the outset it has always been a community of destiny and a forum for nations that are joined together by common values, convictions and basic interests - a political alliance thus, but equipped with military means. Today, at a time when the direct threat to our security has dwindled, its political role is becoming ever more significant.

That role lies
- in the shaping of East-West relations
- in the construction of a new European security architecture
- in steering the arms control process
- in maintaining a healthy transatlantic relationship.

In all these areas the Alliance can and must strive to ensure the development, discussion and formulation of a coordinated Western approach. Where else could this task be carried out, if not in the Alliance? Only the Atlantic Alliance incorporates the United States and Canada as well as important states on the European periphery that are not members of the European Community; and without the North American democracies, European security can neither be built nor maintained.

If the Alliance were to disappear tomorrow, the community of destiny that the Alliance has established between the North American and European democracies would be irreparably damaged. Both continents, whose populations will represent less than 10 % of the world total by the end of the century, would be isolated; and that at a time when their active solidarity will be as necessary to face the challenges of tomorrow as those of yesterday:
- without a close working relationship to North America, how can the European democracies balance the continuing and enormous military might of the Soviet Union which will of course remain a factor even in the cooperative order that we are striving for?
- how could they respond to the immense challenge of social and economic reconstruction in Central and Eastern Europe?
- and, finally, how could they meet the challenges of the North-South agenda I referred to earlier and to which Europe, with its numerous Mediterranean neighbours, and trading economies must perforce be especially sensitive?

Finally the Alliance is altogether indispensable in guaranteeing stability in Europe and even beyond. This is no less true in times of a reduced direct and immediate threat to our security - I would even say more so. For the threat posed by the massive Soviet military presence in Central Europe was in its way predictable and relatively easy to quantify. Now we see new risks to our security that are less easy to predict and to quantify, and which consequently cannot be managed in the same way that we dealt with the European balance of military power in the past.

The new risks therefore are no longer confined to a military attack on our territory but are as likely to originate from a breakdown in regional stability that would either spill over into our Alliance's own area or alternatively be exploited against our interests and solidarity. As, for instance, in using the oil weapon, terrorism or hostages against us.

Over the last two years the Atlantic Alliance has undergone fundamental change. Its centre of gravity is moving from the military to the political role, from confrontation to cooperation, from peace-keeping to peace-building, from the staving off of a clear and present danger to the more long term and prudent provision against future risks, from an Alliance under American leadership to a partnership between North America and Europe.

The London Declaration by the Heads of State and Government of the Atlantic Alliance accordingly states that "security and stability do not lie solely in the military dimension ... We intend to enhance the political component of the Alliance". NATO has always been a political Alliance, as is shown in the political objectives and common values already set out in the Washington Treaty of 1949 and subsequently amplified in the Alliance's intensive political consultations. Yet, this political role is now becoming stronger still. In the future, the Alliance will be called upon more forcefully than up to now to contribute to the construction of a new European security order, and to enhance long term security through new responsibilities : cooperation in the political field, military contacts, confidence-building, disarmament, and verification.

Our main tasks will be :

- First, to build a new European architecture, a new European order of cooperation, to include the Soviet Union and the other countries of Central and Eastern Europe. We must not allow the old East-West ideological division of Europe to be replaced by a new division based on wealth and living standards. This is a major preoccupation of many of the new democratic governments in Central and Eastern Europe, as I know from my recent visits there. Such a gap may be inevitable in the short term but it will undermine our stability if it persists. Equally we must not isolate the Soviet Union from Europe. It has much to contribute and needs our assistance to overcome its immense domestic problems.

Our Alliance concept of a future pan-European architecture of cooperation provides for four supporting pillars on which such a Europe whole and free can securely rest. First there is the European Community, then an institutionalized CSCE process, then the Council of Europe which we hope to make into a parliamentary assembly for the whole of Europe, and last but not least the Atlantic Alliance as the indispensable underpinning of security.

Of course, no-one can deny that since the Helsinki Final Act fifteen years ago, the CSCE process has been a unique success story; it has, without doubt, developed into a key element of any future European structure; and one that will acquire many core security functions in the light of the probable dissolution of the Warsaw Treaty Organisation. The increased institutionalisation of the CSCE process is a common goal of all the Allies. By endowing CSCE with a new system of political consultations and giving it pan-European functions in such fields as information exchange, the observation of unusual military activities, the implementation of arms control agreements, and the resolution of conflicts, we can open a new institutional chapter in the political development of our entire continent. Indeed the proposals of our London Summit Declaration for institutionalizing the CSCE have found broad consensus among the 34. Now that a CFE treaty has been practically agreed, we have the basis for a very successful CSCE Summit in Paris in two weeks time which really should live up to the expectation that it will give birth to a new European architecture.

Yet to infer from this that the collective security system of the Atlantic Alliance will become superfluous - even over the long term - would be a mistake. New CSCE structures can bridge old antagonisms, and can lead to new and common concepts for the enhancement of peace and partnership. However, CSCE cannot provide firm security guarantees against potential future risks. It requires consensus which is difficult to obtain while each of the 34 states has a right of veto, and the CSCE states do not yet share common values or common social systems. Thus for the foreseeable future the CSCE cannot ensure stability and the necessary degree of insurance against risks which is provided uniquely by the collective defence capacities of our Alliance.

The relationship between the Alliance and CSCE must be complementary, not one of either/or. It will be the task of our Alliance to provide stability and to build the basis for cooperation. A cohesive Alliance is thus the prerequisite for a smoothly functioning CSCE. The nations of Central and Eastern Europe have in fact been more explicit than many of our own Western opinion leaders in recognizing that the continuation of NATO as a stabilizing element in a European security structure is indispensable.

The European Community will play a key role in the construction of a new Europe. It is in the interests of the Atlantic Alliance that Europe not only unites economically but also politically. But it is also essential that in striving for such unity, we do not marginalize or exclude nations that wish to be part of this process. All of our future European structures will be stronger and more durable to the extent that they are inclusive, not exclusive. Moreover the political union of Europe is not feasible without the inclusion of security and defence. The Alliance's London Declaration explicitly supports this goal. We want a united Europe. A strong Europe means a strong Atlantic Alliance. Such a European security identity will be achieved within the framework of our Alliance, because even a European defence community - which is still many years away - cannot replace the transatlantic link guaranteed by the Atlantic Alliance. As a result, all ideas and developments related to that European security identity should be coordinated with our Alliance from their inception, so that both institutions reinforce each other. In this context we must preserve NATO's integrated military structure. It is a unique achievement, and ensures that noone will be tempted to renationalize security.

- Second, we must further intensify our growing contacts with the nations of Central and Eastern Europe. The London Summit Declaration sent a powerful message to those nations: that the Cold War and the years of confrontation are over; that the Alliance considers these nations to be friends and potential partners; that it wishes henceforth to work with them to build a new Europe; and that through our diplomatic and military contacts we can build our future security together and according to strategies and doctrines that give maximum reassurance. Certainly the message that the Alliance is changing and will continue to change, which was conveyed in all the overtures we made at the London Summit to the nations of Central and Eastern Europe, has been very well received. For instance this timely message played a key role, just two weeks after the Summit, in persuading the Soviet Union to agree to a united Germany being a full member of the Alliance - perhaps the single most important contribution to stability in Europe. I myself, in visiting the countries of Central and Eastern Europe, have been pleasantly surprised to see how positively our Alliance is now seen, despite years of disinformation and propaganda.

It is this adaptability of our Alliance, reflecting change but also actively shaping that change, which makes me optimistic about the way in which it will fulfil its security mission in the years ahead. The conditions for a new European security structure, that will lastingly guarantee peace by means of a network of cooperative ties, have now been achieved. Provided we proceed sensibly, remain vigilant and use our diplomatic skills to full effect, we can look forward to decades of peaceful evolution in Europe.

Thus our Alliance remains indispensable, regardless of whether the Warsaw Pact is successfully reshaped into a political, democratic alliance or, as seems more likely, disappears from the scene altogether. The role of ensuring stability and a secure defence is one that cannot be transferred from the Atlantic

Alliance to another body. Only NATO will guarantee the presence of the North American democracies in Europe tomorrow, as it has always done in the past. Without this political as well as military presence, Europe could not be certain of stability, at least for the foreseeable future. Finally no other body but the Atlantic Alliance with its military potential can ensure that military force is never again used in Europe. In a nutshell, NATO represents the political co-operation of 16 sovereign democratic nations. If they stick together they can influence the historical process of transformation towards our vision of a Europe whole and free. So politically it is needed.

- Third, we must extend the arms control process in Europe to the point at which defensive postures and transparency make war militarily impossible and politically unthinkable. The signature of a first CFE agreement in Paris in just a few days, although a historic event in the fullest sense of the word, will not by any means represent the culmination of our Alliance efforts to build security and stability through arms control. The immediate consequence of CFE signature will be the initiation of follow-on conventional negotiations, which I expect will focus on manpower issues, and of negotiations on short-range nuclear forces. Linked to these SNF talks will be the proposal we made in London on the elimination of nuclear artillery from Europe. We are also already committed, since London, to longer-term conventional arms negotiations in the 1990s that will go beyond the transitional aim of closing off the vestiges of the Cold War confrontation and will initiate the task of structuring the military configuration of the new era that is opening. And, of course, the START and then START II negotiations and the very important chemical weapons nego-tiations in Geneva are also high on the Alliance's agenda. We are determined to use to the full the more constructive stance we see now from Moscow to secure as much of this agenda as possible.

- Fourth, an important task is without doubt the elaboration of a new military strategy. The London Summit has laid down some guidelines for this exercise, specifically in advocating that the Alliance scale back its military forces, as arms control agreements permit, review its force structures and change its political strategy in line with political change in Europe, especially German unification. We will be seeking over the next few years to move increasingly towards a "reconstitution strategy" based more on multinational units and on the capacity to mobilize sufficient reserves and reinforcements in the event of a potential threat. As part of this review, the Alliance will be looking to rely less on nuclear forces and make the minimal number that will remain in Europe to ensure peace truly weapons of the last resort.

- Fifth, we must, as the US Secretary of State has eloquently suggested, redefine the position of the United States in an undivided Europe so as to form a new transatlantic partnership, "a new Atlanticism". To succeed in this task, the Alliance will also need to provide a framework in which the Western

237

European nations continue to become increasingly aware of their global responsibilities now that their economic strength and political stability make them much more than the fledgling democracies of the immediate post-war period.

- Sixth, we have to cope with the new challenges to our security, as for example the proliferation of missile technology and weapons of mass destruction.

The Alliance is in good shape. Solidarity and cohesion have made it possible for our policies to be successful. And this success has certainly put the wind in our sails. This in turn has further strengthened the unity and resolve of the Alliance. It has successfully passed the test of overcoming the obstacles to the full NATO membership of a united Germany. That too is cause for optimism. At the same time there are bound to be difficulties in our path that we have to avoid or to overcome. But I am certain that we can and will overcome them, as we have always done. Our past success must never lead, however, to complacency and a false sense of self-confidence or indeed a premature and inappropriate feeling of triumphalism. In the future, as much as in the past, determination, leadership quality, courage and perseverance will prove essential if we are to maintain our cohesion and solidarity.

☐

*S*peech before the Hungarian Parliament

Budapest
22 November
1990

Until about eighteen months ago, the visit of the Secretary General of NATO to Hungary as the official guest of your government would have seemed an exercise in futurology. Yet today a new Europe has emerged which makes the once improbable now seem wholly natural; a Europe drawn together by the unfettered aspiration for freedom, democracy and economic prosperity.

Hungary, a nation at the geographical as well as cultural heart of Europe, has played a crucial role in bringing about this historic change. From the outset it was clear that the Hungarian people would never bow to totalitarian rule nor accept permanent isolation from their fellow Europeans. In 1956 your people bravely rose up against oppression, with tragic consequences. In the years that followed, you worked more cautiously but with the same dogged determination to change the system from within. Hungary was always different from other Communist countries, exuding a sense of a Western society itching to break free of a rigid but ultimately fragile corset.

You have not only liberated yourselves but helped decisively to liberate others. The decision of Hungary in the late Summer of 1989 to brave the anger of its Warsaw Pact allies and allow the East Germans to go to the West triggered the collapse of Communist régimes in Central and, later, Eastern Europe. I believe that change was inevitable sooner or later. But Hungary's brave decision accelerated this process and thus made it more peaceful than it might otherwise have been. You have earned the gratitude not only of the German people, but all Europeans.

Therefore it is hardly surprising that Hungary has always been in the vanguard of what is often called "the return to Europe"- the first to establish links with NATO and our parliamentary body the North Atlantic Assembly, the first to approach the European Community with a view to eventual membership and the first of the Central and Eastern European countries to become a full member of the Council of Europe, which happened two weeks ago. Today you are concerned to be part of Europe not only institutionally, but also economically and socially. This will not be easy, as we all know. Reform is not without its social consequences. It will take a combination of sustained reform efforts by you and sustained help from the West before living standards in both halves of Europe are more equal. Together we must make sure that popular enthusiasm and hope for the future are not dented by the inevitable pains and hardships of transition. Certainly your government's dynamism in establishing intensive links with Western nations, and encouraging their industries and enterprises to come to Hungary, bodes well for your ultimate success. Moreover the West's actions thus far demonstrate that you can count on our political support and concrete assistance, whether that be in the group of 24, the European Community or the new European Bank for Reconstruction and Development.

It is, of course, not only in the relations between government and people that the Cold War is over. Also in the relations between nations we see a new spirit of cooperation - a common desire not to be held back by the fears and suspicions that have bedevilled all previous attempts to create a European family of nations. Indeed I would say that never has Europe had such a palpable opportunity to break out of the infernal cycle of peace and war and create a durable order of peace and prosperity. It is the privilege of our generation to have this historically unique opportunity to make a fresh start.

We in the Alliance are determined to seize this opportunity. Certainly, and even with all the changes we see, age-old fears and suspicions, stereotyped images and popular misconceptions, will not be banished overnight. But they can be overcome. The active participation of Hungary in the Pentagonal Initiative, and its interest in building regional stability through a new dialogue with Yugoslavia and other neighbours testify that old divisions can indeed be bridged. We now have a chance to spend our energy, imagination and money on building those democratic, free-market societies that we know are inherently peaceful, and thus our best guarantee of lasting stability, security and prosperity.

I have come to Budapest today with a very simple message. It is a message that is indeed addressed with equal conviction to **all** our former adversaries who are now our partners. We extend the hand of friendship to you. We wish to cooperate with you. The time of confrontation is over. The hostility and mistrust of the past must be buried. We need to work together. Only in this way can we build the Common European Home or the European Confederation or the new European Order, call it what you will. We all know what we mean : a Europe of democracy, human rights and partnership in which the whole sustains the parts and the parts sustain the whole. We must go forward together; or we will be condemned to go backwards separately.

There is a way that leads us beyond confrontation and towards a Europe whole and free :

- through the building of new structures of cooperation, a new European architecture that includes all of us;
- through arms control negotiations to reduce weapons to the minimum, and to increase stability and reassurance;
- through cooperation between us in all fields, political, economic, scientific, cultural.

We need to look afresh at our objectives and tasks. This our Atlantic Alliance has done, and will continue to do. At the London Summit in early July we decided to change our Alliance in the most far-reaching way since its inception forty one years ago. We have no interest in a confrontational system. For NATO has a new, even more valuable role to play as a supporting pillar of a new and peaceful order of cooperation in Europe. In such an order military power will play a lesser role; less dominant, directed at no specific threat or potential enemy and dedicated to the role of reassurance against risks and the prevention of war.

How has NATO changed, you may well ask. Which concrete steps have we taken?

- We are reducing our defence budgets and scaling back our forces;
- we are reviewing our force structures, and changing our military strategy;
- we are reducing the readiness of our active units, reducing training requirements and the number of exercises;
- we are relying less on nuclear forces in Europe and moving to a posture where they will be truly weapons of last resort and the ultimate guarantee of peace; we have proposed to the Soviet Union the elimination from Europe of all nuclear artillery warheads;
- and we have offered to negotiate on short-range nuclear forces in Europe and now that a CFE treaty has been signed, we intend to move ahead in the very near future. Our Alliance's Special Consultative Group has commenced its work with a view to drawing up a mandate for these talks;
- and also, again now that there is agreement on CFE, we intend to proceed immediately to follow-on negotiations to build on that agreement, including measures to limit manpower in Europe.

These changes will be carried out as Soviet forces leave the territories of Czechoslovakia and Hungary, as they have already agreed to do, and also the part of Germany that was formerly the GDR in the transition period up to 1994 that follows German unification. They will also be conditional on the implementation of a CFE treaty which will give all participating states firm guarantees against military aggression or intimidation. Moreover the Atlantic Alliance wishes not only to eliminate tension by reducing weapons, but also by increasing confidence and transparency. Hence our efforts to secure a significant CSBM agreement in time for the Paris Summit last week. The West will continue its efforts between now and the Helsinki Summit in 1992 to achieve even more ambitious CSBMs that will make our military activities fully transparent and restrict the scope for surprise or unusual force deployments. We are still pushing hard for an Open Skies agreement, a domain in which Hungary has also played a leading role. We are proposing further discussions on military strategy and doctrine. Above all we want security to be something that we discuss and decide upon together.

No nation these days can provide for its security alone or in isolation from its neighbours. Nations seeking total security by their own efforts only create insecurity around them. So we must never re-nationalize European security. On the contrary real security can be achieved only through cooperation and sharing.

This does not, of course, mean that NATO or any European nation has to be defenceless. We live in an uncertain world with many risks and instabilities. Indeed the present Gulf crisis has brought this home to us with a vengeance. This crisis is not like previous regional disputes in which the interests of only a few nations were directly at stake; nor is it only, or even primarily about oil. If our principal common objective - which must be the complete Iraqi withdrawal from Kuwait and the release of all hostages - is not fulfilled, the entire international community will be exposed to grave danger. Danger from a new energy crisis with higher oil prices threatening the economic development of many countries, and your own in particular, certainly; but also danger from the precedent of a large, powerful country cynically taking over a smaller neighbour; danger even more ominously from the ambitions that successful aggression will undoubtedly engender in dictatorships that increasingly have access to technologies of mass destruction.

Thus it is of crucial importance not only for Kuwait, and peace in the Middle East, but for our common effort to create a more durable and just international order after the Cold War that the international coalition against Iraq should prevail. We hope very much - and indeed are confident - that the United Nations sanctions against Iraq will work. We in the Alliance are determined to maintain our solidarity, and we will do our utmost to build further on the new-found effectiveness of the United Nations as the guarantor

242

of international law and stability. I salute the robust stance that Hungary has taken on this issue, at great cost to its economic reform programme, and trust that we can continue to work together until we can prove to Iraq - and all potential belligerents - that naked aggression cannot succeed.

Thus in the light of the Gulf crisis, it becomes even clearer to us in the Alliance that we must maintain a secure defence and we expect no less of other nations. NATO will maintain a mix of conventional and nuclear forces in Europe as the ultimate guarantee of peace. Yet our goal is clear : to reduce military forces in Europe to a minimum so that no nation needs to threaten others to feel secure itself. A military posture that gives maximum reassurance is possible. Our Alliance's experience with its integrated defence structure proves this; for could any of you seriously imagine 16 sovereign and democratic states deciding to launch or support an attack? Within our Alliance, the collective approach to defence has enabled old antagonisms, for instance between France and Germany, to be permanently reconciled. So this is an approach that we will seek to promote elsewhere both through the CSCE and an active dialogue between NATO and all countries in Central and Eastern Europe. Thus NATO's integrated military structure, as a proven model of collective defence, can be of indirect benefit to your security.

Our aim is a Europe in which military aggression or threat becomes materially impossible and politically meaningless. At our NATO Summit we moved resolutely ahead to put the structures of such a secure Europe in place.

Firstly in creating a new dialogue with your country and all the other members of the Warsaw Treaty Organisation, whether you decide to remain in that organisation or not. We have invited President Gorbachev to come to Brussels to address the North Atlantic Council - an invitation that I was able to deliver in person in Moscow last July and which he readily accepted. Foreign Minister Jeszenszky came to NATO last June, and Prime Minister Antall was our guest on 18 July last, the first Head of State and Government from this region to be our guest in Brussels. Thus the Hungarian response to our London Declaration has perhaps been the most impressive of all.

We have proposed also the establishment of permanent diplomatic contacts with NATO, to which Hungary has favourably responded. We look also to a multiplication of military as well as diplomatic contacts and exchanges. We have negotiated and agreed a joint declaration on non-aggression between the member states of NATO and of the Warsaw Treaty Organisation.

Secondly in pursuing the arms control process with vigour and deter-mination. If we pushed so hard for a conventional arms control agreement it is because we knew that it would be the key to unlock the syndrome of confrontation among the old adversaries of the two alliances. Thus its achievement is the indispensable first step in building a Europe whole and free. This agreement will lay the basis of cooperation and mutual reassurance that will enable us to create an enduring peace in Europe. It is the secure foundation on which the new European order must be built if it is to last.

The conventional arms control process, coupled with talks on short-range nuclear forces and the agreement on additional confidence building measures, will give all of us in Europe guarantees that change and renewal will not be prejudicial to anyone's legitimate security interests. This is particularly important in the case of the Soviet Union. Understandably that country fears exclusion from the new Europe and is experiencing the impact of change most acutely. So it is essential that we use the arms control process to convince the Soviet Union that it has nothing to fear, but indeed everything to gain from helping a process of change - that it has done so much to initiate - to continue to its natural destination - a Europe whole and free.

Thirdly, and most importantly when we think of the long-term future, there is the CSCE. My visit here takes place one day after the CSCE Summit meeting in Paris. This was a decisive moment in history, producing a number of results which will all be key elements in this future European architecture of peace and cooperation. A CFE treaty, and an initial package of CSBMs, the endorsement of the results of the 2+4 talks on German unity, the Joint Declaration on peaceful relations between the members of NATO and of the Warsaw Treaty Organization; and, finally, all those new perspectives that are subsumed in the term "institutionalization" of the CSCE process : regular high-level consultations among member governments; CSCE review conferences once every two years; a small CSCE secretariat; a CSCE Centre for the Prevention of Conflict; and a parliamentary Assembly of Europe.

Clearly the CSCE Summit has lived up to the ambitious expectations we set for it when we announced these initiatives in our London Summit Declaration last July. We recognized that in the fifteen years since the Helsinki Final Act, CSCE has been a unique success story. Yet it also has scope to do more than only its traditional roles of upholding human rights and enhancing military transparency. For since the Bonn and Copenhagen meetings earlier this year, for the first time in the Helsinki process all CSCE states will proceed from an agreed basis of democratic and market principles. So in our preparations for the Paris Summit, we stressed ways to strengthen the Helsinki principles and give them more operational content : initiatives such as the right to free and fair elections, commitments to uphold the rule of law, guidelines for economic and environmental cooperation, and a role for CSCE in tackling some of the problems involved in the transition to efficient market economies. In applying very early on and successfully to become a member of the Council of Europe, Hungary has demonstrated that it attaches the same importance to these values as we do in our Alliance.

Our Alliance will be supportive of the CSCE process and help it to bring its stabilizing influence to bear on the larger pan-European process. We will be actively encouraging further steps to make that process even more efficient in the future.

Will you, however, permit me to sound on the subject of CSCE just one note of caution? Some see CSCE as a replacement for the existing security organisations, some in the short term, others in the long term. I will not comment on the Warsaw Treaty Organisation for its continuation is clearly dependent on the free choice of its members. Yet NATO will remain an essential supporting pillar of a successful CSCE.

The CSCE can certainly enhance security. But it cannot substitute for the Atlantic Alliance. It does not have the means to take sanctions or ensure their implementation. The interests of each of its members, their social structures and value systems, at least for the foreseeable future, are in all likelihood too diverse to enable them to act collectively to preserve security in the event of crisis. This does not in any way diminish the importance of CSCE as a framework for creating confidence and promoting cooperation. It can, for instance, contribute to the peaceful resolution of disputes between states arising from problems with national minorities. We indeed see already how much instability they can cause in Central and Eastern Europe. In this respect the introduction into law of those commitments on human rights contained in the Helsinki Final Act can be a useful step forward. At the same time, we can and will develop confidence building measures and information exchanges that will enable us to live more harmoniously together. Yet, in the final analysis, CSCE will live up to its promise only if it is complementary to a strong Atlantic Alliance on which it can rely. Consequently, it will be all the more successful to the extent that we do not burden it with unrealistic expectations from the outset.

The existence of a strong and coherent new Atlantic Alliance is in the interest of Hungary as much as of any other European nation. Perhaps there is more explicit recognition of this fact in your country than in many others in Central and Eastern Europe. It provides stablility for change and maintains the transatlantic link with the United States of America and Canada. This is indispensable for peace, and the freedom and security of the whole of Europe.

Yet even such a well-established and resilient institution as NATO cannot shoulder alone the burden of ensuring cooperation, prosperity and peaceful progress across Europe. Fortunately for this purpose we also have the European Community. It is the other essential component in our Western institutional framework and it too is undergoing a process of change and renewal in its striving to achieve an ever closer union of its members. While NATO provides the reassuring credible means of defence through its integrated system and the transatlantic link, the European Community provides dynamism, creativity and the basis of an ever more fruitful economic inter-dependence. Together with an expanded role for the CSCE and an enlarged Council of Europe, both a strong NATO and a strong European Community are the prerequisites for a Europe of progress and prosperity. Indeed a future European defence identity within our Alliance will bind these institutions even more closely together. If you leave any of these institutions out of the architecture, it would be much less stable and efficient. Thus none can succeed without the others. Our future task will be to make these institutions more complementary and interlocking so that although they each have their specific functions, each takes over where the other leaves off.

At a time when the entire international system is being transformed, no government or alliance can fully control the powerful forces that make change inevitable. But by working together we can steer that change and produce an outcome in which there are no losers, only winners. I am vastly more hopeful in this respect now that agreement has been reached on membership of a united Germany in our Alliance. This will increase stability for all. It is the gateway to overcoming division, and to establishing a partnership between Western Europe and the newly democratising nations which will be a key factor in their economic and social modernization.

In short, NATO sees its future role as putting in place new structures of cooperation across Europe that will make it impossible for a situation like the Cold War ever to return. We want to work together with you in helping to manage the two crucial tasks in Europe today :

- to promote constructive change;
- to provide stability so that change can take place in optimal conditions, with diminished risk of setbacks and reversals.

Here in Budapest I hardly need to emphasize the benefits that cooperation between us will bring. The 21st century will bring new challenges, some of which could threaten our survival even more than nearly half a century of Cold War. You too are aware as we are of the destabilizing potential of such things as drugs, hunger, population growth and the proliferation of immensely destructive military technologies in the Third World. Thus a dynamic Europe of advanced industrial economies and technological inter-dependence is not only essential for our material prosperity, but also for our security and stability at home and abroad. Without such cohesion Europe could well be the victim of these global challenges; together we can help to solve them.

Although Hungary looks West, Budapest has always been for us Westeners the gateway to Eastern Europe. My visit today symbolizes a new era; but it is also a concrete invitation : to work together using our combined resources and ingenuity to create a new world, a world of cooperation where none of us feel threatened. We cannot escape the responsibility that this unique opportunity brings. Hungary which has contributed so much to our European political and intellectual culture, is a key partner in the building of a new Europe and a more just and equal world order. Let us therefore make today the start of that new relationship and work for that brighter future with trust and imagination.

□

Discours au Parlement Hongrois

Budapest
22 novembre
1990

Il y a encore dix-huit mois environ, la visite du Secrétaire général de l'OTAN à Budapest en qualité d'invité officiel du gouvernement hongrois eût semblé relever de la futurologie. Pourtant, nous assistons aujourd'hui à l'émergence d'une Europe nouvelle, dans laquelle ce qui était naguère improbable paraît maintenant tout à fait naturel; cette Europe est réunie par une aspiration, sans entrave, à la liberté, à la démocratie et à la prospérité économique.

Située au coeur à la fois géographique et culturel de l'Europe, la Hongrie a joué un rôle crucial dans la réalisation de ce changement historique. Dès le début, il était clair que le peuple hongrois n'allait jamais s'incliner devant la loi du totalitarisme, ni accepter d'être isolé en permanence des autres Européens. En 1956, votre peuple s'est révolté avec bravoure contre l'oppression, et cette révolte a eu des conséquences tragiques. Dans les années qui ont suivi, vous vous êtes employés, plus prudemment, mais avec la même opiniâtreté, à changer le système de l'intérieur. La Hongrie a toujours été différente des autres pays communistes, car elle laissait transparaître l'image d'une société occidentale impatiente de se délivrer d'un corset rigide, mais finalement fragile.

Non seulement vous vous êtes libérés, mais vous avez apporté une contribution déterminante à la libération d'autres peuples. La décision de la Hongrie, vers la fin de l'été 1989, de braver la colère de ses alliés du Pacte de Varsovie en permettant aux Allemands de l'Est de rejoindre l'Occident a déclenché l'effondrement des régimes communistes en Europe centrale, puis en Europe orientale. Je suis persuadé que ce changement se serait inévitablement produit, tôt ou tard, mais la courageuse décision de la Hongrie a accéléré ce processus et l'a ainsi rendu plus pacifique qu'il n'aurait pu l'être dans d'autres conditions. Vous avez donc mérité la gratitude, non seulement du peuple allemand, mais de tous les Européens.

Il n'est, dès lors, guère étonnant que la Hongrie ait toujours été à l'avant-garde de ce que l'on appelle souvent "le retour à l'Europe". Elle a été le premier des pays d'Europe centrale et orientale à établir des liens avec l'OTAN et son organe parlementaire, l'Assemblée de l'Atlantique Nord, à entreprendre une démarche auprès de la Communauté européenne en vue d'y adhérer finalement, et à devenir membre à part entière du Conseil de l'Europe, ce qu'elle a fait il y a deux semaines. Vous avez aujourd'hui le souci d'appartenir à l'Europe, non seulement sur le plan des institutions, mais aussi dans les domaines économique et social. Nous savons tous que cela ne sera pas facile. La réforme ne va pas sans conséquences d'ordre social. Le rapprochement des niveaux de vie des deux moitiés de l'Europe exigera que les efforts soutenus que vous déploierez sur la voie de la réforme soient accompagnés d'une aide soutenue des pays occidentaux. Il nous faut veiller ensemble à ce que l'enthousiasme populaire et les espoirs mis dans l'avenir ne soient pas entamés par les dures épreuves que la transition implique inévitablement. Il est certain que le dynamisme qu'a montré votre gouvernement en établissant des liens intensifs avec les pays occidentaux, et en encourageant leurs industries et leurs entreprises à venir en Hongrie, est de bon augure pour votre succès final. Par ailleurs, les actions que l'Ouest a menées jusqu'ici montrent que vous pouvez compter sur notre soutien politique et sur une aide concrète de notre part, que ce soit au Groupe des 24, à la Communauté européenne ou à la nouvelle Banque européenne pour la reconstruction et le développement.

Ce n'est pas, bien entendu, seulement dans les relations entre le gouvernement et le peuple que la Guerre froide est terminée. Nous voyons aussi dans les rapports entre nations un nouvel esprit de coopération, un désir commun de ne pas être prisonnier des craintes et des suspicions auxquelles se sont heurtées toutes les précédentes tentatives de création d'une famille de nations européenne. Je dirais même que l'Europe n'a jamais eu une occasion aussi tangible de sortir du cycle infernal de la paix et de la guerre et de créer un ordre durable de paix et de prospérité. Notre génération a le privilège de voir s'offrir à elle cette occasion, unique dans l'Histoire, de prendre un nouveau départ.

Nous, les membres de l'Alliance, sommes résolus à saisir cette occasion. Certes, et même avec tous les changements auxquels nous assistons, les craintes et les suspicions du fond des âges, les images stéréotypées et les idées fausses ancrées dans la mémoire populaire ne vont pas disparaître du jour au lendemain. Il est cependant possible d'en triompher. La participation active de la Hongrie à l'Initiative pentagonale et l'intérêt qu'elle montre pour la réalisation d'une stabilité régionale par un nouveau dialogue avec la Yougoslavie et d'autres pays voisins attestent qu'il est bel et bien possible de jeter des ponts surmontant les vieilles divisions. Nous avons à présent une chance de consacrer notre énergie, notre imagination et nos ressources financières à l'édification de ces sociétés démocratiques à économie de marché qui, nous le savons, sont pacifiques par nature, et nous offrent ainsi la meilleure garantie d'une stabilité, d'une sécurité et d'une prospérité durables.

Je suis venu à Budapest aujourd'hui porteur d'un message très simple. Il s'agit d'un message que nous adressons en fait avec une égale conviction à **tous** nos anciens adversaires, qui sont désormais nos partenaires. Nous vous offrons notre amitié. Nous souhaitons coopérer avec vous. Le temps de la confrontation est révolu. Il faut enterrer l'hostilité et la méfiance du passé. Nous devons travailler ensemble. C'est de cette façon seulement que nous pourrons édifier la Maison commune européenne, ou la Confédération européenne, ou le Nouvel ordre européen - peu importe le nom qu'on lui donne. Nous savons tous ce que nous entendons par là : une Europe de la démocratie, des droits de l'homme et du partenariat, dans laquelle le tout renforce les parties et les parties renforcent le tout. Nous devons avancer ensemble; sinon, nous serons condamnés à reculer séparément.

Il existe une voie qui nous conduit, au-delà de la confrontation, vers une Europe entière et libre :

- par l'édification de nouvelles structures de coopération, d'une nouvelle architecture européenne qui englobe chacun de nous;
- par des négociations sur la maîtrise des armements en vue de réduire au maximum nos arsenaux et d'accroître la stabilité et la confiance mutuelle;
- par une coopération entre nous dans tous les domaines - politique, économique, scientifique, culturel.

Nous devons considérer d'un oeil nouveau nos objectifs et nos tâches. C'est ce que notre Alliance atlantique a fait, et continuera de faire. Lors du Sommet que nous avons tenu à Londres au début du mois de juillet, nous avons décidé de modifier notre Alliance de la façon la plus profonde depuis sa création, il y a quarante et un ans. Un système de confrontation n'offre pour nous aucun intérêt. Car l'OTAN a un rôle nouveau, encore plus important, à jouer : celui de pilier d'un ordre de coopération européen nouveau et pacifique. Dans le cadre d'un tel ordre, la puissance militaire jouera un rôle moindre; elle sera moins prépondérante, ne sera dirigée contre aucune menace ni aucun ennemi potentiel en particulier et aura pour vocation de fournir des assurances contre les risques et de prévenir la guerre.

Comment l'OTAN a-t-elle changé, me demanderez-vous? Quelles mesures concrètes avons-nous prises?

- Nous réduisons nos budgets de la défense et le niveau de nos forces;
- nous réexaminons nos structures de forces et modifions notre stratégie militaire;
- nous abaissons le niveau de préparation de nos unités d'active, en réduisant les normes d'entraînement et le nombre des exercices;
- nous tablons moins sur les forces nucléaires en Europe, et nous nous orientons vers un dispositif où celles-ci seront véritablement des armes de dernier recours et la garantie ultime de la paix; nous avons proposé à l'Union soviétique l'élimination de toutes les ogives d'artillerie nucléaire présentes sur ce continent;
- nous avons aussi offert de négocier sur les forces nucléaires à courte portée en Europe et, maintenant qu'un traité sur les FCE a été signé, nous avons l'intention d'aller de l'avant dans un avenir très proche; le Groupe consultatif spécial de notre Alliance a commencé ses travaux pour élaborer un mandat en vue de ces pourparlers;
- par ailleurs et, encore une fois, maintenant qu'un accord sur les FCE a été conclu, nous avons l'intention de passer immédiatement à de nouvelles négociations dans le prolongement de cet accord, notamment sur des mesures de limitation des effectifs en Europe.

Ces changements interviendront à mesure que les forces soviétiques quitteront le territoire de la Tchécoslovaquie et de la Hongrie, comme l'URSS l'a déjà accepté, ainsi que le territoire de la partie de l'Allemagne qui constituait l'ancienne RDA, au cours de la période de transition allant jusqu'en 1994 qui suit l'unification allemande. Ces changements dépendront également de la mise en oeuvre d'un traité sur les FCE qui offrira à tous les Etats participants de solides garanties contre l'agression et l'intimidation militaires. En outre, l'Alliance atlantique n'entend pas éliminer les tensions par la seule réduction des armements : elle veut aussi, pour cela, accroître la confiance et la transparence. D'où nos efforts pour obtenir un accord significatif sur des MDCS à temps pour le Sommet de Paris la semaine dernière. L'Ouest poursuivra ses efforts, d'ici au Sommet d'Helsinki en 1992, pour faire adopter des MDCS encore plus ambitieuses qui rendront nos activités militaires entièrement transparentes et réduiront les possibilités de surprise ou de déploiements de forces inhabituels. Nous continuons de tout mettre en oeuvre pour obtenir la conclusion d'un accord sur le régime du "Ciel ouvert", domaine dans lequel la Hongrie a aussi joué un rôle de pointe. Nous proposons l'ouverture de nouvelles discussions sur la stratégie et la doctrine militaires. Nous souhaitons avant toute chose que la sécurité soit débattue et définie en commun.

Aucun pays ne peut aujourd'hui assurer sa sécurité à lui seul ou en s'isolant de ses voisins. Les pays qui recherchent une sécurité absolue par leurs propres moyens ne font que créer l'insécurité autour d'eux. Nous ne devons donc jamais ramener la sécurité européenne au niveau purement national. La véritable sécurité ne peut, au contraire, s'obtenir que par la coopération et le partage.

Il ne faut pas en déduire, évidemment, que l'OTAN ou un pays européen quelconque doivent rester sans défense. Nous vivons, en effet, dans un monde fait d'incertitudes, qui comporte de nombreux risques et facteurs d'instabilité. L'actuelle crise du Golfe nous le rappelle on ne peut plus clairement. Elle ne s'apparente pas aux précédents conflits régionaux où seuls les intérêts de quelques pays étaient directement en cause; il ne s'agit pas davantage d'une crise dont le pétrole est l'enjeu exclusif ni même essentiel. Si notre principal objectif commun - qui doit nécessairement être le retrait complet des forces irakiennes du Koweït et la libération de tous les otages - n'est pas atteint, c'est l'ensemble de la communauté internationale qui se trouvera exposé à un grave danger. Danger d'une nouvelle crise de l'énergie, où le renchérissement des produits pétroliers menacera le développement économique de nombreux pays, et le vôtre en particulier, certainement; mais aussi danger du précédent créé par un pays, grand et puissant, qui annexe avec cynisme un pays voisin plus petit; danger, plus inquiétant encore, d'une agression victorieuse qui ne manquera pas de nourrir les ambitions de dictatures qui ont de plus en plus accès aux technologies de destruction massive.

Il est donc crucial, non seulement pour le Koweït, et pour la paix au Moyen-Orient, mais aussi pour notre action commune qui vise à instaurer un ordre international plus durable et plus juste au lendemain de la Guerre froide, que la coalition internationale contre l'Irak l'emporte. Nous espérons vivement - nous l'escomptons même avec confiance - que les sanctions imposées par les Nations Unies à l'encontre de l'Irak seront suivies d'effets. Tous les pays de l'Alliance sont déterminés à préserver leur solidarité, et nous mettrons tout en oeuvre pour unir toujours plus nos efforts à ceux de l'Organisation des Nations Unies, qui a retrouvé son efficacité comme garant du droit international et de la stabilité à l'échelle mondiale. Je salue la ferme attitude que la Hongrie a adoptée face à la crise, quoi qu'il en coûte à son programme de réforme économique, et je ne doute pas que nous pourrons continuer d'oeuvrer ensemble pour prouver à l'Irak - et à tous les autres belligérants potentiels - que l'agression brutale est vouée à l'échec.

Ainsi, à la lumière de la crise du Golfe, il nous apparaît encore plus clairement que notre Alliance doit maintenir une défense solide, et nous n'en attendons pas moins des autres pays. L'OTAN conservera en Europe une combinaison de forces conventionnelles et nucléaires qui sera l'ultime garant de la paix. Notre but est cependant clair : nous voulons réduire les forces armées en Europe à un niveau minimum, de telle sorte qu'aucun pays ne doive plus en menacer d'autres pour se sentir en sécurité. Il est possible d'arriver à un dispositif militaire qui offre les meilleures assurances de sécurité mutuelle.

Notre Alliance en a d'ailleurs fait l'expérience positive avec sa structure de défense intégrée; qui, parmi vous, pourrait sérieusement imaginer que seize Etats souverains et démocratiques décident un jour de lancer une attaque ou de la soutenir? A l'intérieur de notre Alliance, l'approche collective de la défense a permis d'effacer définitivement de vieux antagonismes, par exemple entre la France et l'Allemagne. C'est donc une approche que nous chercherons à promouvoir ailleurs, à la fois par les mécanismes de la CSCE et par un dialogue actif entre l'OTAN et tous les pays d'Europe centrale et orientale. Constituant ainsi un modèle de défense collective qui a fait ses preuves, la structure militaire intégrée de l'OTAN peut donc être pour vous, indirectement, un facteur de sécurité.

Notre objectif est une Europe dans laquelle l'agression ou la menace militaires deviendront matériellement impossibles et politiquement dénuées de sens. A la réunion au sommet de l'OTAN, nous sommes allés résolument de l'avant pour mettre en place les structures propres à garantir cette sécurité de l'Europe.

D'abord, nous voulons instaurer un nouveau dialogue avec votre pays et tous les autres membres de l'Organisation du Traité de Varsovie, que vous décidiez de rester ou non dans cette organisation. Nous avons invité le président Gorbatchev à prendre la parole devant le Conseil de l'Atlantique Nord, à Bruxelles; j'ai eu le plaisir de lui transmettre personnellement cette invitation à Moscou, au mois de juillet, et il l'a volontiers acceptée. Monsieur le ministre des affaires étrangères Jeszenszky s'est rendu à l'OTAN en juin dernier, où nous avons également reçu le 18 juillet Monsieur Antall, premier chef d'Etat et de gouvernement d'un pays de cette région à être notre hôte à Bruxelles. La promptitude de cette réponse de la Hongrie aux initiatives lancées dans notre Déclaration de Londres n'a pas manqué de nous impressionner.

Nous avons en outre proposé l'établissement de contacts diplomatiques permanents avec l'OTAN, proposition à laquelle la Hongrie a répondu tout aussi favorablement. Nous comptons également multiplier les contacts et les échanges militaires aussi bien que diplomatiques. Nous avons négocié et adopté une déclaration commune de non-agression par les pays membres de l'Alliance atlantique et ceux de l'Organisation du Traité de Varsovie.

Ensuite, nous poursuivons le processus de maîtrise des armements avec vigueur et détermination. Si nous avons tant poussé à la conclusion d'un accord sur la maîtrise des armements conventionnels, c'est parce que nous savions qu'il permettrait aux anciens adversaires des deux alliances de se débarrasser du syndrome de la confrontation. L'aboutissement de notre effort constitue donc la première étape indispensable vers l'édification d'une Europe entière et libre. Cet accord jettera les bases de la coopération et de la confiance mutuelle grâce auxquelles nous pourrons construire une paix durable en Europe. Il sera le fondement solide sur lequel devra nécessairement reposer le nouvel ordre européen si l'on veut en assurer la pérennité.

Le processus de maîtrise des armements conventionnels, combiné avec des pourparlers sur les forces nucléaires à courte portée et avec un accord sur des mesures de confiance supplémentaires, donnera à tous les pays européens la garantie que le changement et le renouveau ne porteront atteinte aux intérêts légitimes de personne en matière de sécurité. Ceci est particulièrement important dans le cas de l'Union soviétique. On peut comprendre que ce pays craigne de se voir exclu de l'Europe nouvelle, et il subit les effets du changement d'une manière particulièrement aiguë. Il est donc essentiel que nous nous servions du processus de maîtrise des armements pour convaincre l'Union soviétique qu'elle n'a rien à craindre, mais au contraire tout à gagner d'un processus de changement dont elle est d'ailleurs l'un des principaux initiateurs et qu'elle peut aider à conduire vers sa destination naturelle : une Europe entière et libre.

Enfin et surtout, lorsque nous envisageons le long terme, la CSCE s'impose à notre esprit. Ma visite à Budapest a lieu le lendemain même de la réunion au sommet de la CSCE, à Paris. Cette réunion a marqué un instant décisif de l'histoire de notre continent. Ses résultats seront autant d'éléments clés dans cette architecture européenne future de paix et de coopération : signature d'un traité sur les forces conventionnelles en Europe, adoption d'un premier ensemble de mesures de confiance et de sécurité, prise en compte des résultats des pourparlers "2+4" sur l'unité allemande, déclaration commune sur les relations pacifiques entre les membres de l'OTAN et ceux de l'Organisation du Traité de Varsovie, et aussi ouverture de diverses perspectives nouvelles que recouvre le terme "institutionnalisation" du processus de la CSCE, avec, en l'espèce, des consultations régulières de haut niveau entre les gouvernements des Etats membres, des conférences-bilans de la CSCE tous les deux ans, un secrétariat léger, un centre pour la prévention des conflits et une assemblée parlementaire de l'Europe.

De toute évidence, le sommet de la CSCE a bien répondu aux aspirations ambitieuses que nous formions à son sujet en annonçant ces différentes initiatives dans notre Déclaration de Londres, au mois de juillet dernier. Nous avons reconnu que, pour la CSCE, le bilan des quinze années écoulées depuis la publication de l'Acte final d'Helsinki avait été exceptionnellement positif. Mais on peut aussi en attendre plus que le simple accomplissement de son rôle traditionnel de gage du respect des droits de l'homme et de l'accroissement de la transparence militaire. En effet, depuis les réunions de Bonn et de Copenhague qui se sont déjà tenues cette année, tous les Etats participant au processus de la CSCE vont pour la première fois pouvoir partir d'une même base convenue de valeurs démocratiques et de règles du marché. C'est pourquoi, en préparant le sommet de Paris, nous avons mis l'accent sur les moyens de renforcer les principes d'Helsinki et de leur donner un contenu plus concret, avec par exemple la reconnaissance du droit à des élections libres et loyales, l'engagement de maintenir la primauté du droit, des directives pour la coopération dans les domaines de l'économie et de l'environnement et l'attribution à la CSCE d'un rôle dans la recherche de solutions à certains des problèmes que pose le passage à des économies de marché performantes. En demandant très tôt son adhésion au Conseil de l'Europe, point sur lequel elle a obtenu satisfaction, la Hongrie a démontré qu'elle attache la même importance que les membres de notre Alliance à ces valeurs.

Notre Alliance s'emploiera à favoriser le bon déroulement du processus de la CSCE et l'aidera à exercer une influence stabilisatrice sur le processus paneuropéen dans son ensemble. Nous encouragerons activement l'adoption d'autres mesures destinées à rendre ce processus encore plus efficace à l'avenir.

Je voudrais cependant, si vous me le permettez, faire une mise en garde s'agissant de la CSCE. Certains considèrent en effet que la CSCE est appelée à se substituer aux organisations de sécurité existantes, à brève échéance pour les uns, à longue échéance pour les autres. Je m'abstiendrai de parler de l'Organisation du Traité de Varsovie, dont le maintien dépend naturellement du libre choix de ses membres. Mais je tiens à souligner que l'OTAN, pour ce qui la concerne demeurera un pilier essentiel sur lequel la CSCE devra fonder sa réussite.

La CSCE peut certainement accroître la sécurité. Mais elle ne saurait remplacer l'Alliance atlantique. Elle n'a pas les moyens de prendre des sanctions, ni d'en assurer l'application. Les intérêts de chacun de ses membres, leurs structures sociales et leurs systèmes de valeurs resteront, du moins dans l'avenir prévisible, trop divers pour qu'ils puissent, selon toute probabilité, agir collectivement afin de préserver la sécurité en cas de crise. Cela ne diminue en rien l'importance de la CSCE comme cadre de l'instauration de la confiance et de la promotion de la coopération. Elle peut, par exemple, contribuer au règlement pacifique de différends surgissant entre Etats à la suite de problèmes concernant des minorités nationales. De fait, nous voyons déjà à quel point ceux-ci peuvent engendrer l'instabilité en Europe centrale et orientale. A cet égard, l'introduction dans les textes de loi des engagements sur les droits de l'homme contenus dans l'Acte final d'Helsinki peut marquer un réel progrès. Dans le même temps, nous allons, car nous le pouvons, élaborer des mesures de confiance et développer des échanges d'informations qui nous permettront de vivre ensemble dans une plus grande harmonie. Mais, en dernière analyse, la CSCE ne tiendra ses promesses que si elle est complémentaire d'une Alliance atlantique forte, sur laquelle elle puisse se reposer. Elle aura, par conséquent, des chances de succès d'autant plus grandes si nous n'y mettons pas, dès le départ, des espoirs irréalistes.

L'existence d'une nouvelle Alliance atlantique forte et cohérente est de l'intérêt de la Hongrie tout autant que de n'importe quel autre pays européen, et ce fait est peut-être plus explicitement reconnu dans votre pays que dans beaucoup d'autres pays d'Europe centrale et orientale. Elle permet le changement dans la stabilité et maintient le lien transatlantique avec les Etats-Unis d'Amérique et le Canada, ce qui est indispensable à la paix, comme à la liberté et à la sécurité de l'ensemble de l'Europe.

Cependant, même une institution aussi solidement établie et aussi capable d'adaptation que l'OTAN ne peut supporter à elle seule la charge d'assurer la coopération, la prospérité et le progrès pacifique dans toute l'Europe. Heureusement, il y a encore, pour cela, la Communauté européenne. C'est l'autre composante essentielle de notre cadre institutionnel occidental, et elle connaît, elle aussi, un processus de changement et de renouveau dans l'action qu'elle mène pour parvenir à une union toujours plus étroite entre ses membres. Si l'OTAN fournit le moyen de défense crédible et rassurant que représente son système intégré et préserve le lien transatlantique, la Communauté européenne apporte le dynamisme, la créativité et la base d'une interdépendance économique toujours plus fructueuse. Avec une CSCE dotée d'un rôle accru et un Conseil de l'Europe à la participation élargie, une Alliance atlantique forte et une Communauté européenne forte sont les conditions préalables pour une Europe de progrès et de prospérité. Et l'émergence future d'une identité européenne en matière de défense dans le cadre de notre Alliance liera plus étroitement encore ces institutions entre elles. Si l'une quelconque de celles-ci n'était pas intégrée à l'architecture globale, elle perdrait beaucoup de sa stabilité et de son efficacité. En conséquence, aucune ne peut réussir sans les autres. Il nous faudra à l'avenir rendre ces institutions plus complémentaires et plus largement imbriquées, de façon que, même si elles ont chacune leurs fonctions spécifiques, elles puissent toutes prolonger l'action des autres.

A un moment où se transforme l'ensemble du système international, aucun gouvernement, aucune alliance ne peut parfaitement maîtriser les puissantes forces qui rendent le changement inévitable. Mais, en oeuvrant ensemble, nous pouvons orienter ce changement de manière que, à son terme, il n'y ait pas de perdants, et que tous gagnent. Je suis infiniment plus optimiste à cet égard maintenant qu'il y a accord sur l'appartenance d'une Allemagne unie à notre Alliance. Cette solution est de nature à accroître la stabilité pour tous. Elle ouvre la voie à l'élimination de la division et à l'établissement d'un partenariat entre l'Europe occidentale et les pays ayant récemment engagé un processus de démocratisation, partenariat qui sera un facteur clé dans la modernisation économique et sociale de ces pays.

En bref, l'OTAN voit son rôle futur comme la mise en place, dans toute l'Europe, de nouvelles structures de coopération qui rendront à jamais impossible le retour à une situation semblable à celle de la Guerre froide. Nous voulons

travailler avec vous à la gestion des deux tâches cruciales qui s'imposent à l'Europe d'aujourd'hui :
- promouvoir un changement constructif;
- assurer la stabilité pour que ce changement puisse se dérouler dans des conditions optimales, avec un moindre risque de retours en arrière et de revirements.

Il n'est guère besoin que je souligne ici, à Budapest, les bénéfices qu'apportera la coopération entre nous. Le 21ème siècle nous placera devant de nouveaux défis, dont certains pourraient menacer notre survie encore plus gravement que ne l'avait fait près d'un demi-siècle de Guerre froide. Vous savez comme nous l'effet de déstabilisation que peuvent avoir des phénomènes tels que la toxicomanie, la famine, l'accroissement de la démographie et la prolifération de technologies militaires potentiellement dévastatrices dans le Tiers-monde. Ainsi, une Europe dynamique, composée de pays industriellement avancés et technologiquement interdépendants, est essentielle non seulement pour notre prospérité matérielle, mais aussi pour notre sécurité et pour la stabilité dans nos propres pays et à l'extérieur. Sans une telle cohésion, l'Europe pourrait bien être la victime de ces problèmes planétaires; ensemble, nous pourrons contribuer à les résoudre.

Bien que la Hongrie regarde vers l'Ouest, Budapest a toujours été pour nous, Occidentaux, la porte de l'Europe de l'Est. La visite que je fais aujourd'hui symbolise une ère nouvelle; mais elle représente aussi une invitation concrète à mettre en commun nos ressources et notre ingéniosité pour bâtir un monde nouveau, un monde de coopération où aucun d'entre nous ne se sente menacé. Nous ne pouvons nous dérober à la responsabilité que cette occasion unique nous impose. La Hongrie, qui a tant apporté à notre culture politique et intellectuelle européenne, est un partenaire clé dans l'édification d'une Europe nouvelle et d'un ordre mondial marqué par plus de justice et plus d'égalité. Faisons donc d'aujourd'hui le début de cette nouvelle relation entre nous, et employons-nous à préparer cet avenir meilleur avec confiance et imagination.

*A*ddress given at the 36th Annual Session of the North Atlantic Assembly

London
29 November
1990

When we last met in Rome, the Berlin Wall had not yet fallen, German unification was a hopeful but still distant prospect, the Soviet Union did not seem likely to withdraw soon from its strategic position in the heart of Europe and a CFE agreement was still the subject of some very hard bargaining. So, my focus then was on how the Alliance could bring about these essential first objectives in achieving its ultimate aim : a Europe whole and free, prosperous and secure. Now they have all been realised, more rapidly and smoothly than we would have dared to dream. At our London Summit, NATO drew the consequences from these seismic changes. Our transformed Alliance ushered in a new era of cooperation supported by concrete actions. The hand of friendship we extended to all the nations of Central and Eastern Europe has been accepted. Europe is rapidly recovering not only its political but also its strategic unity. Now everybody is asking : What next? What is the new agenda? How conceptually does the Atlantic Alliance fit into a new architecture which does not need to address a single, collective and overwhelming threat?

Three views are often put forward in the debate regarding NATO's future.

A first view sees the Alliance as the victim of its own success. It has realised a long-standing dream of creating a Europe in which politico-military alliances such as NATO would no longer be necessary. Most people do not of course go so far as to argue that security is no longer a basic need, but they believe it is now easier and cheaper to obtain; or no longer needs a military component, so that it can be handled just as well by a body such as CSCE which lacks a common defence structure.

259

A second view sees our Alliance losing its political importance, becoming more a technical organization that would manage the integrated defence structure and oversee the implementation and verification of arms control agreements. In this view, NATO should stick to what it knows and does best : fostering military cooperation among its 16 members. High politics - the nurturing of transatlantic relations, the coordination of Western policies towards Central and Eastern Europe and the Soviet Union, the building of a new European architecture and the response to the new global challenges are seen to move either to the CSCE or to the emerging bilateral EC/US relationship, or to a mixture of both. Holders of this view often believe that a stronger European political and defence union is incompatible with a strong Atlantic Alliance. Thus, in order to survive, NATO should adopt a low profile and emphasize its military dimension.

The third view is that our Alliance is playing and should play not only a military but also a more important political role. It should adapt to changing circumstances and deal with new challenges to the security of Alliance member countries.

Who is right? The protagonists of a minimal role for NATO or the protagonists of an enhanced role, directed to the management of change and the maintenance of stability? To answer this question we have to examine two things. Firstly, what are the security tasks that remain now that the Cold War is over? And then, secondly, who can best deal with these tasks? Is it NATO or can others do it better?

We have now to come to terms with a transformed European landscape of security in which the direct threat by a massive Soviet aggression has disappeared and the staving off of an imminent threat has become less urgent. With day to day peace keeping no longer our overriding preoccupation, we have an opportunity to lay the foundations of a more secure, durable and constructive peace. The political conditions for success are clear: we must maintain and develop the partnership between the European and North American democracies, we must help the nations of Central and Eastern Europe to build solid democracies and viable market economies, we must tie the Soviet Union to Europe through new structures of cooperation, and we must put in place a new security system that gives all states firm guarantees against aggression. A new European architecture that does not manage all four tasks simultaneously, or some less well than others, will not serve our interests.

A more peaceful world means a more prosperous and interdependent global economy with our societies pursuing a creative economic competition instead of a sterile military confrontation. But a more interdependent world is also a more fragile one, more vulnerable to threats and blackmail. The Gulf crisis underscores that the West is almost as vulnerable to a prolonged oil crisis today as to a military threat in Europe yesterday; and the Central and Eastern European countries are in an even more precarious position. So clearly we need a security policy to enjoy the fruits of interdependence without the dangers. Without the assurance of security no-one will make the investments or the forward planning on which our continuing prosperity depends.

Then clearly the passing of Cold War confrontation has not eliminated uncertainty. Where is the Soviet Union going? We are less sure today than ever. Despite our active support for the twin process of democratization and market reforms in Central and Eastern Europe, we cannot tell if these reforms will be successful. We must recognize the enormous burdens that transformation will place on these countries. Domestic instability and a new division of Europe along wealth lines could reopen nationalist options and foment ethnic strife to an explosive degree. Already the spectre of massive migratory flows of people away from these areas of tension and towards the West has been raised. It will take a very long time and a combination of sustained reform efforts by these countries and sustained help from the West before living standards in both halves of Europe are more equal. Together we must make sure that popular enthusiasm and hope for the future are not dented by the inevitable pains and hardships of transition.

Equally we cannot afford just yet to write off Soviet military power. Whatever happens tomorrow to the Soviet Union, it will remain militarily the most powerful European nation. Who is going to balance it, for we know that power cannot be contained only through diplomatic, economic or even institutional ties? Reductions there have been, but also significant modernizations, particularly in the nuclear field. Defence production is down but still at a level that exceeds reasonable Soviet defence requirements and far ahead of anything that NATO nations, individually or collectively, are doing. I do not doubt Gorbachev's peaceful intentions. Indeed we no longer base our planning on worst case scenarios for we are convinced that long term Soviet interests lie in stability, cooperation and peaceful interaction with our Alliance countries. We trust the present leadership of the Soviet Union and are assisting them on their way towards reform. But that does not mean that there may not be setbacks and reversals along the way. So our relationship with the Soviet Union is bound to preserve for the foreseeable future a dual character. Our offer is sincere: we want the Soviet Union to become a partner and even a friend in organizing security and protection together. But the Soviet Union will take a long time to find a new, stable shape and its immense strategic mass will need to be balanced. In the meantime, the residual security risk from Soviet military power will keep alive the need for insurance and a certain vigilance.

Finally we are now more aware of the importance of challenges from outside our Alliance's territory. Risks can arise from new and unexpected quarters. Moreover, the trend toward disarmament and reduced military spending in the industrialized world magnifies the significance of Third World arsenals that also now include ballistic missiles and technologies of mass destruction, and gives smaller states a new, undesirable leverage. So we in the West cannot renounce a coherent defence. Along the southern perimeter of Europe there is to some extent an arc of tension from the Maghreb to the Middle East. Tensions are exacerbated not only by the ambitions of dictators like Saddam Hussein, but also by population growth, resource conflicts, migration, underdevelopment, religious fundamentalism and terrorism. Clearly threats to NATO's territorial integrity from beyond Europe cannot be downplayed as out-of-area threats. Turkey is directly threatened, and our Southern Region is an area where the collective interests of all Allies are engaged.

So security remains important because there are still risks and instabilities - some of which are already emerging, others still latent but ominous. Increasingly our Alliance must factor these risks into its defence planning. Nor can we afford to sit back and wait for these risks and instabilities to develop into direct threats that could trigger military conflicts. Most of these risks cannot be managed by national defence policies only. They require a collective response and a renewed focus on long-term crisis prevention.

Yet there is another reason why we need a collective approach to security. One of NATO's unique historical achievements has been the integrated defence structure. It has given our Alliance nations a security they could never have achieved alone. And it has provided a deterrence in excess of the forces actually allotted to it in peacetime. Without the underpinning of an effective and integrated security structure, the security guarantees of the Alliance would sooner or later be seen to be illusory. An obvious principle of a future European architecture must therefore be to maintain collective defence where it exists, which means maintaining NATO's integrated defence structure, albeit with reduced forces and a different military strategy. This is not simply because that structure maintains the nuts and bolts of a functioning defence capability. Nations that merge their defence signal their wish to act together in a common unity of purpose.

The alternative would be to renationalize security. Europe would run the risk of returning to the shifting alliances, rivalries and power politics of the past. Certainly there would be no question of the North American democracies providing a security force if Europe were to return to a pre-1914 situation.

If the integrated defence structure were allowed to dissolve, how could we recreate it later when we needed it? Only painfully, if at all. Moreover we would have needlessly sacrificed the capacity of that integrated defence structure to prevent conflicts and not only respond to them. So the collective approach to security is not only the most cost-effective; it is also the safest and the fairest - the only way to share the roles, risks and responsibilities of our Alliance equitably. In an age when we cannot precisely quantify future risks, NATO's collective security is by far the most sensible insurance policy against every kind of uncertainty.

Can other institutions handle this new concept of security just as well as NATO or even better? Can, for instance, a European defence identity arising from European political integration, or a collective, pan-European security system like the CSCE process in institutionalised form replace NATO? Both these developments are in the interest of NATO but both of them are far from being able to offer solid security guarantees. They are not alternatives to the Atlantic Alliance.

A European political and security identity is a long-standing goal of our Alliance. With the current dynamism of the European Community we are obviously closer today to the twin-pillar Alliance that President Kennedy envisaged in the early sixties. Security cooperation among the Twelve of the European Community is now firmly back on the agenda. There are specific proposals as to how Europe should organize a common security policy. I repeat this is natural and desirable.

Yet a European security and defence identity must be organized within the framework of our Alliance. It would be neither realistic nor sensible to develop a completely independent European defence capability. If the Europeans decide to go it alone, the North American democracies will receive the message that their contribution is neither necessary nor any longer wanted. It would thus be difficult to prevent a total withdrawal of their forces from Europe which we know would be destabilizing, particularly as America's extended nuclear deterrence is unlikely to remain in place either. What has kept the peace in Europe for nearly half a century and helped to bring about change is as much the physical presence of US and Canadian forces in Europe, as the political commitment of these two nations, one of which is the world's greatest industrial power, to democracy and stability on our continent. A purely European security organisation could neither balance the Soviet Union militarily nor provide the same kind of political stability.

Nonetheless those who affirm that you cannot have a united Europe without a common European defence are right. Thus it is important for NATO and the European Community that we throw the right switches now and establish a concept for a European pillar that can be harmoniously integrated into the Alliance. A binary relationship - North America versus Europe - or which prevents **all 16** members from participating fully in Alliance activities is unacceptable. For if we cannot maintain a sense of a transatlantic community, then the Alliance will fail. If the United States believes that it is being asked to play only a military balancing role in Europe, its engagement could disappear as rapidly as the receding Soviet threat. There has to be the sense of a "commonality of destiny and values" between North America and Europe, such as our Alliance has created and nurtured since its inception. Therefore this newly emerging European identity should not be one of distinctness but should contribute to greater Alliance harmony, cohesion and influence. We can handle this evolution pragmatically, through close contacts between NATO, the European Community and WEU, avoiding competitive stances. Our institutions are complementary. Yet if we do not coordinate our policy from the outset, we run the risk of weakening our organizations rather than reinforcing them.

The other institution that is sometimes mooted as an alternative to our Alliance is the Conference on Security and Cooperation in Europe, or CSCE.

Since the Helsinki Final Act fifteen years ago, the CSCE process has been a unique success story. The manifold achievements of last week's Paris Summit, and the common democratic and market commitments enshrined in the Charter of Paris for a New Europe have now taken CSCE a quantum leap forward, and made it into a key element of any future European structure. Undoubtedly, and in the light of the probable dissolution of the Warsaw Treaty Organisation, the CSCE will acquire many important security responsibilities. The increased institutionalisation of the CSCE process has been a common goal of all the Allies. By endowing CSCE with a new system of political consultations and giving it pan-European functions we have fulfilled the objectives of our London Declaration and opened a new institutional chapter in the political development of our entire continent.

Yet to infer from this that the collective security system of the Atlantic Alliance will become superfluous - even over the long term - would be a mistake. New CSCE structures can bridge old antagonisms, and can lead to new, and common concepts for the enhancement of peace and partnership. However, CSCE requires consensus which is difficult to obtain while each of the 34 states has a right of veto, and the CSCE states do not yet share common values or common social systems. Nor is there any kind of enforcement mechanism. Thus for the foreseeable future the CSCE alone cannot ensure stability and the necessary degree of insurance against risks which is provided uniquely by the collective defence capacities of our Alliance.

The relationship between the Alliance and CSCE must be complementary, not one of either/or. NATO will serve as a back-up for CSCE. We will also seek to establish a dynamic interaction with CSCE in its everyday work. For NATO serves not only to provide direct defence for its member states but will also serve indirectly to stabilize the CSCE system. The nations of Central and Eastern Europe have in fact been more explicit than many of our own Western opinion leaders in recognizing this important future role of our Alliance.

This leads me to say a word about the North Atlantic Assembly. Over many years it has not only made an exemplary contribution to the cohesion of, and public response to, our Alliance, especially as a fiduciary of the transatlantic link - it has also been the trail-blazer of relations with the Central and Eastern European countries. Even before the phase of free elections in these countries, it cultivated and encouraged those who were fighting for freedom and democracy. When elections could finally be held, it established close co-operation with parliamentarians from these new republics, who have now been given "associate delegate" status. It has then paved the way for a coming-about of our common Europe and has helped to anchor it in public consciousness. This task will remain highly topical and I see no competition or conflict between the parliamentary assembly of all CSCE states, which the Paris Summit has proposed, and the ongoing work of this body. True enough, if parliamentarians from all CSCE nations respond to the call of their governments at the Summit, the CSCE assembly, yet to be defined in all its functions, will have important work to do. However, here, as in the other domains of the CSCE, this specific body, concerned with the security issues of our Alliance and of the larger Europe, will continue to shape the debate with the excellence of its reports, the density of discussions in specialised working groups and the long-standing co-operation and good comradeship they have developed among their members and their regular guests and observers over so many years. I am certain that a new CSCE parliamentary assembly will appreciate the highly professional contribution which will not cease to flow from the North Atlantic Assembly.

Here and elsewhere, then, there is no identity crisis of NATO, nor are we desperately in search of new tasks now that the classical threat has disappeared. There is a new European landscape full of opportunities, but also full of risks and uncertainties. The battle for freedom and economic recovery is not yet finally won. If you listen to the leaders of the Central and Eastern European countries, you know: the most difficult years, which will decide the fate of democracy and prosperity, lie ahead. What is needed in such a situation is, on the one hand, the determination to actively promote and manage change, make use of the opportunities, shape history and, on the other hand, the ability to cope with the risks and provide the process of change with the necessary stability, preventing the use of force. Who else could do that if not our Alliance which is by far the most cohesive, solid and powerful political and military community on this globe?

So, NATO is indispensable:
(a) as the only functioning, collective security and defence structure which can ensure stability and insure its member nations against threats and risks to their security and territorial integrity from whatever direction they may come;
(b) as the tested political partnership and community of values between 16 sovereign and democratic nations on both sides of the Atlantic which enables them to define and put in place a new relationship with

the Soviet Union and with the new democracies in Eastern Europe, to shape an emerging European system and to determine what the relations within that new Europe should be, both internally and with North America;

(c) as the only institutional forum which binds together North America and Europe and which offers the main and most suitable channel for managing the future evolution of the relationship.

Of course, the NATO of the nineties will not be the NATO of the eighties, as the NATO of today is not the NATO of yesterday. Our Alliance is evolving: we are adapting to the new circumstances and will continue to do so as we shape European history. Our Alliance in the future will shift its emphasis from the military to the political, from peace-keeping to peace-building, from the staving off of an imminent threat to the insurance against future risks, from an Alliance led by the United States to an equal partnership between North America and a more united Europe.

We are reforming our military strategy along the lines of our London Summit Declaration. Clearly, in present day Europe, a massive in-place defence is not as much needed as before. We will need instead to be able to reconstitute forces as rapidly as new threats may arise. Thus, a coherent defence will require less but still substantial forces with more multinational units. Of course, a future defence will also allow reductions in defence budgets. But, these reductions should be done in a way which allows us to maintain a coherent defence planning. An over-hasty rush towards a peace dividend may prove to be counter-productive in terms of real economics and even dangerous. Equally, we will significantly reduce further the numbers of nuclear weapons and reduce our reliance on them, so as to make them truly weapons of last resort. But we must continue to have them in our Alliance strategy as the ultimate and indispensable guarantee of peace.

Another important change will be what I would call a greater Europeanisation of our Alliance. This, of course, is not a question just for the European Allies, but rather a question for all the Allies to address together. It concerns on the one hand the problem of NATO's internal re-balancing; an increased European share in the decision-making process will only come about as a result of an increased European share in responsibilities, risks and burdens. On the other hand, there is the problem of dealing with the European defence structure, if and when the Europeans decide to create it. We have to ensure that such a development would take place in the best possible conditions and in a way not detrimental to NATO. Through early consultation, we have to devise ways in which we can fit an emerging European security structure into our overall political and military Alliance structures. I am confident - even sure - that it is possible.

There are, however, two essentials which we have to safeguard through all the changes. One is the political role of our Alliance, and the other is the military role. Our Alliance will survive neither as a purely military organization, nor as a purely political consultative body. Both elements are vital. We have to deal with all political questions related to security in a broader sense and we have to maintain our integrated military structure.

What then are the major tasks which our Alliance has to tackle in the next decade?

The first of these is to promote democracy and prosperity throughout Europe. As Alexis de Tocqueville pointed out 150 years ago, "democracies are inherently peaceful" and thus more predictable and reassuring to their neighbours. A policy of economic and technical assistance to the reforming nations of Central and Eastern Europe is our best long-term security policy. It is not primarily NATO's task to provide such aid; but by helping to establish new multinational structures of cooperation in Europe and extending the arms control process to embrace all 34 CSCE nations, NATO can create the climate of stability and confidence that will encourage a dynamic Western support and investment programme in all those new democracies that are willing to create the necessary conditions.

The next new task arising naturally from the end of the Cold War is to build a new European security system. Unlike a confrontational situation, members of such a community regard security as a common good that cannot be enjoyed at the expense of other parties.

The first step in establishing a future European security system is to design a new political and strategic relationship with the Soviet Union and the nations of Central and Eastern Europe, whether they remain its Warsaw Pact allies or not. This process is already well in hand. At our London Summit last July we announced a transformed Alliance that extended the hand of friendship and cooperation to our former adversaries. Their diplomats maintain liaison with NATO Headquarters and come regularly for briefings and exchanges; our officials go to Moscow and other capitals; theirs visit us. In Paris, a few days ago, we signed a joint declaration on peaceful relations with the Warsaw Pact nations. Through arms control negotiations beyond CFE and seminars on military doctrines we aim to redimension the military factor in the East-West relationship, making it ever more cooperative and reassuring. We must establish a new kind of military balance at lower levels but equally capable of containing any individual or collective concentration of military forces in Europe. Arms control must stabilize a balance at lower levels, and enhance defence efficiency while progressively eliminating attack options. This will take time but we are moving ahead.

Security cooperation will also be another way of drawing the Soviet Union into Europe, helping it to overcome its sense of isolation and cultural and economic marginalization. We can also smooth the path by building further on the good cooperation that we have established with the Soviet Union within the United Nations, especially during the Gulf crisis. Soviet interests, as this crisis shows, are at stake as much as ours from the spread of dangerous military technologies, or from any economic dislocation of the Western economies and of economic reform in Central and Eastern Europe in the wake of a new oil shock.

This brings us to the question of what a future all-European security system would look like. We cannot yet envisage the precise form of such a system, for this will evolve over time like the various stages of a cathedral rather than be imposed from the outset. Yet certain building principles of this construction are already clear.

If NATO is still our only real possibility for **peace-keeping**, it cannot handle all by itself our other essential security task of today which is obviously **peace-building**. This task is naturally much more complex. It cannot be handled by one single "super-institution" addressing financial, economic, military, arms control, human rights and cultural tasks all at once. So our future European architecture will rest on a system of different organisations, sometimes overlapping, but interlocking and each with a different focus. I foresee four essential pillars of such an architecture : the European Community as the source of economic dynamism and political integration, including the organisation of the security interests of its members, the Council of Europe to emphasize the human and social dimension, the CSCE which is the pan-European forum of cooperation and, last but not least, NATO as the framework of stability and the link to the United States and Canada. Our task will be to develop increasingly complementary relations among these four institutional pillars in ways which make them mutually reinforcing and stabilising to the overall architecture as such.

Another important task which we cannot afford to neglect is to deal effectively with those global challenges which directly affect the security of our member nations and the stability of the pan-European system.

Let me highlight just two.

One concerns risks from adjacent areas. Our Alliance's contribution to the international effort in the Gulf has been criticized by some, in my view unfairly. There has been more Alliance solidarity than in any previous out-of-area conflict and a greater material contribution by the Europeans. Indeed all Allies have done something. The United States is by no means standing alone. Yet there is a widespread feeling that some Allies and the Alliance as a whole can and should do more. After the Gulf crisis is over, there will be a debate - but I hope not before, as we must concentrate now on maintaining our well established solidarity.

When this debate opens we must draw the lessons of the Gulf crisis to improve both our crisis management and crisis prevention machinery. Na turally there is no question of NATO trying to become a global policeman or taking on every security problem. That would overtax our structures to nobody's benefit. But because we cannot do everything, we should not conclude we cannot do more. The Washington Treaty commits us to work for a more peaceful international order and does not limit the scope of our security planning or coordination; nor does it exclude all joint action. There are many interesting ideas on the table which do not imply collective military action in extra-European conflicts - something that, of course, would need the consensus of all member nations. For instance could we not develop an internal Alliance understanding whereby, in a spirit of solidarity, the degree of engagement in dealing with a given problem might vary from Ally to Ally, but the assets of the Alliance would be available for coordination and support. This would operate where there is a clear need for common Alliance interests to be defended.

At the same time, we must recognize that there is a new threat to our security from the proliferation of weapons of mass destruction and ballistic missile technologies beyond the traditional East-West axis. It is imperative for us to do more to prevent this proliferation and establish a more rational code of conduct for arms and technology transfers to the Third World. This is a domain where our Alliance in cooperation with the Soviet Union and working closely with the United Nations can play a useful role.

Thus the Alliance is no less important as during the days of the Cold War: in part because old functions - like balancing Soviet power and maintaining the transatlantic link - remain essential; in part because only with and through the Alliance can we handle the new security tasks occasioned by the melting of the confrontational ice in Europe and the looming challenges related to the establishment of a new, more just and stable world order. Because we have NATO, the Western nations are able to exercise their responsibility and historic opportunity :
- to promote change;
- to provide stability for that process to succeed over the long-term.

Discours prononcé à la 36ème session annuelle de l'Assemblée de l'Atlantique Nord

Londres
29 Novembre
1990

Lors de notre dernière rencontre, à Rome, le mur de Berlin ne s'était pas encore effondré, l'unification allemande restait une perspective séduisante, mais lointaine, l'Union soviétique ne paraissait pas prête à se retirer bientôt de sa position stratégique au coeur de l'Europe, et un accord sur les FCE donnait toujours lieu à des marchandages très serrés. Mon premier souci était alors de déterminer comment l'Alliance pourrait promouvoir ces premiers objectifs essentiels en atteignant son but ultime : une Europe entière et libre, prospère et sûre. Tous ont maintenant été réalisés, plus vite et plus facilement que nous n'aurions osé l'imaginer. A notre Sommet de Londres, l'OTAN a tiré les conséquences de ces changements sismiques. Notre Alliance rénovée a inauguré une ère nouvelle de coopération, grâce à des mesures concrètes. Les pays d'Europe centrale et orientale ont accepté l'amitié que nous leur offrions à tous. L'Europe retrouve rapidement son unité politique, mais aussi son unité stratégique. Chacun se demande à présent : quelle sera l'étape suivante ? Quel est le nouveau programme ? Comment, au niveau conceptuel, l'Alliance atlantique s'insère-t-elle dans une nouvelle architecture qui ne doit pas faire face à une seule menace, collective et redoutable ?

Dans le débat sur l'avenir de l'OTAN, trois conceptions sont fréquemment exprimées.

La première présente l'Alliance comme la victime de son propre succès. Elle a réalisé un vieux rêve, la construction d'une Europe dans laquelle les alliances politico-militaires, comme l'OTAN, ne seraient plus nécessaires. La plupart ne vont naturellement pas jusqu'à prétendre que la sécurité n'est plus une nécessité fondamentale, mais ils pensent qu'il est devenu

271

plus facile et moins coûteux de l'obtenir, ou qu'elle n'a plus besoin de composante militaire, de sorte qu'elle peut être assurée tout aussi bien par un organisme comme la CSCE, qui n'a pas de structure de défense commune.

La deuxième thèse est que notre Alliance va perdre de son importance politique, et devenir davantage un organisme technique appelé à gérer la structure de défense intégrée et à surveiller la mise en oeuvre et la vérification des accords de maîtrise des armements. Dans cet esprit, l'OTAN devrait s'en tenir à ce qu'elle connaît et à ce qu'elle fait le mieux : promouvoir la coopération militaire entre ses seize membres. La haute politique - le développement des relations transatlantiques, la coordination des politiques occidentales envers l'Europe centrale et orientale et envers l'Union soviétique, la mise en place d'une nouvelle architecture européenne et la conduite à tenir face aux nouveaux défis mondiaux - se déplacerait alors, soit vers la CSCE ou les mécanismes bilatéraux qui se créent entre la Communauté européenne et les Etats-Unis, soit vers une combinaison des deux. Les tenants de cette thèse pensent souvent qu'une union européenne politique et de défense plus étroite n'est pas compatible avec une Alliance atlantique forte. Pour survivre, l'OTAN devrait donc adopter un profil bas, et privilégier sa dimension militaire.

La troisième conception est que notre Alliance joue, et devrait jouer, non seulement un rôle militaire, mais aussi un rôle politique plus important. Elle devrait s'adapter à l'évolution de la situation et relever les nouveaux défis pour la sécurité de ses pays membres.

Qui a raison ? Les partisans d'un rôle minimal pour l'OTAN, ou les tenants d'un rôle accru, axé sur la gestion du changement et le maintien de la stabilité ? Pour répondre à cette question, il faut se demander, d'une part, quelles sont les tâches de sécurité qui subsistent maintenant que la Guerre froide est terminée, et, d'autre part, qui peut le mieux les assumer. Est-ce l'OTAN, ou d'autres organisations peuvent-elles se montrer plus efficaces?

Nous devons maintenant nous adapter à la transformation du paysage de la sécurité en Europe, dans laquelle la menace directe d'une agression massive de l'Union soviétique a disparu et la prévention d'un danger imminent est devenue moins urgente. A présent que le souci quotidien du maintien de la paix n'occupe plus toutes nos pensées, nous avons la possibilité de jeter les bases d'une paix plus sûre, plus durable et plus constructive. Les conditions politiques du succès sont claires : nous devons maintenir et renforcer le partenariat entre les démocraties d'Europe et d'Amérique du Nord, nous devons aider les pays d'Europe centrale et orientale à édifier des démocraties solides et des économies de marché viables, nous devons ancrer l'Union soviétique à l'Europe par de nouvelles structures de coopération, et nous devons mettre en place un nouveau système de sécurité qui donne à tous les Etats des garanties fermes contre l'agression. Une nouvelle architecture européenne qui ne permettrait pas de gérer ces quatre tâches simultanément et de manière égale ne servirait pas nos intérêts.

Un monde plus pacifique signifie une économie mondiale plus interdépendante et plus prospère, dans laquelle nos sociétés se livreront une concurrence économique fructueuse et renonceront à une confrontation militaire stérile. Mais un monde plus interdépendant est aussi plus fragile, plus vulnérable aux menaces et au chantage. La crise du Golfe montre bien que l'Ouest est presque aussi vulnérable aujourd'hui à une crise pétrolière prolongée qu'hier à une menace militaire en Europe; les pays d'Europe centrale et orientale se trouvent dans une situation plus précaire encore. Il est clair, dans ces conditions, que nous avons besoin d'une politique de sécurité pour recueillir les fruits de l'interdépendance sans en courir les risques. Si la sécurité n'est pas assurée, nul ne consentira les investissements ou l'effort de prospective dont dépend le maintien de notre prospérité.

Ensuite, il est évident que la fin de la Guerre froide et de ses confrontations n'a pas balayé les incertitudes. Où va l'Union soviétique ? Nous le savons moins que jamais. Malgré le soutien actif que nous apportons au double processus de démocratisation et de réforme du marché en Europe centrale et orientale, nous ne pouvons pas dire si ces réformes aboutiront. Nous devons considérer les charges énormes qu'une telle transformation va imposer à ces pays. L'instabilité au plan intérieur et une nouvelle division de l'Europe fondée sur la richesse pourraient rouvrir des options nationalistes et fomenter des luttes ethniques jusqu'à un point d'explosion. Déjà, le spectre de flux migratoires massifs de ces zones de tension vers l'Ouest a été évoqué. Il faudra beaucoup de temps, et aussi des efforts de réforme soutenus de la part de ces pays, accompagnés d'une aide soutenue de l'Occident, pour que les niveaux de vie des deux moitiés de l'Europe se rapprochent. Nous devons, ensemble, veiller à ce que l'enthousiasme populaire et les espoirs mis dans l'avenir ne soient pas entamés par les dures épreuves que la transition implique inévitablement.

De même, il est encore trop tôt pour faire table rase de la puissance militaire de l'Union soviétique. Quoi qu'il advienne demain dans ce pays, il restera le plus puissant d'Europe sur le plan militaire. Qui lui fera contrepoids ? Car nous savons que les liens diplomatiques, économiques ou même institutionnels ne peuvent, à eux seuls, contrebalancer la puissance. S'il y a bien eu des réductions, les modernisations ont été significatives, notamment dans le domaine nucléaire. La production pour la défense est en baisse, mais reste à un niveau qui est supérieur aux besoins raisonnables de la défense de l'URSS et qui dépasse de loin ce que font les pays de l'OTAN, ensemble ou séparément. Je ne mets pas en doute les intentions pacifiques de M. Gorbatchev. Nous ne fondons d'ailleurs plus nos plans sur les pires hypothèses, car nous sommes convaincus que les intérêts à long terme des Soviétiques résident dans la stabilité, la coopération et une interaction pacifique avec les pays de notre Alliance. Nous faisons confiance à la direction actuelle de l'Union soviétique, et nous l'aidons dans son cheminement vers la réforme. Mais cela ne veut pas dire qu'il ne pourra pas y avoir de retours en arrière et de revirements en cours de route. Aussi nos relations avec l'Union soviétique demeureront-elles nécessairement, dans l'avenir prévisible, placées sous le signe de la dualité. Notre offre est sincère : nous voulons que l'URSS devienne un partenaire, et même un ami, avec qui organiser sécurité et protection. Cependant, elle mettra longtemps à trouver une forme nouvelle et stable, et il faudra faire équilibre à son énorme masse stratégique. Dans l'intervalle, le risque résiduel que la puissance militaire soviétique représente pour la sécurité va faire subsister la nécessité de prendre des assurances et d'observer une certaine vigilance.

Enfin, nous sommes désormais plus conscients de l'importance des défis extérieurs au territoire de notre Alliance. Des risques peuvent venir de directions nouvelles et inattendues. En outre, la tendance au désarmement et à la réduction des dépenses militaires dans les pays industrialisés ne donne que plus de poids aux arsenaux des pays du Tiers monde, où entrent aussi maintenant des missiles balistiques et des technologies de destruction massive, et elle offre aux Etats plus petits des moyens de pression nouveaux et peu souhaitables. Nous ne pouvons donc pas, en Occident, renoncer à une défense cohérente. Le long du périmètre sud de l'Europe existe, dans une certaine mesure, un arc de tension qui va du Maghreb au Moyen-Orient. Les tensions sont exacerbées, non seulement par les ambitions de dictateurs comme Saddam Hussein, mais aussi par la croissance démographique, les conflits qu'engendre le problème des ressources, les migrations, le sous-développement, le fondamentalisme religieux et le terrorisme. A l'évidence, on ne saurait minimiser les menaces pour l'intégrité territoriale de l'OTAN qui ont leur origine au delà de l'Europe en les considérant comme des menaces hors zone. La Turquie est directement menacée, et notre région Sud est une zone où sont en jeu les intérêts collectifs de tous les Alliés.

La sécurité garde donc son importance, car des risques et des facteurs d'instabilité subsistent - certains se manifestent déjà, tandis que d'autres, à l'état latent, menacent. Notre Alliance devra de plus en plus intégrer ces risques dans ses plans de défense. Nous ne pouvons pas nous permettre d'attendre sans rien faire que ces risques et ces facteurs d'instabilité dégénèrent en menace directe capable de déclencher des conflits militaires. La plupart de ces risques ne peuvent être gérés par les seules politiques nationales de défense. Ils exigent une riposte collective et une relance de la prévention des crises à long terme.

La nécessité d'une approche collective de la sécurité est également dictée par une autre raison. La structure de défense intégrée a été l'une des réussites historiques et exceptionnelles de l'OTAN. Elle a donné aux pays de notre Alliance une sécurité qu'ils n'auraient jamais pu obtenir séparément. Elle a assuré une dissuasion dont le niveau dépasse celui des forces qui lui sont réellement affectées en temps de paix. Sans le soutien d'une structure de sécurité efficace et intégrée, les garanties de sécurité de l'Alliance seraient, tôt ou tard, perçues comme des garanties illusoires. De toute évidence, une future architecture européenne doit donc avoir pour principe de maintenir une défense collective là où elle existe, et préserver ainsi la structure de défense intégrée de l'OTAN, quoique avec des forces moins nombreuses et une stratégie militaire différente. Ce n'est pas seulement parce que cette structure maintient le potentiel de défense en état de fonctionner. Des pays qui intègrent leur défense manifestent leur volonté d'agir de concert, unis par un même objectif.

L'autre solution consisterait à renationaliser la sécurité. L'Europe courrait alors le risque de revenir aux renversements des alliances, aux rivalités et à la politique de puissance du passé. Il ne serait certainement pas question que les démocraties nord-américaines fournissent une force de sécurité si l'Europe devait revenir à une situation comme celle qui existait avant 1914.

Si nous laissions se défaire la structure de défense intégrée, comment pourrions-nous la rétablir en cas de nécessité ? A grand-peine, ou même pas du tout. En outre, nous aurions sacrifié inutilement la capacité de cette structure de prévenir les conflits, et pas uniquement d'y réagir. L'approche collective de la sécurité n'est donc pas seulement la plus rentable; elle est aussi la plus sûre et la plus juste - la seule façon de partager équitablement les rôles, les risques et les responsabilités au sein de notre Alliance. A une époque où il nous est impossible d'évaluer avec précision les risques futurs, la sécurité collective de l'OTAN est de loin l'assurance la plus raisonnable contre toute forme d'incertitude.

D'autres institutions sont-elles en mesure de gérer ce nouveau concept de la sécurité aussi bien que l'OTAN, ou même mieux ? Une identité européenne dans le domaine de la défense, résultant de l'intégration politique européenne, ou un système paneuropéen de sécurité collective comme le processus institutionnalisé de la CSCE, peuvent-ils par exemple remplacer l'OTAN ? Ces deux formules vont dans le sens des intérêts de l'OTAN, mais l'une et l'autre sont loin de pouvoir offrir de solides garanties de sécurité. Elles ne sauraient se substituer à l'Alliance atlantique.

L'affirmation d'une identité européenne dans le domaine de la politique et de la sécurité est depuis longtemps un objectif de notre Alliance. Grâce au dynamisme dont fait preuve actuellement la Communauté européenne, nous sommes, à l'évidence, plus proches aujourd'hui de la conception d'une Alliance à deux piliers, à laquelle le président Kennedy songeait au début des années soixante. La coopération entre les douze pays de la Communauté européenne dans le domaine de la sécurité est revenue en force à l'ordre du jour de cette institution. Des propositions spécifiques ont été formulées concernant la façon dont l'Europe devrait organiser une politique de sécurité commune. Je le répète, cette évolution est naturelle et souhaitable.

Cependant, une identité européenne dans le domaine de la sécurité et de la défense doit absolument être organisée dans le cadre de notre Alliance. Il ne serait ni réaliste ni rationnel que l'Europe cherche à se doter d'un potentiel de défense entièrement indépendant. Si les Européens décident de faire cavalier seul, les démocraties d'Amérique du Nord y verront un message signifiant que leur contribution n'est pas nécessaire et n'est plus souhaitée. Il serait dès lors difficile d'empêcher un retrait total des forces nord-américaines d'Europe, retrait dont nous savons qu'il aurait un effet déstabilisateur, d'autant que le dispositif de dissuasion nucléaire avancé de l'Amérique ne serait probablement pas maintenu non plus. Ce qui a permis le maintien de la paix en Europe pendant près d'un demi-siècle et favorisé le changement, c'est autant la réalité physique de la présence de forces des Etats-Unis et du Canada en Europe que l'engagement politique de ces deux pays, dont l'un est la plus grande puissance industrielle du monde, en faveur de la démocratie et de la stabilité sur notre continent. Une organisation de sécurité purement européenne ne pourrait ni contrebalancer militairement l'Union soviétique ni apporter le même genre de stabilité politique.

Néanmoins, ceux qui affirment qu'il ne peut y avoir d'Europe unie sans une défense européenne commune ont raison. Il est donc important pour l'OTAN et pour la Communauté européenne que nous prenions maintenant les mesures appropriées et que nous établissions un concept permettant d'intégrer harmonieusement le pilier européen dans la structure de l'Alliance. Une relation binaire qui mettrait l'Amérique du Nord et l'Europe face à face, ou qui empêcherait **la totalité des seize** pays membres de participer pleinement aux activités de l'Alliance est inacceptable. En effet, si nous ne pouvons maintenir un sens de la communauté transatlantique, l'Alliance est vouée à l'échec. Si les Etats-Unis en viennent à penser qu'on leur demande de jouer un rôle uniquement de contrepoids militaire en Europe, leur engagement pourrait disparaître aussi vite que la menace soviétique s'éloigne. Il doit exister entre l'Amérique du Nord et l'Europe un sens de la "communauté de destin et de valeurs" semblable à celui que notre Alliance a fait naître dès sa fondation et qu'elle n'a cessé de nourrir depuis lors. Cette identité européenne qui commence à s'affirmer ne devrait donc pas tendre vers une différenciation, mais contribuer à donner plus d'harmonie, plus de cohésion et plus d'influence à notre Alliance. Nous pouvons gérer cette évolution de façon pragmatique, grâce à des contacts étroits entre l'OTAN, la Communauté européenne et l'UEO, en évitant de nous poser en concurrents les uns des autres. Nos institutions sont complémentaires. Mais, si nous ne coordonnons pas nos politiques dès le départ, nous courons le risque d'affaiblir nos organisations au lieu de les renforcer.

L'autre institution dont on entend parfois dire qu'elle pourrait remplacer notre Alliance est la Conférence sur la sécurité et la coopération en Europe, la CSCE.

Depuis la signature de l'Acte final d'Helsinki, il y a quinze ans, le processus de la CSCE a connu un développement remarquable et unique en son genre. Le bilan extrêmement riche du Sommet de Paris, la semaine dernière, et les engagements communs pris par les signataires de la Charte de Paris pour une nouvelle Europe en faveur de la démocratie et de l'économie de marché ont permis à la CSCE de franchir une étape décisive et en ont fait un élément clé de toute structure européenne future. La CSCE est appelée sans nul doute à assumer de nombreuses responsabilités essentielles en matière de sécurité, du fait aussi de la dissolution probable de l'Organisation du Traité de Varsovie. Accroître l'institutionnalisation du processus de la CSCE est depuis un certain temps un but commun à tous les Alliés. En dotant la CSCE d'un nouveau système de consultation politique et en lui conférant des fonctions paneuropéennes, nous avons atteint les objectifs de notre Déclaration de Londres et ouvert un nouveau chapitre institutionnel dans l'évolution politique de notre continent tout entier.

En déduire que le système de sécurité collective de l'Alliance atlantique deviendra superflu - même à long terme - serait toutefois une erreur. L'établissement de nouvelles structures dans le cadre de la CSCE peut permettre de surmonter de vieux antagonismes et d'arriver à de nouveaux concepts communs touchant le renforcement de la paix et du partenariat. Mais la CSCE fonctionne selon la règle du consensus, consensus qui paraît difficile à réaliser tant que chacun des 34 Etats membres dispose d'un droit de veto et que, comme maintenant, ces Etats n'ont pas tous en commun les mêmes valeurs et les mêmes systèmes sociaux. Il n'existe pas non plus le moindre mécanisme permettant de faire exécuter les décisions. Aussi la CSCE ne sera-t-elle pas, dans l'avenir prévisible, en mesure de garantir à elle seule la stabilité et le nécessaire degré d'assurance contre les risques qui ne peuvent être apportés que par le potentiel de défense collectif de notre Alliance.

La relation entre l'Alliance et la CSCE doit être une relation de complémentarité, et non pas d'exclusion mutuelle. L'OTAN servira d'appoint et de soutien à la CSCE. Nous chercherons à établir des liens d'interaction dynamique avec la CSCE dans l'exécution de ses activités courantes. L'OTAN, en effet, a non seulement pour fonction de pourvoir à la défense directe de ses membres, mais elle aura également celle, indirecte, de stabiliser le système de la CSCE. Les pays d'Europe centrale et orientale ont d'ailleurs reconnu, de façon plus explicite que bon nombre de personnalités influentes dans nos propres pays, l'importance de ce rôle futur de notre Alliance.

Ceci m'amène à évoquer l'Assemblée de l'Atlantique Nord. Depuis de nombreuses années, l'Assemblée a contribué de façon exemplaire à renforcer la cohésion de notre Alliance et à faire réagir l'opinion publique à son action, surtout en étant le gage et l'incarnation du lien transatlantique, mais elle a aussi été le pionnier des relations avec les pays d'Europe centrale et orientale. Avant même que des élections libres ne puissent être organisées dans ces pays, elle a noué des liens avec ceux qui combattaient pour la liberté et la démocratie et elle les a encouragés à poursuivre leur lutte. Lorsque des élections ont finalement pu avoir lieu, elle a établi une coopération avec les parlementaires de ces nouvelles républiques, auxquels est maintenant accordé le statut de "délégué associé". Votre Assemblée a ensuite ouvert la voie à ce qui va devenir notre Europe commune et elle a aidé à faire entrer cette aspiration dans la conscience collective. Cette tâche restera d'une grande actualité, et je ne vois pour ma part ni concurrence ni conflit entre ce que fera l'Assemblée parlementaire de tous les Etats de la CSCE, proposée au Sommet de Paris, et les travaux que poursuit votre institution. Certes, si les parlementaires de tous les pays de la CSCE répondent à l'appel que les gouvernements de leurs pays ont lancé au sommet, l'Assemblée de la CSCE, dont les diverses fonctions restent à définir, aura un travail important à faire. Mais, là comme dans les autres domaines de la CSCE, votre Assemblée, qui se préoccupe des problèmes de sécurité de notre Alliance et de l'Europe élargie, continuera d'infléchir le cours du débat par la grande qualité de ses rapports, la haute tenue des délibérations de ses groupes de travail spécialisés et l'esprit de coopération et d'amitié qui s'est instauré depuis tant d'années entre ses membres et les personnalités qu'elle invite régulièrement à ses sessions en qualité d'orateur ou d'observateur. Je suis certain qu'une nouvelle assemblée parlementaire de la CSCE appréciera la contribution que l'Assemblée de l'Atlantique Nord ne cessera d'apporter en remplissant sa tâche avec une telle compétence.

Il n'y a donc pas, ici ou ailleurs, de crise d'identité de l'OTAN, et nous ne sommes pas non plus désespérément à la recherche de tâches nouvelles maintenant que la menace traditionnelle a disparu. Nous avons devant nous un nouveau paysage européen, riche de possibilités, mais aussi lourd de risques et d'incertitudes. La bataille pour la liberté et le redressement économique n'est pas encore définitivement gagnée. Il suffit d'écouter les dirigeants d'Europe centrale et orientale pour savoir que les années les plus difficiles, qui décideront du sort de la démocratie et de la prospérité, sont encore à venir. Ce qu'il faut dans une telle situation c'est, d'une part, la volonté d'agir pour promouvoir et gérer le changement, de mettre à profit les possibilités qui se présentent, de façonner l'histoire et, d'autre part, la capacité de faire face aux risques et de donner au processus de changement la stabilité nécessaire, en empêchant tout recours à la force. Qui pourrait le faire si ce n'est notre Alliance, communauté politique et militaire de loin la plus soudée, la plus solide et la plus puissante de la planète ?

Ainsi, l'OTAN est indispensable :

(a) parce qu'elle est la seule structure de sécurité et de défense collective qui fonctionne effectivement et qui peut assurer la stabilité et garantir ses pays membres contre les menaces et les risques, quelle qu'en soit l'origine, qui viseraient leur sécurité et leur intégrité territoriale;

(b) parce qu'elle représente pour seize nations souveraines et démocratiques, de part et d'autre de l'Atlantique, une forme de partenariat politique et une communauté de valeurs qui ont fait leur preuve et qui permettent aux Alliés de définir et de mettre en place de nouvelles relations avec l'Union soviétique et avec les nouvelles démocraties d'Europe orientale, ainsi que de déterminer quel système européen ils souhaitent voir apparaître et quelles devraient être les relations de la nouvelle Europe, aussi bien sur le plan interne qu'avec l'Amérique du Nord;

(c) parce qu'elle constitue le seul cadre institutionnel où se trouvent liées l'Amérique du Nord et l'Europe, en même temps que l'instrument le plus important et le plus approprié pour gérer l'évolution future de leurs relations.

Il va de soi que l'OTAN des années quatre-vingt-dix n'est pas l'OTAN des années quatre-vingts, tout comme l'OTAN d'aujourd'hui n'est pas l'OTAN d'hier. Notre Alliance est en train se transformer : nous nous adaptons à la nouvelle conjoncture et nous continuerons de le faire tout en nous attachant à façonner l'histoire de l'Europe. Notre Alliance fera passer l'accent, dans ses activités futures, du côté militaire au côté politique, du maintien de la paix à la construction de la paix, de la prévention d'un danger imminent à l'assurance contre les risques futurs, d'une Alliance dirigée par les Etats-Unis à un partenariat sur un pied d'égalité entre l'Amérique du Nord et une Europe plus unie.

Nous nous employons actuellement à remodeler notre stratégie militaire comme le prescrivait la Déclaration du sommet de Londres. Il est clair que dans l'Europe d'aujourd'hui, garder en place un énorme dispositif de défense n'est plus aussi nécessaire qu'avant. Il nous faudra plutôt pouvoir reconstituer des forces aussi rapidement que pourraient apparaître de nouvelles menaces. Une défense cohérente exigera donc des forces moins nombreuses, mais encore importantes, avec parmi elles davantage d'unités multinationales. Certes, en organisant une défense future selon ce schéma, il sera possible de réduire aussi les budgets de la défense. Encore faudrait-il que ces réductions s'opèrent de telle façon que la planification de notre défense puisse rester cohérente. Trop de hâte à toucher les dividendes de la paix pourrait compromettre les possibilités d'économies réelles, et même nous exposer à des dangers. Parallèlement, nous réduirons encore dans des proportions sensibles le nombre de nos armes nucléaires et nous chercherons à moins tabler sur elles, en en faisant véritablement l'arme du dernier recours. Mais nous devons continuer à faire entrer dans la stratégie de l'Alliance ces armes représentant l'ultime et indispensable garantie de la paix.

Un autre changement important marquera notre Alliance, c'est ce que j'appellerais : une plus nette européanisation. C'est là, naturellement, une question qui n'intéresse pas seulement les Alliés européens, mais bien une question que tous les Alliés auront à examiner ensemble. Elle pose, d'abord, le problème du rééquilibrage interne de l'Alliance; les Européens ne pourront avoir une part accrue dans le processus de décision que s'ils assument une part accrue des responsabilités, des risques et des charges. Ensuite, il s'agit de savoir comment traiter le problème de la structure européenne de défense dès lors que les Européens auront décidé de la créer. Il nous incombe de faire en sorte que l'évolution dans ce sens se déroule dans les meilleures conditions possibles, sans que l'OTAN en subisse le moindre préjudice. En nous consultant à un stade précoce, nous devons ainsi concevoir des formules qui permettent à une structure de sécurité européenne naissante de trouver sa place dans les structures militaires et politiques globales de l'Alliance. Je suis persuadé, et même tout à fait persuadé, que cela est possible.

Il y a cependant deux points essentiels auxquels nous devons absolument veiller à travers tous ces changements. Je veux parler du rôle politique de notre Alliance et de son rôle militaire. Notre Alliance ne pourra se perpétuer ni comme organisation exclusivement militaire ni comme organe consultatif exclusivement politique. Les deux éléments sont vitaux. Nous devons aborder toutes les questions politiques liées à la sécurité en nous plaçant dans un contexte plus large et nous devons maintenir notre structure militaire intégrée.

Quelles sont donc les principales tâches auxquelles notre Alliance doit s'attaquer au cours de la prochaine décennie?

La première de ces tâches est de promouvoir la démocratie et la prospérité dans toute l'Europe. Comme le soulignait Alexis de Tocqueville il y a 150 ans, les démocraties sont pacifiques par nature, et donc plus prévisibles et plus rassurantes pour leurs voisins. Une politique d'assistance économique et technique aux pays d'Europe centrale et orientale engagés dans la voie des réformes est notre meilleure politique de sécurité à long terme. Il n'incombe pas au premier chef à l'OTAN de fournir une telle assistance, mais en aidant à l'établissement de nouvelles structures multinationales de coopération en Europe, et en élargissant le processus de maîtrise des armements à l'ensemble des 34 Etats participant à la CSCE, l'OTAN peut créer le climat de stabilité et de confiance qui encouragera la réalisation par les Occidentaux d'un programme dynamique d'aide et d'investissement dans toutes les nouvelles démocraties qui seront disposées à créer les conditions nécessaires.

Il y a ensuite la nouvelle tâche, découlant naturellement de la fin de la

Guerre froide, qui consiste à édifier un nouveau système de sécurité pour l'Europe. A la différence de ce qui se passait au temps de la confrontation, les membres d'une telle communauté considèrent la sécurité comme un bien commun dont aucun d'eux ne saurait jouir aux dépens des autres.

Pour établir un futur système de sécurité européen, il faut d'abord concevoir de nouvelles relations politiques et stratégiques avec l'Union soviétique et les pays d'Europe centrale et orientale, que ceux-ci restent ou non les alliés de Moscou dans le cadre du Pacte de Varsovie. Ce processus est déjà bien engagé. A notre Sommet de Londres, en juillet dernier, nous avons annoncé l'émergence d'une Alliance rénovée, offrant son amitié et sa coopération à ses anciens adversaires. Des diplomates de ces pays entretiennent des liaisons avec le siège de l'OTAN, où ils assistent régulièrement à des exposés et à des échanges de vues; nos responsables se rendent à Moscou et dans d'autres capitales, et les leurs nous rendent visite. A Paris, il y a quelques jours, nous avons signé une déclaration commune sur des relations pacifiques avec les pays du Pacte de Varsovie. Par la poursuite de négociations sur la maîtrise des armements au-delà des FCE et la tenue de séminaires sur les doctrines militaires, nous entendons donner une autre dimension au facteur militaire dans les relations Est-Ouest, pour les placer toujours davantage sous le signe de la coopération et de la confiance. Nous devons établir un nouveau genre d'équilibre militaire, qui se situe à des niveaux plus bas, mais qui offre les mêmes possibilités d'endiguer toute concentration, individuelle ou collective, de forces armées en Europe. La maîtrise des armements doit stabiliser un équilibre à des niveaux plus bas, et accroître l'efficacité de la défense tout en éliminant progressivement les risques d'attaque. Cela prendra du temps, mais nous allons de l'avant.

La coopération dans le domaine de la sécurité sera aussi un autre moyen d'attirer l'Union soviétique dans l'Europe, en l'aidant à surmonter son sentiment d'isolement et de marginalisation économique et culturelle. Nous pourrons également aplanir les difficultés en continuant à tirer parti de la bonne coopération que nous avons établie avec l'URSS dans le cadre des Nations Unies, spécialement pendant la crise du Golfe. Comme cette crise le montre, les intérêts des Soviétiques sont mis en jeu autant que les nôtres par la prolifération des technologies militaires dangereuses, ou par toute perturbation des économies occidentales et des réformes économiques en Europe centrale et orientale provoquée par un nouveau choc pétrolier.

Ceci nous amène à la question de savoir comment se présenterait un futur système de sécurité paneuropéen. Nous ne pouvons pas encore envisager la forme précise d'un tel système, car elle évoluera avec le temps comme varie l'architecture dans l'édification d'une cathédrale, plutôt qu'elle ne sera imposée au départ. Cependant, certains des principes de cette construction apparaissent déjà clairement.

Si l'OTAN demeure notre unique possibilité réelle d'assurer le **maintien de la paix**, elle ne peut faire face, à elle seule, à l'autre tâche fondamentale qui est aujourd'hui la nôtre en matière de sécurité : je veux parler, bien entendu, de la **construction de la paix**. Il s'agit, évidemment, d'une tâche beaucoup plus complexe. Elle ne peut être accomplie par une "superinstitution" unique qui aborderait à la fois les aspects financiers, économiques et militaires, et ceux qui concernent la maîtrise des armements, les droits de l'homme et le domaine culturel. Notre architecture européenne future reposera donc sur un système composé d'organisations différentes, dont les activités se chevaucheront parfois, mais qui s'imbriqueront et dont chacune sera axée sur un domaine différent. J'envisage quatre grands piliers pour une telle architecture : la Communauté européenne, en tant que source du dynamisme économique et de l'intégration politique, y compris l'organisation des intérêts de sécurité de ses membres, le Conseil de l'Europe, pour mettre en relief la dimension humaine et sociale, la CSCE, qui est l'instance de coopération paneuropéenne, et, dernier élément, mais non le moindre, l'OTAN, cadre de la stabilité et lien avec les Etats-Unis et le Canada. Notre tâche consistera à développer entre ces quatre piliers institutionnels des relations de plus en plus marquées par la complémentarité, de façon à leur permettre de se renforcer mutuellement et de stabiliser l'architecture globale elle-même.

Une autre tâche importante que nous ne pouvons nous permettre de négliger consiste à répondre efficacement aux défis mondiaux qui touchent directement la sécurité de nos pays membres et la stabilité du système paneuropéen.

Je voudrais mettre ici en lumière deux de ces défis.

L'un concerne les risques venant de zones adjacentes. D'aucuns ont critiqué, injustement à mon sens, la contribution de l'Alliance à l'effort international mené dans le Golfe. Les Alliés ont fait preuve, en la circonstance, d'une solidarité plus grande que dans n'importe lequel des conflits hors zone antérieurs, et les Européens ont apporté une contribution matérielle plus importante. En fait, tous les Alliés ont joué un rôle. Les Etats-Unis ne sont nullement isolés. Pourtant, on s'accorde à considérer que certains Alliés, et l'Alliance dans son ensemble, peuvent et doivent faire davantage. Nous procéderons à un débat une fois la crise du Golfe terminée - mais, je l'espère, pas avant, étant donné que nous devons maintenant nous concentrer sur le maintien de notre solidarité bien établie.

Lorsque ce débat s'ouvrira, nous devrons tirer les leçons de la crise du Golfe afin d'améliorer les mécanismes dont nous disposons aussi bien pour la gestion des crises que pour leur prévention. Naturellement, il n'est pas question que l'OTAN cherche à devenir un "gendarme du monde" ou prenne en main tous les problèmes de sécurité. Une telle démarche imposerait à nos structures une surcharge qui ne profiterait à personne. Mais ce n'est pas parce que nous ne pouvons pas tout faire que nous ne pouvons pas faire davantage. Le Traité de Washington nous engage à oeuvrer pour un ordre international plus pacifique et ne limite pas la portée de nos plans ni la coordination de nos efforts en matière de sécurité. Il n'exclut pas non plus toute action conjointe. On a avancé beaucoup d'idées intéressantes qui n'impliquent pas une action militaire collective dans des conflits extra-européens - ce qui, évidemment, exigerait le consensus de tous les pays membres. Ne pourrions-nous pas, par exemple, arriver à une entente interne à l'Alliance aux termes de laquelle, dans un esprit de solidarité, le degré d'engagement face à un problème donné pourrait varier d'un Allié à l'autre mais les moyens de l'Alliance seraient là pour permettre la coordination et le soutien ? Un tel système fonctionnerait lorsqu'il serait manifestement nécessaire de défendre des intérêts communs de l'Alliance.

En même temps, nous devons être conscients du fait qu'il existe, pour notre sécurité, une nouvelle menace née de la prolifération des armes de destruction massive et des technologies associées aux missiles balistiques au delà du traditionnel axe Est-Ouest. Il nous faut absolument faire plus pour empêcher cette prolifération et établir un code de conduite plus rationnel pour les transferts d'armes et de technologie au Tiers monde. C'est là un domaine où notre Alliance, en coopération avec l'Union soviétique et en étroite collaboration avec les Nations Unies, peut utilement jouer un rôle.

L'Alliance n'est donc pas moins importante qu'à l'époque de la Guerre froide. D'une part, ses fonctions du passé, comme celles consistant à contrebalancer la puissance soviétique et à maintenir le lien transatlantique, demeurent essentielles. D'autre part, ce n'est qu'avec et par l'Alliance que nous pourrons faire face aux nouvelles tâches de sécurité découlant de la fonte des glaces de la confrontation en Europe et aux défis que laisse entrevoir l'établissement d'un nouvel ordre mondial, plus juste et plus stable. C'est grâce à l'OTAN que les nations occidentales sont en mesure d'exercer leur responsabilité et de saisir cette occasion historique de promouvoir le changement et d'assurer la stabilité qu'exige la réussite à long terme de ce processus.

* * *

Artwork and layout
by NATO Graphics Studio

Conception et réalisation
par le Studio Graphique de l'OTAN

0004-91